THE
EXPERIENCE
OF
MODERNISM

For Brian Goodey

THE
EXPERIENCE
OF
MODERNISM

Modern architects and the future city,
1928–53

John R. Gold
Oxford Brookes University

E & FN SPON
An Imprint of Thomson Professional

London · Weinheim · New York · Tokyo · Melbourne · Madras

Published by E & FN Spon, an imprint of Thomson Professional, 2–6 Boundary Row, London SE1 8HN, UK

Thomson Science and Professional, 2–6 Boundary Row, London SE1 8HN, UK

Thomson Science and Professional, Pappelallee 3, 69469 Weinheim, Germany

Thomson Science and Professional, 115 Fifth Avenue, New York, NY 10003, USA

Thomson Science and Professional, ITP-Japan, Kyowa Building, 3F, 2-2-1 Hirakawacho, Chiyoda-ku, Tokyo 102, Japan

Thomson Science and Professional, 102 Dodds Street, South Melbourne, Victoria 3205, Australia

Thomson Science and Professional, R. Seshadri, 32 Second Main Road, CIT East, Madras 600 035, India

First edition 1997
© John R. Gold

Typeset in 10/12pt Meridien by Photoprint, Torquay
Printed in Great Britain at The University Press, Cambridge

ISBN 0 419 20740 6

∞ Printed on permanent acid-free text paper, manufactured in accordance with ANSI/NISO Z39.48-1992 and ANSI/NISO Z39.48-1984 (Permanence of Paper).

CONTENTS

LIST OF TABLES AND FIGURES

PREFACE

In April 1962 Ilford Borough Council, shortly afterwards reborn as the Council of the London Borough of Redbridge, unveiled plans for its new town centre. There was nothing unusual about this event. During the 1950s and 1960s, many councils decided that their town centres were badly congested and needed replacing by something truly modern. Nor was there anything particularly unusual about the scheme itself. The old High Street shops and surrounding area would be swept away and replaced by a shopping precinct and civic complex. The new buildings would be placed on a deck 12 feet above ground level, with parking, services and storage space beneath. The drawings and models suggested gleaming buildings of concrete and glass with striking geometric shapes. Narrow but intimate alleyways would open up into shared civic spaces, dominated by a circular council chamber.

In design and underlying intent, it was a typical action by a local authority that wished to assert its progressive outlook as well as retain the competitiveness of its shops and services in an age of change. It would be many years before I realised that the scheme itself had some architectural interest, not least because its co-designer was the same Frederick Gibberd who was the master-planner of Harlow and the architect of Liverpool's Roman Catholic Cathedral. Nevertheless, it was my introduction to architectural modernism at the urban scale. This was the era of comprehensive redevelopment. Although scarcely mentioned then by the media, for whom such occurrences were commonplace, a swathe of housing had to be cleared to make way for the new town centre. The houses were unexceptional late-Victorian terraces. Tall and brick-built with slate roofs, they were typical of many areas of housing developed speculatively by private-sector builders in towns along the line of the Great Eastern Railway. Their most attractive feature, perhaps, was their long plots that supplied narrow but substantial gardens where a child could get on with things unobserved by interfering adults. One of them was our family home.

The saga that followed was an ingredient of everyday life throughout my teenage years. The immediate local response after the publication of the plans was collective outrage. The area displayed signs of hitherto unsuspected community spirit. Petitions were signed, protest marches organised. The air was rife with residents' claims about the Council's megalomania and the Council's counter-claims about short-sighted people who stood in the way of progress. An alderman earned himself considerable opprobrium by appearing on television and blithely announcing that the houses were 'slums' and that clearance was 'in the best interests of the town'.

What happened next exemplified much of what went wrong when translating the Modern Movement's ideas about the future city into practice. The visionary master plan foundered when confronted by the politics and economics of urban development. Houses were boarded up and the slates removed from their roofs to keep out squatters. Once they were suitably derelict, they could be cleared piecemeal, leaving islands of inhabited dwellings surrounded by dereliction masquerading as temporary car parks. Street repairs halted and infestations of mice and other vermin were experienced. Graffiti appeared on walls and no-one bothered to clean it off. The area started to feel insecure.

Faced with this seemingly relentless process, the residents' fighting talk of solidarity and standing firm quickly evaporated. Those who had the resources quickly cut their losses, accepted a selling price based on 'site-value only' and moved out. Those who could not afford alternative housing, like my parents, eventually accepted rehousing in a block of high-rise council flats some miles distant.

The irony was that the town centre itself, like many similar schemes, was never built. Lack of resources, changing design ideas and a decade of plain indecision led to the abandonment of any comprehensive concept for the redevelopment of central Ilford. Today the area has acquired a bleak appearance; a patchwork of ill-coordinated developments and windswept open spaces that can justifiably be regarded as much worse than anything that existed previously.

All this may sound like a prelude to yet another blanket denunciation of the Modern Movement and its ideas, but that is emphatically not the aim of this book. Quite apart from the fact that there are already sufficient texts with that as their central theme, it would only represent part of my experience. Despite the negative character of the events that I have described, I distinctly remember visiting the Public Library to gaze at the scale models that were displayed there when the

town centre scheme was first announced. My initial and
lasting impression was how splendid and logical everything
looked. Quite simply, it *did* look like a scheme that would
have propelled the town into the twenty-first century. It
might well have been what I would have wanted if only we
had lived a few streets further away, outside the clearance
zone.

That sense of ambiguity, that pervading fascination with the
bold lines of the initial vision as well as knowledge of the
doomed end product, remain with me. It would strain the
limits of credulity to assert that this episode kindled a deep
and enduring interest in modernism that I have never lost. No
twelve-year-old – at least, not of my acquaintance – is ever
that single-minded. Nevertheless, this book expresses an abid-
ing fascination with the ideas that contributed to the greatest
transformation in the urban landscape seen in modern times.
Certainly, the themes contained here are ones on which I
have actively worked since starting my doctorate in the late
1970s.

Over that period, I have tried to develop a viewpoint that
avoids the repeated historiographic problem of interpreting
the past from what is known at the present. I wanted to learn
about the challenge of a world where planners and architects
were faced by large tracts of cities in urgent need of redevelopment and where exciting and untarnished visions of possible futures were on offer. I wanted to explore the fascination
that modernism had for its advocates as well as identifying
elements that later represented its pitfalls.

As the project developed, I came to realise that the triumph
of modernism was far from the inevitability that a generation
of architectural historians had insisted. To my surprise, I found
that even as late as the mid-1950s there was still widespread
disappointment that the Modern Movement had not achieved
more. I also found that there was little understanding of how
a set of ideas generally considered international in origin
worked their way into national practice. There were few
studies of how such a process of transference came about or
what amalgam of international *and* local factors might be
involved.

This book represents the first part of my investigations into
these and related matters. It aims to build an understanding of
how modern architects thought about the future city, and
how they believed their ideas might contribute to the reshaping of the city. It takes the ideas and work of British modern

architects as the central case-study, but always tries to locate their thinking and practices within the wider international scene. The specific period considered is the quarter-century between 1928 and 1953, a time when visions remained largely uncompromised by prolonged encounters with reality. A subsequent volume is intended to extend the story through the roller-coaster ride of dreams and dashed hopes of the ensuing years.

Throughout this project, I have employed two major sources of primary data to collect evidence. One was the documentary record of memoirs, press-cutting files, films, correspondence and memorabilia that have survived the astonishing neglect that surrounds this unfashionable and derided period of recent urban history. The other was interviews with those who were 'there'; architects and planners who practised in the years when the Modern Movement's ideas about city design were first developed. Neither of these major sources has priority in establishing a definitive interpretation of ideas and events. Documents are selectively retained and sometimes subject to considerable archival restrictions. Personal testimony, especially when dealing with events of 50 years or more ago, can be wholly unreliable. Either can mislead, yet the two taken together provide the best prospect that we have of building an understanding that moves past the limitations of the current historical writings.

The Introduction contains more formal discussion of the sources of data and methodology employed. Meanwhile, I would like to thank the many individuals who gave up considerable amounts of their time to be interviewed and freely and trustingly loaned me irreplaceable documents. Above all, it was their cooperation and active encouragement that made this project not just possible but also a joy to undertake.

There are many others to whom I also owe a debt of gratitude, although the length of time that I have been interested in this subject poses considerable problems of recall for someone whose memory has never been famed for its accuracy. I must begin by thanking Oxford Brookes University for instituting its enlightened sabbatical policy and my colleagues in the Geography Department for being prepared to cover for my absence. Without the essential availability of time, things would never have started at all. My warm thanks in this respect go to David Pepper, Martin Haigh, Alan Jenkins, Judy Chance, Peter Keene and Derek Elsom for their

support and, to borrow David Pepper's elegant word, com-
radeship. An additional debt of gratitude goes to George Revill
and Pyrs Gruffudd who – much as it will surprise them to
know it – caused me to start thinking again after a long period
in which I managed to get by without feeling the need to do
so.

Continuing the theme of debts incurred from sabbaticals,
sincere thanks go to Derek Diamond of the Department of
Geography, London School of Economics, David Canter and
David Uzzell then of the Department of Psychology at the
University of Surrey, and Philip Ogden, Murray Gray and
Roger Lee of the Department of Geography, Queen Mary and
Westfield College (University of London). All were more than
generous hosts during short periods of leave spent at their
institutions.

Next come a series of individuals who, in various ways, all
had a material impact on this book. Caroline Mallinder was a
helpful and encouraging editor with whom it was a pleasure
to work. Chris Plews converted my old Amstrad PCW disks so
that I could read their files on my IBM-PC, a favour that saved
me more time than I could ever have imagined. Thanks also
go to the following for suggesting lines of research or for
showing me how to proceed on the many occasions when I
got stuck on this or that: Colin Boyne, the late Gordon Cherry,
Jon Coaffee, Laura Cohn, Birgit Cold, Anthony Ferguson,
Margaret Gold, Dennis Hardy, Michael Hebbert, Bob Jarvis,
Valerie Karn, Paul Lehane, Eric Mumford, Barbara Smith,
Mike Thomas, Stephen Ward and Chris Watson. As ever, the
deficiencies that remain are entirely down to me.

Thanks must also be recorded to the following libraries and
their staff for their for their assistance: the British Library,
Royal Institute of British Architects, Architectural Association,
Senate House (University of London), the Library of Congress,
Harvard University, the British Film Institute, Queen Mary
and Westfield College (University of London), the Canadian
Centre for Architecture and Oxford Brookes University. The
illustrations were derived from many sources, but I would like
to convey my particular thanks to Christian Digby Firth for
giving me access to his late father's scrapbooks. These not only
revealed a treasure trove of architectural illustrations but also
ensured that the drawings and photographs reproduced here
accurately represent things seen and discussed at the time.

Special debts of gratitude in this respect also go to Shirley
Hind, former curator of the photographic archive at the

Architectural Press; Mary F. Daniels, Curator of the Special Collections Archive at the Graduate School of Design, Harvard University; and Jane Collins, Robert Elwall and the staff of the Drawings Collection, all at the Royal Institute of British Architects. By way of small recompense, it is anticipated that the transcripts of my interviews will be deposited with the RIBA's British Architectural Library Manuscripts and Archives Collection on completion of this study.

Thanks as ever to Margaret, Jennifer and Iain for putting up with me, not always the easiest thing to do despite my incessant propaganda to the contrary. Finally, one of the privileges of authorship is being allowed to acknowledge deep debts of gratitude in print. For reasons too many to mention, it is a great pleasure to dedicate this book to my friend and colleague Brian Goodey.

West Ealing, London
March 1997

ACKNOWLEDGEMENTS

The author and publishers would like to thank the following individuals, organizations and publishers for permission to reproduce copyright material. We have made every effort to contact copyright holders, but if any errors have been made we would be happy to correct them at a later printing.

Sources

2.1   Sert Collection, Frances Loeb Library, Harvard University.

2.2   Sert Collection, Frances Loeb Library, Harvard University.

2.3   Photographs Collection, Royal Institute of British Architects.

2.4   Hoffman, D. (1970) 'The Setback Skyscraper of 1891: an Unknown Essay by Louis H. Sullivan', *Journal of the Society of Architectural Historians*, 29, p.185.

2.5   Photograph courtesy of BFI Stills, Posters and Designs.

2.6   Photograph courtesy of BFI Stills, Posters and Designs.

2.7   Sert Collection, Frances Loeb Library, Harvard University.

2.8   Velez, D. (1982) 'Late Nineteenth-Century Spanish Progressivism: Arturo Soria's Linear City', *Journal of Urban History*, 9, p.135.

2.9   Johnson-Marshall, P.E.A. (1966) *Rebuilding Cities*, Edinburgh: Edinburgh University Press, p.132.

2.10 Johnson-Marshall, P.E.A. (1966) *Rebuilding Cities*, Edinburgh: Edinburgh University Press, p.132.

2.11 Johnson-Marshall, P.E.A. (1966) *Rebuilding Cities*, Edinburgh: Edinburgh University Press, p.138.

2.12 Photographs Collection, Royal Institute of British Architects.

2.13 Johnson-Marshall, P.E.A. (1966) *Rebuilding Cities*, Edinburgh: Edinburgh University Press, p.139.

3.1   Photographs Collection, Royal Institute of British Architects.

3.2   Photographs Collection, Royal Institute of British Architects.

3.3   Sert Collection, Frances Loeb Library, Harvard University.

3.4   Drawings Collection, Royal Institute of British Architects.
4.1   *The Home Owner*, August 1939, pp.30–1.
4.2   Photographs archive, *The Architectural Review*.
4.3   McDonald, J.D.H. (1931) *Modern Housing*, Glasgow: Carson & Nicol for the author.
4.4   McDonald, J.D.H. (1931) *Modern Housing*, Glasgow: Carson & Nicol for the author.
4.5   Author's collection.
4.6   Photographs Collection, Royal Institute of British Architects.
4.7   Sert Collection, Frances Loeb Library, Harvard University.
4.8   Scrapbooks belonging to the late Francis Digby Firth.
4.9   Author's collection.
4.10 Photographs Collection, Royal Institute of British Architects.
4.11 Scrapbooks belonging to the late Francis Digby Firth.
4.12 Photographs Collection, Royal Institute of British Architects.
4.13 Photographs archive, *The Architectural Review*.
4.14 Scrapbooks belonging to the late Francis Digby Firth.
4.15 Scrapbooks belonging to the late Francis Digby Firth.
5.1   Photographs Collection, Royal Institute of British Architects.
5.2   Photographs Collection, Royal Institute of British Architects.
5.3   MARS Group (1938) *New Architecture*, London, New Burlington Galleries, p.4.
5.7   Johnson-Marshall, P.E.A. (1966) *Rebuilding Cities*, Edinburgh: Edinburgh University Press, p.138.
5.8   Photographs Collection, Royal Institute of British Architects.
5.9   Yorke, F.R.S. and Breuer, M. (1937) 'A Garden City of the Future', in J.L. Martin, B. Nicolson and N. Gabo (eds), *Circle*, London, Faber & Faber, p.183.
6.1   Personal Papers, W.E. Tatton Brown.
6.2   Personal Papers, W.E. Tatton Brown.
6.3   Personal Papers, W.E. Tatton Brown.
6.4   Personal Papers, Professor A.G. Ling.
6.5   Drawn by the author.
6.6   Sharp, T.W. (1940) *Town Planning*, Harmondsworth: Penguin, p.63.

6.7   Korn, A. and Samuely, F.J. (1942) 'A Master Plan for
       London', *The Architectural Review*, 91, p.150.
6.8   Fry, E.M. (1944) *Fine Building*, London, Faber, facing
       p.94.
6.9   Fry, E.M. (1944) *Fine Building*, London, Faber, facing
       p.96
7.1   Drew, J.B. (ed.) (1945) *Architects' Year Book*, London:
       Paul Elek, p.69.
7.2   Johnson-Marshall, P.E.A. (1966) *Rebuilding Cities*,
       Edinburgh: Edinburgh University Press, p.138.
7.3   Drawings Collection, Royal Institute of British
       Architects.
7.4   Pierce, S.R. (1943) 'Excerpts from a Post-War Guide to
       the Metropolis of Britain', *Architect and Building News*,
       p.69.
7.5   *Proud City* (1945). Photograph courtesy of BFI Stills,
       Posters and Designs.
7.6   Abercrombie, P. (1945) *Greater London Plan, 1944*,
       London: HMSO.
7.7   Abercrombie, P. (1945) *Greater London Plan, 1944*,
       London: HMSO.
7.8   Drawings Collection, Royal Institute of British
       Architects.
7.9   Drawings Collection, Royal Institute of British
       Architects.
8.1   Forshaw, J.H. and Abercrombie, P. (1943) *County of
       London Plan*, London: Macmillan.
8.2   Photographs Collection, Royal Institute of British
       Architects.
8.3   Photographs Collection, Royal Institute of British
       Architects.
8.4   Photographs Collection, Royal Institute of British
       Architects.
8.5   Drawings Collection, Royal Institute of British
       Architects.
8.6   Drawings Collection, Royal Institute of British
       Architects.
8.8   Drawn by the author.
8.9   Drawings Collection, Royal Institute of British
       Architects.
9.1   Photographs Collection, Royal Institute of British
       Architects.
9.2   Johnson-Marshall, P.E.A. (1966) *Rebuilding Cities*,
       Edinburgh: Edinburgh University Press, p.228.

9.3   Sert Collection, Frances Loeb Library, Harvard University.
9.4   Ministry of Housing and Local Government (1953) *Design in Town and Village*, London: HMSO, p.70.
9.5   Photographs by the author.
9.6   Drawings Collection, Royal Institute of British Architects.
9.7   Smithson, A. and Smithson, P. (1970) *Ordinariness and Light: Urban Theories 1952–1960 and Their Application in a Building Project 1963–1970*, London: Faber & Faber, p.58.
9.8   Ministry of Housing and Local Government (1953) *Design in Town and Village*, London: HMSO, p.68.
9.9   Arts Council of Great Britain (1964) *The Shakespeare Exhibition*, London: Arts Council, p.102.

Illustration credits

Abbey National: 4.9
The Architectural Review: 4.13, 5.4, 5.5, 5.6, 6.7
Richard Bryant: 4.2
Central Office of Information: 7.5
Chicago Historical Society: 2.4
Faber & Faber: 5.9, 6.8, 6.9, 9.7
Fox-Movietone: 2.6
Halifax Building Society: 4.1
Harvard University: 2.1, 2.2, 3.3, 4.7, 8.7, 9.3
The late Percy Johnson-Marshall: 2.9, 2.10, 2.11, 2.13, 5.7, 7.2, 9.2
Arthur Ling: 6.4
Macmillan: 8.1
F.-W. Murnau-Stiftung/Transit Film GmbH: 2.5
Penguin Books: 6.6
Royal Insitute of British Architects: 2.3, 2.12, 3.1, 3.2, 3.4, 4.6, 4.12, 5.1, 5.2, 5.8, 7.3, 7.8, 7.9, 8.2, 8.3, 8.4, 8.5, 8.6, 8.9, 9.1, 9.6
Sage Publications: 2.8
The late William Tatton Brown: 6.1, 6.2, 6.3

All other illustrations come from the author's own collection or are his own photographs.

Some parts of Chapters 3, 5 and 6 have appeared in previous articles in *Town Planning Review* and *Planning Perspectives*.

1   INTRODUCTION

An ideology which states that the world is essentially mean-
ingless but that we ought to strive, suffer and fight for it is
unlikely to be powerful because of the essential contradiction
among its components. . . . An ideology by contrast which has
a clear image of a significant and exciting future and a clear
view of what people have to do in order to achieve this future
is likely to be powerful whether or not it is true.

Kenneth Boulding[1]

Story-telling has enormous cultural significance. Traditional
story-tellers memorised epic tales from the Golden Age and
recounted them to new audiences with consistent content and
inflection, thereby transmitting values and social memory.
Their present-day equivalents may often use technological
media to reach far-flung audiences but their actions have
many parallels. Stories provide the structure into which detail
inserts itself. They order the flux of events, resolve ambiguity,
reduce the disorienting effects of change, and help to clothe
the world with meaning, linking together isolated events
and experiences with 'bridges' of causal analysis.[2] Above all,
they retain their age-old function of identifying heroes and
villains.

The word 'story' suggests informality, but story-telling also
pervades the formal construction of historical knowledge,
most notably through 'Grand Narratives'. These are stories
with unifying properties that shape historiography and act as
taken-for-granted frameworks into which, consciously or
otherwise, new knowledge is fitted.[3] They thrive whenever it
is credible to resist plurality and merge experience into a
single thread. Moreover, they gain strength from appeal to
profound moral principles. A Grand Narrative does not just
offer seamless explanation for events. It also carries the sanc-
tion of relating the flow of those events to high ideals such as
the triumph of Good over Evil, the struggle for liberation, or
the path to ultimate redemption.

Powerful advocacy by their supporters lends Grand Narratives an aura of permanence but they eventually lose their
hold as circumstances place them under pressure. Prevailing
myths are challenged by events that yesterday they accommodated effortlessly. Statements of self-apparent truths become

ideological assertions. Freshly won freedoms turn out to be
old oppressions in disguise. Revered authorities suddenly
acquire feet of clay. Sequences of occurrences once considered
evidence of dogged persistence on the road to final success are
reinterpreted as pride before an inevitable fall.

Modernism and Grand Narratives

Few branches of historical study reveal the operation of Grand
Narratives more clearly than the history of modern architecture. Over the last 70 years, two Grand Narratives have
codified knowledge about the origins, development and purpose of architectural modernism. Both became the unques-
tioned framework for scholarship in their day, even though
they reached opposite conclusions about the historical trajectory of the Modern Movement. The first looked at the origins
and development of modernism, celebrated its rise to prominence and heralded the imminent fulfilment of its historic
mission. The second reappraised matters in the light of subsequent knowledge, chronicling modernism's dramatic fall from
grace and searching for who was to blame.

   The first Grand Narrative formally appeared in the late
1920s and dominated interpretations of the history of architectural modernism for more than four decades. While it held
sway, historians selectively identified key thinkers and
mapped chains of events to show modern architecture as the
outcome of a long and continuous process of evolution.
Embracing deep social commitment, purged of applied ornamentation and other 'paraphernalia of historical reminis-
cence',[4] modern architecture arose from the rational
application of technology to building and construction. As
such, it was regarded as the only authentic contemporary
architecture in that it employed the materials and constructional methods specific to that age and matched built forms to
the functions that they served.

   When substantiating that point, historians emphasised
those antecedents that heralded the emergence of a rationalist
approach to modern architecture. By contrast, they downplayed the rival attractions of the organic tradition within
modernism and marginalised modernist architectural movements not conforming to the idea of continuous evolution.
The German Expressionist movement, for instance, was dis-

missed either as a 'regrettable, but luckily temporary, Mannerist interpretation of rationalist tendencies' or as a historic dead-end.[5] Only much later was Expressionism's place in the intellectual melting pot of Weimar Germany recognised, not least for its influence on leading figures at the Bauhaus – the institution usually taken as the hearth of rationalist thought.

Justification for this blatant selectivity primarily rested on the *Zeitgeist* ('Spirit of the Age'), an idea devised by Romantic philosophers and elaborated by art historians such as Heinrich Wölfflin. The *Zeitgeist* was first applied to the history of architectural modernism by writers such as Henry-Russell Hitchcock, Nikolaus Pevsner and Sigfried Giedion.[6] According to this perspective, every age generated a new expression of collective humanity, characterised by a spirit that invalidated all previous traditions and cultural patterns. For their part, architects were committed 'to the revelation of the essential spirit unique to their time, morally superior to all others and tending towards ever more advanced development'.[7]

Exactly how that revelation came about was open to debate. Pevsner's account suggested that the architect, as the individual with aesthetic awareness and expertise, was the person who uncovered the spirit of the age. Others depicted architects acting as the tools of the superhuman and elusive *Zeitgeist*.[8] The precise mechanism at stake, however, made little real difference to the overall belief that modern architecture gained its validity from facing up to the challenge of modern times. Art Deco, Neo-Classicism, National Romanticism and other contemporary non-modernist movements lacked that validity, even though each in its day attracted far more adherents than modernism. Popularity was no guide to historic mission.

In due course, this Grand Narrative crumbled under pressure from two distinct directions. One source came from developments in historical scholarship (see below). The other, and more powerful source of pressure lay outside academic circles since, regardless of their intrinsic intellectual appeal, Grand Narratives are most plausible when validated by events taking place in the outside world. Widespread adoption of modernist principles in urban reconstruction programmes seemingly authenticated the historic triumph of modernism. Twenty years later, popular discontent with the products of those principles made that position untenable. Concern about the dysfunctional consequences of supposedly functional architecture led to sustained critical analysis of issues like the death of the street, social isolation and pathology, the constructional and structural failings of public housing, and the ambiguities of control in semi-public space. The self-referential and spartan aesthetics of modernist buildings were derided as boring; the associated urban planning denounced as autocratic. Even the derided slums were redesignated as homely and of human scale.[9] As the evidence stacked up, it became progressively less feasible to treat difficulties as representing either teething troubles or poor applications of visionary principles by less-gifted architects.

A new Grand Narrative grew out of this sea-change in attitudes. This version traced chains of causation that linked the *deficiencies* of recently designed urban environments back to the flawed visions of pioneering modern architects. Those supporting this view reappraised buildings and environments once warmly greeted as affirmations of social progress and a brighter future as hugely expensive follies foist on an unsuspecting population. They recognised that the associated problems were persistent rather than transitory. They seriously questioned the results of applying abstract philosophies, especially functionalism and aesthetic minimalism, to public housing. Perhaps more damagingly, they decried the humanism and social engineering embraced by many modern architects as megalomania. Judged in moral terms – the hallmark of a Grand Narrative – the damage inflicted on the human and physical fabric of the city was taken as the melancholy consequence of high-handed arrogance. The culprits were a small coterie of radical European architects and their supporters.

It is easy to find commentators on the urban environment who have expressed this view. Alice Coleman[10] blamed the pathology of high-rise public housing estates directly on the design deficiencies of a flawed visionary utopia. Robert Hughes[11] censured modern architecture for a utopianism that disastrously attempted to remake cities in the light of fanciful ideals. Christopher Booker[12] sought to show how:

> a certain image of the city . . . [an] image of colossal buildings and restless traffic, first came to haunt a number of science-fiction writers and architects more than fifty years ago and how their ideas became the orthodoxy which hovered over the wholesale reconstruction of many of Britain's cities in the Sixties and early Seventies.

Alison Ravetz, in a more measured analysis, drew connections between an 'increasingly dominant' modern style that developed in Britain after 1950 and 'images not yet built'. Prominent among them were 'Le Corbusier's *Ville Radieuse* from the 1930s and, beyond that, the ferro-concrete *cité industrielle* of Tony Garnier, published in 1917'.[13]

The French-Swiss architect, Le Corbusier, features remarkably often in these accounts, even in the popular media. Peter Popham, for instance, noted how designers of high-rise flats were under 'the inspiration of Le Corbusier and CIAM'. The latter acronym (standing for *Les Congrès Internationaux d'Architecture Moderne*) received no explanation other than the inaccurate claim that it was 'the modern movement's ruling council'. Their vision, it was said, led to a 'stark and simple' solution to housing needs. This comprised 'huge slabs or towers of housing rising majestically and disdainfully above the old towns, set in sprawling parkland and totally divorced from the historical fabric'.[14]

Beatrix Campbell took that theme further in her reflections on the fate of four high-rise blocks of flats in Glasgow's Gorbals district known as 'the Queenies'. Although only built in the 1960s, the estate's severe structural and social problems prompted the local authority to demolish the flats in September 1993 rather than commit any further resources for repairs and modifications. Campbell primarily blamed the architect, Sir Basil Spence, and his mode of working for the resulting disaster. Spence did not consult the community. Rather, he visited France, 'consulted Le Corbusier's Unité flats and brought his brutalism back to one of the most optimistic and needy neighbourhoods in Western Europe'. The unfortunate Spence was not alone in falling into this trap, since the Conservative governments of the time were similarly 'bewitched by the promise of Le Corbusier's utilitarian urbanism'.[15]

The crucial role of Le Corbusier also figures in formal accounts of town planning history. Peter Hall equated Le Corbusier's influence over the creative imagination of modern architects with the malign hold that Rasputin exerted over the Russian royal family.[16] His account presented a sequence of schemes designed or influenced by Le Corbusier to illustrate the progress of modernist ideas of city form and planning from utopian ambition to popular disillusionment. In chronological order the examples included the Ville Contemporaine, the

Ville Radieuse, the city of Chandigarh in India, Brasilia, Shef-field's Park Hill and Glasgow's 'Queenies'.

Similarly, Jules Lubbock allotted Le Corbusier a central place in his study of the relationship between politics and architecture in Britain. Le Corbusier's work, covering the spectrum between interior design, housing and city planning, exemplified the enlarged role played by the architect. Lubbock noted that 'architect-planner-designers' had exercised great influence from the 1940s until the early 1980s. Their position was sustained by a permissive framework of planning law and aesthetic control. As a result, they exercised 'almost dictatorial powers and immunity from interference either by the owners or residents of private property or by the general public who opposed the new projects'.[17]

These interpretations were not confined to European writers. James Howard Kunstler,[18] for example, blamed modernism for impoverishing the American environment by 'promoting a species of urbanism that destroyed age-old social arrangements and with them, urban life as a general proposition'. His argument rested on a set of reciprocal trans-Atlantic influences that had shaped architectural practice. During the early twentieth century, America influenced Europe. European architects became enamoured with built forms that originated in North America, notably industrial architecture and the new metal-framed skyscrapers, and copied aspects of their construction and aesthetics. Later, as many architects fled to the USA to escape from Nazi persecution, they effectively reimported the results.

Quickly finding their way into leading roles in academic institutions, the refugees became 'part of the cultural establishment . . . practically overnight'. From that base, Gropius, Breuer, Mies and the rest had a major impact on built forms, while Le Corbusier's 'particular brand of urbanism', promoted by the refugees, dominated the thinking of the planning profession. The Radiant City appealed to architects, property developers, and city authorities alike and its combination of tall buildings and super-highways were imitated in housing projects all over America. The defects of the concept were quickly apparent but that hardly stopped anyone from building these estates, so powerful was the ostensible hegemony of the 'Formgivers'. Their failure to create a social utopia was ultimately recognised, but not before they did 'tremendous damage to the physical setting for civilization'.

In praise of complexity

These examples are neither atypical nor taken out of context. They give insight into the arguments, style of language and the certainties expressed. Collectively, they show the existence of a credible and persuasive story that directly associates present-day disasters with the beguiling visionary prototypes of a previous era. Nevertheless, closer examination reveals the importance of recognising the *ideological* context of writings about modern architecture. 'Ideology' is an inescapable part of the process by which people come to terms with the world around them. Defined here as the pervasive set of ideas, values, images and stories that groups employ to make the world more intelligible to themselves, an ideology is a frame that makes sense of experience, past and present, and maps hopes for the future. More often than not, it also serves to advance the interests of a particular group, placing them in the centre of the narratives that they share.[19]

Applying this analysis to the history of modernism, we see how ideology helps to promote tendencies towards conceptual tidiness, stripping away complexity and ambiguity in favour of simple deterministic sequences and readily identifiable outcomes. Pevsner, Giedion, Hitchcock and others who first wrote the 'official' history of early modernism actively promoted the movement that they studied: indeed it is fair to say that they saw no special distinction between the work of the architect and the historian in that both were actively engaged in the creation of a theory of architectural practice.[20] They lionised the accomplishments of leading modern architects, who were often friends and colleagues. They constructed doctrines, such as the notoriously 'elastic' notion of functionalism,[21] that included architects regarded as motivated by the 'right spirit' and excluded those who failed to meet those exacting standards. For their part, the architects aided the historians by publishing those works recognisably permeated by modernism even though, in reality, they could fit almost any progressive historical narrative. A careful veil was drawn over early works supposedly marred by compromises or regional influences.[22]

If ideological factors were involved in lionising the pioneers, they were equally implicated in the way in which modernism was subsequently denigrated. Critics are frequently advocates of alternative visions. Supporters of community architecture or renewal of Garden City ideals, for instance, have vested interests in portraying modernism as a movement that led inexorably to monumental solutions to urban reconstruction that crushed the individual. By doing so, they promote a conveniently adverse picture of modernism that contrasts unfavourably with the 'human-scale' quality of their own ideals. Similarly, commentators interested in postmodernism generally restrict modernism to a readily identifiable, historically bounded set of principles, styles and built forms. This strategy has two advantages. First, a more specific definition of modernism makes it possible to achieve more coherent definitions of *post*modernism – no mean feat in itself. Secondly, this strategy supplies proponents of postmodernism with a stable adversary against which to propose and justify the various conceptual and stylistic departures that they favour.

Nevertheless, other stories were possible. These looked beyond the unifying tendencies of the Grand Narratives and recognised 'the living matter of architecture, the myths and symbols, the personalities and pressure-groups [that] have been left out'.[23] A new wave of scholarship indicated the divergent trends and experiences within modernism. Although led by writers like Reyner Banham, Charles Jencks and Manfredo Tafuri, this period of architecture's history is no longer solely the province of architectural historians. The emergence of critical perspectives from, among others, cultural historians, construction and design historians, feminist historians, and historical geographers has opened new approaches to the study of the Modern Movement and substantially widened the empirical basis of inquiry.[24]

The new stories rest on two broad premises: that there were many histories of modernism rather than one; and that the flow of events did not resemble a strip cartoon moving tidily from frame to frame.[25] Rather than view early modernism through the lens of convergence around shared ideas and beliefs, its history was reconceptualised to reveal untidy diversity. Ambiguities and exceptions continually appeared as research penetrated the masking blanket of internationalism and paid closer attention to national experience. The complex history of modernism saw groups emerging at different times in the widely varying cultural and political contexts of Europe and the USA. The relations between and within such groups reveal tensions between globalism and parochial ethnocentrism, between universalism and class privilege.[26] Their ideas on issues like city-planning or building styles might converge, but apparent consensus between groups could conceal deep underlying disagreements.

Having said this, it is important not to overstate matters by denying the extent of shared thinking. There were many elements that gave the Modern Movement a genuine sense of collective identity to set alongside the fissiparous tendencies. The strong urge to associate with others for mutual support, for instance, arose from the fact that to identify oneself with modernism in the early days meant taking up an adversarial position with no shortage of enemies. The resulting associations were sometimes short-lived, but they supplied a sympathetic forum for developing ideas and projects. Their continued existence was bolstered by assuming the mantle of the *avant-garde* – cultural innovators who stood out against 'bourgeois' tastes in pursuit of a vision of the way ahead. Admission to the avant-garde was jealously guarded, but once individuals had negotiated the rites of passage, they drew strength from being surrounded by those of like mind. These feelings persisted long after modernism had made the transition from the margins of professional architecture to centre-stage. They were part and parcel of the experience of modernism in the period studied here.

Aims and sources

The need to construct narratives that recognise these layers of complexity provides the rationale for this book. Its subject is imagery of the future city and its impact on, and expression in, architectural thought. More specifically, this book examines the 'urban imagination' – the anticipation of future urban forms and patterns of city life – of the Modern Movement between 1928 and 1953. Its central assumption is that the most appropriate way to resolve disputes about interpretations of images of the future city is to study what they meant to those individuals who participated in the early days of modernism. Put another way, critical assessment of the nature and purpose of this imagery requires building an accurate understanding of the *experience* of modernism for those who were 'there'.

The key evidence needed to address that goal came from two sources. The first, as with any empirically based historical study, was extensive recourse to the documentary record. Relevant sources included correspondence and scrapbooks held in private hands, archival collections, press-cutting files, published autobiographies, private memoirs and documentary films. These have many advantages in establishing the chronology of events and in providing the flavour of contemporary thinking, but suffer from a variety of problems. Press-cutting files rely on the categories and interpretations imposed by their compilers. Archives offer astonishingly patchy coverage given the recency of the events concerned and suffer from varying rights of access afforded to researchers. Memoirs and autobiographies suffer from having to live uneasily between the secrets of the diary and the mask of the novel.[27]

Visual imagery poses even greater problems. The plans and drawings with which this book is concerned were executed, for the most part, by young people actively experimenting with novel ideas. Relegated to the fringes of their profession by prejudice or choice, they freely exercised their imaginations without the restraint of having to implement the projects that they designed. Paper is cheap. It is not obligatory to think through every detail before picking up the drafting pen. Many projects also contained critical and promotional dimensions, being intended to indicate the poor conditions of the present day as much as inviting people to contemplate the wonders of the future. Their designers were not even obliged to be serious. Some illustrations lovingly preserved in archives were never more than lightly discarded first sketches. Moreover, it is important to realise that drawings and scale models were seldom created by a single hand, particularly once an architect's practice was fully established. They might well reflect the anonymous contributions and teamwork of junior members of the office as much as, if not more than, the distinguished architect with whom they are normally associated.

To counter these limitations and provide greater sensitivity of analysis, documentation was supplemented wherever possible by in-depth interviews. This was achieved by using the membership lists of British architectural associations sympathetic to the development of modernism during the quarter-century studied here. As such, the most significant membership lists used here were those of the Modern Architectural Research (MARS) Group. Founded in 1933 to support the cause of modern architecture, the MARS Group always had close links with the wider Modern Movement and a deep interest in town planning. Indeed, throughout its existence, MARS was the accredited English branch of CIAM and organised two of its post-war Congresses.[28] It claimed the membership of many modern architects working in Britain, as well as many who later became leading figures in town planning. It immediately attracted Continental European refugee architects when they arrived in Britain in the 1930s. Certainly no group is more appropriate for interpreting the development of modernist thought about the future city or for discerning the balance of local and international influences in the formative phase of British modernism.

The resulting interviews had a semi-structured format, guided by a standardised schedule that was arranged into major sections. This format focused the interview on a given set of topics, but was sufficiently flexible to allow both the respondent or interviewer to develop other relevant themes wherever appropriate. Each interview explored aspects of the individual's career and activities in depth, with the average interview taking between $1\frac{1}{2}$ and 2 hours. The results were tape-recorded, fully transcribed and revised by respondents whenever they felt that the transcript was insufficiently clear or misleading. These interviews eventually yielded more than 120 000 words of agreed transcript.

Naturally interviews, too, have their shortcomings. There is clearly truth in Anthony Howard's dictum that there is 'no more flawed source for recalling the events of yesterday than human recollection'.[29] As one respondent, apologising for his fading memories of the inter-war years, said to the author:

> In the last few years, I have largely lost track of the events of that period which is a great pity because it was a most interesting time. What I felt at that time . . . may not be what I feel now and I may also be wrong about the value of it.[30]

To some extent, checking material gained from different interviews against itself as well as against available documentation helps to eliminate some problems caused by *ex post facto* rationalisation and self-justification, but revisiting past futures is a difficult art. Put simply, the interviews dealt with futures that now belong to the past. However constructed, it is impossible to avoid the fact that the interview takes place at a moment when the fate of so many promising ideas is known. Rather than requesting respondents to try to divorce themselves from such knowledge, it made greater sense to recognise that these elements of hindsight are today an inseparable part of the experience of modernism.

Throughout the ensuing study, there is an important relationship between national and international experience. The experience of modernism varied from country to country, yet internationalism is part of both the myth and reality of its development. Each informed the other. The international theme here starts with the Weissenhof exhibition at Stuttgart in 1927, the first truly international exposition of modern architecture at the urban scale. It then continues with the story of CIAM, the body that nurtured the convergence of modern architecture and town planning. Its activities are followed from its foundation in 1928 through to its ninth Congress at Aix-en-Provence in 1953.

The insights into wider currents of ideas and rivalries glimpsed in CIAM's activities combine with the important detail available from a national case-study. The latter involves urban-scale projects associated with modern architects in Great Britain. This part of the story begins with the earliest stirrings of interest in modernism in the late 1920s. As the narrative unfolds we look at specific plans and exhibitions, pipedreams and realised projects, private commissions and municipally sponsored schemes. The account ends at the point when decisive change had started to occur. With post-war urban reconstruction gathering pace, the visionary future seemed, for the first time, within the grasp of modern architects even if there remained dissatisfaction about the lack of tangible progress. Moreover, the Modern Movement was itself changing. The uncertainties of the early days and the powerful urge to associate in mutually supportive groups had passed. There was a growing generational split between the pioneers, ironically now representing architectural orthodoxy, and their successors who wished to set off in new directions.

Three interwoven threads are emphasised as the account unfolds. The first concerns the intellectual origins of the discourse of modern architects about the future city and its society, identifying not only what they wanted to achieve but also what they were reacting against. When looking back to the antecedents of visionary plans, it identifies the broad mix of ideas that architects gradually absorbed. In the process, it recognises that aspects of their underlying imageries were often shared with groups whose ideas about the future city were quite different.

The second thread involves the anatomy of the diverse imagery that was proposed by modern architects. It is emphasised throughout that there was no programmatic manifesto for the future. Rather, the imagery comprised a loose constellation of different elements, worked and reworked to produce plausible ideas about the shape of the future. In addition, the visionary designs for the future city were supported by an alluring, but seldom explicitly stated imagery of the society likely to live there. Consciously or otherwise, the latter imagery was not simply an anticipation of the urban society of the coming age. Rather, it served a vital function within the edifice of modernist theory by legitimising the imagery of physical form.

The third, and related, thread consists of the mutually reinforcing relationship between these images of the future and the ideology of the Modern Movement. By virtue of being a loose constellation of elements rather than a programmatic blueprint, the broad vision of the future allowed individuals to adhere to an ideologically significant consensus based on general principles without opening up underlying divergences of opinion and belief. From an ideological standpoint, too, the Modern Movement's images of the prospective city impart more than just anticipations of desired futures. In part, as suggested earlier, they communicate their designer's critical appraisals of the state of existing cities and disapproval of the social order that had produced them. Moreover, they reveal the personal and collective aspirations of modern architects to extend their professional interests into the realm of town planning.

Defining terms

Before discussing the structure of the ensuing study, it is worth clarifying terminology since almost every major term connected with describing and analysing the experience of modernism is fiercely contested. *Modernity*, the quality or condition of being modern, is perhaps the one least tied to the present era. People in every generation experience living in 'modern times' and ideas about what constitutes being 'modern' date quickly. Modernity implies the 'ephemeral, the fugitive, the contingent', the flip side to 'the eternal and the immutable'.[31]

The aspect of modernity that changes least is the persistent tension between tradition and innovation. This has been ever-present since the Romans copied built forms and social practices from the Greeks and then fought off the insinuation that copying was uncreative. As Lowenthal observed, the conflict sharpened during the post-Renaissance dispute between 'Ancients' and 'Moderns'. The former insisted that antique excellence had no equal, the latter argued that observation and experiment unfettered by tradition could generate insights that transcended those inherited from Antiquity.[32]

These disputes took a new slant during the Age of Enlightenment when modernity became allied to *progress* – belief in the possibility and desirability of improvement in the human condition. That alliance itself came under strain in the nineteenth century through the emergence of *modernisation*. Broadly speaking, modernisation describes the wider-ranging changes that occurred in the wake of demographic upheaval, industrialisation and technological change, especially mechanisation. These changes included an increase in social mobility, a loosening of boundaries between the classes, the growth of education, new processes of industrial negotiation, and the emergence of social services.[33]

Modernism developed against this background of upheaval and dislocation. Although it meant different things even to its practitioners, modernism is best understood at two distinct levels – representational and personal. On the one hand, it was a search for forms of representation that truly expressed the needs and challenges of modern times. Seen in this way, modernism was defined primarily by the forms and aesthetics adopted in the many different media that modernism influenced. These included atonal music, abstract art, free verse in poetry, streams of consciousness in novels, and the 'expressive language of simple, floating volumes and clear-cut geometries' of early architectural modernism.[34] At another level, modernism comprised a radical set of personal attitudes that underpinned the search for new representations: attitudes towards the past, towards society, towards the arts and industry, and towards the conduct of everyday life. Modernism, thus, was not just a matter of learning to paint, sculpt or design buildings in new ways, it also signified that the individual had adopted new moral positions guided by the 'right spirit'.

The precise historical moment at which modernism emerged is impossible to state with any accuracy, since the times when its traces became discernible vary according to the nation and the branch of the arts under consideration. What can be said with reasonable certainty, however, is that modernism achieved critical mass in Western and Central Europe during the first three decades of the twentieth century and that it was primarily a metropolitan phenomenon. Cities like Paris, Vienna, Berlin, Milan, Barcelona, Zurich and New York acted as magnets for the emerging Modern Movement. They offered liberating and receptive environments that fostered exchange of ideas and creativity. In addition, they supplied an essential subject matter. There was widespread agreement that addressing the realities of modern life meant addressing urban life. It was in the city and, increasingly, through the city that the challenge of modernity would be met.

Having said that, opinion divided sharply about the potential impact of the metropolis on its inhabitants. Many French artists and literati embraced an intellectual outlook coloured by 'cultural despair'.[35] The writings of Baudelaire and Flaubert, the poetry of de Vigny and the paintings of Manet and Degas neither expressed the wonders of technology nor marvelled at the profound transformation brought by Baron Haussmann's dramatic reconstruction of Paris. Instead, they focused on the fragmentation, anonymity and underlife of the city and the way in which it ruptured the individual's traditional relationship with nature. Their concerns were with 'images of the anguish and vacuity of the capital' and with the 'new anguish and alienation of French society'. For them, the city undermined the soul.[36]

German writers such as Ferdinand Tönnies, Oswald Spengler, Max Weber and Georg Simmel reinforced these arguments. In their bleak prognoses, modern life was inherently superficial, sterile and empty of human possibilities. Witnessing the rapid modernisation of cities within the newly unified Germany, they emphasised the apparent dangers of the urban environment for personal and communal health. Tönnies, for instance, took the view that the city broke down traditional pre-industrial social structures, replacing *Gemeinschaft* (community) with *Gesellschaft* (society). The result was that the formalised, contractual and impersonal relations of the *Gesellschaft* replaced the warm primary social relationships of the *Gemeinschaft*. For his part, Simmel concentrated on the social psychology of urban life. He believed that the town bombarded the individual with stressful stimuli not experienced in rural life. Coping with these stimuli required conscious, calculated strategies, involving detachment or avoidance. The end product was a metropolitan personality, differentiated by a blasé attitude towards other people.

Others, who included most modern architects, were more optimistic. They detected intrinsic qualities in the urban environment that encouraged them to believe that cities could act as agents of social redemption. Quite apart from anything else, their own experience supported that view. Many had recently been attracted to the city by the positive attributes of metropolitan life. As a result they found it inherently plausible to turn the city's role as a modernising agent to society's advantage. Adopting a philosophy that celebrated human voluntarism, creativity and courage, many looked 'to the future like a predator eying its prey'.[37] Their task was to visualise and campaign for the built forms that might take advantage of a historic opportunity.

Significantly, these prospective built forms were neither tied to any specific perception of the relationship between technology and the built environment nor to any particular moral or political agenda. Modern architects on the right or left could appropriate the same pristine imageries as part of their representations of the new age. This had a short-term tactical advantage. Divergencies in the thinking that generated those imageries were effectively camouflaged, providing the grounds for consensus. In the long run, however, the malleability of the imagery virtually guaranteed conditions for schism and conflict.

Structure and organisation

The interrelationship of these terms and the conceptual debates that underpin them recur constantly in the chapters that follow. Chapter 2 examines patterns of anticipations about the future city on both sides of the Atlantic, sampling the range of visionary urban prototypes that were on offer to modern architects. Chapter 3 deals with modern architects' attempts to stake their claim to the province of town planning. The first part of this chapter deals with large-scale projects that showed the concern of the new architecture with housing. The second half shows the importance of city planning in the formation of CIAM. It discusses the founding ideals of CIAM and notes how its original preoccupation with housing issues evolved into interest in the shape of the wider city. It ends by presenting, for the first time, the full story of the creation of the Athens Charter, CIAM's most famous town planning document.

Chapter 4 examines the emergence of modern architecture in Britain and provides a bridge between the international and

British contexts. After explaining why modern architecture was marginal to the British architectural scene until the 1930s, it discusses various initiatives made to stimulate greater interest. It then outlines the ideas that brought adherents of modernism together, particularly with regard to their ideas about the future city and its society.

The next two chapters discuss parallel aspects of the promotion of modernism in the inter-war period. Chapter 5 considers early exhibition projects that attempted, in a pre-televisual age, to convey the urban imagination of the Modern Movement to the wider public. These include the abortive plans for a Twentieth Century Group exhibition in 1931, the Unit One Exhibition (1935), and the exhibition projects associated with the MARS Group (1934 and 1938). Chapter 6 provides a companion to this discussion by focusing specifically on endeavours to devise urban plans. The first sections highlight several fragmentary efforts to generate new urban forms in the shape of competition entries and student projects. Its main emphasis, however, is on the complexities and compromises involved in generating one specific plan, namely, the MARS Group's Master Plan for London (1942). Collectively, these varied projects show the inherent plurality and experimentation that marked the Modern Movement's thinking about the shape of the future city in the inter-war period.

The rise of fascism, the proscription of modern architecture and the onset of war scattered the European Modern Movement and removed normal channels for meeting and exchange of ideas. As the war progressed, thoughts of reconstruction acted as a catalyst for new ideas. Chapter 7 investigates the various attempts to fly the flag for modernism in war-time through holding exhibitions, the activities of educational associations and publishing ventures. It also discusses the work of the advisory plans drawn up for many British cities in the mid-1940s. Although none was modernist in the strict sense, they contained an edgeways penetration of modernist ideas about design and society, primarily through the sympathies of the personnel appointed to the planning teams, which allowed the plans to be adopted for discussion by modernists. This point is illustrated in particular by reference to Patrick Abercrombie's plans for London (1943).

Chapter 8 considers the progress of the Modern Movement's involvement in town-planning matters in the immediate post-war years. It shows that the end of hostilities brought no immediate change in the prospects of realising influence over the reconstruction of cities. Although easy to find work, it was hard to promote visionary ideas in an age of economic austerity and materials shortage. Although there was a resurgence of internationalism in modern architecture, as shown by the reconstitution of CIAM, there was a real failure of modern architects on the domestic front to make a significant contribution to shaping the future city – a point made by the experience of the British New Towns. At best, it was a period of marking time.

The concluding chapter (9) focuses on the Festival of Britain, two further CIAM Congresses and new initiatives that sought to restore the cutting edge of modernism as a force for urban and social transformation. When reflecting on the position reached by 1953, this chapter notes that the success of modernism as a force in remaking cities was still elusive. Nevertheless, the visionary ideals of the previous era were being absorbed into consensual approaches shaped by the specific circumstances of reconstruction. Although this represented rather less than the desired breakthrough, the essential groundwork was now, at least, in place.

2 ANTICIPATIONS

In the centre of Fedora, that grey stone metropolis, stands a
metal building with a crystal globe in every room. Looking
into each globe, you see a blue city, the model of a different
Fedora. These are the forms the city could have taken if, for
one reason or another, it had not become what we see today.
In every age someone, looking at Fedora as it was, imagined a
way of making it the ideal city, but while he constructed his
miniature model, Fedora was already no longer the same as
before, and what had until yesterday a possible future became
only a toy in a glass globe.

Italo Calvino[1]

Ideal cities and urban utopias

In his extensive analysis of the history of the future, Fred
Polak argued that two types of images have repeatedly
inspired people to take collective action.[2] One, the eschato-
logical, presents the prospect of an eventual paradise that
must be patiently awaited. Human attempts to replicate that
blessed state are at best futile, at worst heretical. The other
category, the utopian, offers at least tangential engagement
with the material world. Production of utopian schemes is
generally associated with times of socioeconomic or political
stress; times when individuals feel a pressing need to search
for something better. A utopia is a comprehensive vision of an
ideal condition of human affairs radically different from and,
it is believed, inherently better than that pertaining at the
time.

Defined in this way, utopias have two important characteristics. First, they gain their vividness from their juxtaposition
with the material conditions that they seek to replace. In
much of the ensuing study, utopianism gains its strength from
the haunting images of poverty, deprivation and alienation
associated with the Victorian industrial city (Figure 2.1). Secondly, while often mute about the mechanisms for the transformation, utopian schemes invariably imply creation of
conditions for the Good Life. Precisely what comprises the
Good Life, however, provides the fault-lines along which
many well-intentioned schemes fracture.

Figure 2.1
Street scene in
Bermondsey, London,
around the turn of the
twentieth century.

Historically, architects made little contribution towards devising utopian schemes. Although treatises from Plato's *The Republic* to Edward Bellamy's *Looking Backward* saw the city as a crucible for social transformation, the art of ideal city planning, to which architects did subscribe, remained separate from that of utopianism.[3] Part of the reason lay in the architect's dependence on the patronage of wealthy clients. Most of the stirring geometric city plans of Renaissance Europe, for example, were produced at the behest of auto-crats, either to confer aggrandizement on their regimes or create strongholds for their defence. The architects' plans effectively supported the established order, scarcely hinting at the social transformation that lies at the heart of utopianism. Moreover, while historians have made much of the deeper social and cosmological meanings of geometrically harmoni-ous designs, the partiality to symmetric shapes, grids, axes and regulating lines often stemmed from little more than the architect's traditional attachment to draughtsmanship.[4] Only rarely did architects strive to use architecture as a vehicle to bring about the Good Life.

In the nineteenth century, Augustus Welby Pugin, John Ruskin and William Morris were instrumental in bringing

architecture into the utopian camp. Each believed that architecture played a role in forming social conditions and could
serve as an agent of social redemption. In due course, modern
architects followed their lead, allying ideal city planning with
utopian thought. It was a propitious moment for that alliance.
Modernism developed against a background of war, revolution and social dislocation: circumstances in which it was easy
to discern the problems of the existing order. Moreover modern architects occupied the archetypal social position of
utopians. Whether by choice or through ostracism, they were
excluded from the Establishment of their profession with few
prospects of change. It was hardly surprising, therefore, that
they eagerly consumed radical ideas about social betterment
and the reorganisation of society.

In this chapter, we survey contributions dating from the late
nineteenth century through to the 1930s that had an impact
on the early Modern Movement's urban imagination. Collectively these schemes contained an astonishing array of ideas
for future cities, coupled with a heady cocktail of sociological
notions. There is no attempt here to synthesise this miscellany
in any manner that implies a common agenda. Quite simply,
there was neither consensus about the shape of the future city
nor agreement about how the tenets of modernism would
translate into urban form. Early modernists freely ransacked
historical precedent and emerging trends to locate possible
sources of inspiration. Sometimes schemes developed on similar lines without their instigators being aware of the fact.
Equally, ideas developed by one architect could be consciously
adopted by another but applied in a quite different manner.

Nevertheless, it is possible to identify common themes.
Most schemes stressed the importance of rationally conceived
comprehensive or 'master' plans. These often favoured layouts that embraced geometric harmony, with sharp boundaries between different zones of land-use and between the city
and its rural surroundings. Abhorring the haphazard internal
structures of the cities of the day, master planning sought to
rationalise matters by separating out land-uses, in particular
separating the home from the workplace. Transport systems,
especially roads, were recognised as a key parameter in the
functioning of the city. Their efficient operation involved
segregating traffic by its different types and requisite flows,
introducing high-density channels for high demand, and
remoulding transport and radically redesigning road layouts
and junctions. Such plans alone should act as the basis for the

Table 2.1 Early sources of the Modern Movement's urban imagination

Date	Centralist	Decentralist
Pre-1900	Sullivan	Ciudad Lineal
1900–9	Cité Industrielle	
1910–19	Città Nuova	Roadtown
1920–9	Ville-Tour	Crystal Cities
	Ville Contemporaine	Social Condensers
	Hochhausstadt	
	Metropolis of Tomorrow	
1930–5		Ville Radieuse
		Rio and Algiers plans
		Rush City Reformed
		Broadacre City

new urban order. The mistakes of the past – a phrase that could embrace almost any aspect of the existing urban environment that met with disapproval – should not stand in the way of this process.

Table 2.1 supplies an initial approximation of the guiding principles of design embraced by these schemes. For convenience, they are differentiated into two broad categories: centralist schemes that capitalised on the dynamics of metropolitan growth; and decentralist schemes that exploited the potential of mass transportation. The prime example of the former was 'the city of towers' (*la ville-tour*), a geometrically arranged, high-density agglomeration with a pronounced vertical dimension. The latter was best exemplified by 'linear cities' arranged in corridors along high-speed transport lines.

These broad ideas were complemented by another loosely articulated set of notions that concerned the future urban society. Again not tied to any specific political or moral agenda, they were culled from sources as varied as fringe religious groups, humanist and socialist philosophers, Social Darwinists, environmentalists, health cults, popular science writers and science-fiction illustrators. These gave rise to an imagery that found ready expression in the conventions of architectural illustration. A figure quietly contemplating a proposed vista of housing or the subtle depiction of artefacts that hint at life-style were not there just to lend a sense of scale. Rather, these emblems of the future society were an essential part of the visual vocabulary of architectural modernism. At one level, they provided an air of reassuring normality, with a sense of the continuity of everyday life within the new surroundings. At another, they symbolised transformation and the belief that the new city could be the setting for, indeed the agent of, a better society: more productive, more leisured and more harmonious. As this and subsequent chapters will show, that multivalent meaning served an important function in the urban imagination of the Modern Movement.

Trans-Atlantic influences

Manhattan, as Rem Koolhaus observed, was the twentieth century's Rosetta Stone.[5] Between 1890 and 1940, a series of technological innovations backed by plentiful corporate capital helped to transform Chicago and various East Coast cities, but none was recast more decisively than New York. The city of New York acquired the most vivid urban skyline in the world. The imagery of the city's skyscrapers and canyon-like streets, the cliff-like buildings stepping down to the wharves on the Hudson excited and appalled observers in equal amounts (Figure 2.2). Whatever their response, most observers felt confident that they were seeing the city of the future.

The skyline symbolised the dramatic changes taking place in the American economy and society. Developments in technology, industrial production, construction and personal trans-

Figure 2.2
The New York skyline in 1935, with the SS *Normandie* in harbour.

Figure 2.3
Temples of the new machine: Ford Factory at night.

portation all held potential to transform the American urban scene. The advent of Fordism, named after the system introduced by the car manufacturer Henry Ford in his factories after 1914, transformed industrial production (Figure 2.3).[6] Ford's ideas of mass production and industrialised systems, with their implementation of F.W. Taylor's ideas about labour management, fascinated those who pioneered architecture's Modern Movement since the same ideas might be applied to building and construction.[7] Industrial architecture, especially grain silos and railway coal staithes, also served as prototypes for possible adoption. Their use of structural steel and reinforced concrete showed the strength of these materials which, when introduced into the design of factory or office buildings, allowed larger window area and far greater use of natural lighting than was previously possible.

In the cities, the combination of load-bearing metal frames, passenger lifts and the telephone system for communication made skyscrapers economically as well as technically viable structures. It also challenged architects and others to work through the implications of concentrations of high buildings for urban form. As early as 1891, the Chicago-based architect,

Louis Sullivan published a newspaper article that envisaged a cityscape of setback skyscrapers.[8] The engraving that accompanied the article (Figure 2.4) depicted Gothic-style skyscrapers characterised by pronounced and progressive diminution of floor area in their upper storeys but gave no clue as to the precise magnitude of the resulting city. At best, it suggested blocks of high buildings situated on a grid of wide highways.

Yet almost as soon as some observers were sketching visionary plans of elegant tall cities, other were suggesting that New York contained all the ingredients necessary for severe congestion. Sir Raymond Unwin, for instance, calculated that the day-time population of the Woolworth Building in New York would occupy $1\frac{1}{4}$ miles of footway 20 feet wide on both sides of the street if walking to work at the same time. Furthermore, if just one in ten workers brought their cars to work, then parked cars would occupy the entire width of the 100 foot-wide roadway for the distance of almost one mile.[9]

One favoured solution to this problem lay in making beneficial use of verticality. Given the lack of room to widen highways and thoroughfares, multilevel circulation systems could accommodate higher-density flows. Drawings completed by Harvey Wiley Corbett in 1913, for instance, showed

Figure 2.4
Louis Sullivan's setback skyscraper concept.

a future New York with pedestrian walkways placed above a triple-decker scheme designed to ease street congestion. This would have vehicles at street-level and subways and goods railways underground. High above this arrangement was a systematic network of overhead bridges linking the sky-scrapers.[10]

The architectural illustrator and renderer Hugh Ferriss explored another range of possibilities. Ferriss was perhaps the foremost proponent of a genre that assimilated sky-scrapers into a romantic and mystic imagery. The perspective drawings in his book *The Metropolis of Tomorrow* depicted a landscape of deep-toned monumental stone skyscrapers and super-highways, resembling a landscape of mountains and canyons. The accompanying text also compared the sky-scrapers to huge crystals:

> Buildings like crystals.
> Walls of translucent glass.
> Sheer glass blocks sheathing a steel grill.
> No Gothic branch: no Acanthus leaf: no recollection of the plant world.
> A mineral kingdom.[11]

As a critic of simple-minded projection of trends for building height, his vision spaced the huge skyscrapers some distance apart with low-rise districts between them. The plan itself was dominated by a triangle at the vertices of which would be situated the Business Centre, the Art Centre and the Science Centre.

Ferriss's scheme remained rooted in the free market com-mercial ethos of late 1920s America. Despite the brilliance of the draughtsmanship, the underlying vision was soon eclipsed by the Depression and overtaken by the import of European modernist ideas in the post-war years (see Chapter 1). While it was perhaps the last time that the existing New York was seen by architects as the prototype for the ideal city of the future, the notion lived on in the popular media.

Around the turn of the century, H.G. Wells's book *When The Sleeper Wakes*[12] had depicted London in the year 2100 as a domed super-city housing 33 million people. Its imagery drew in equal measures on New York and on a retrospective glance at the Crystal Palace built for London's Great Exhibition (1851). By the 1920s the oppressive city of vast scale, with huge buildings rising above cavernous roadways, high-level bridges and thoroughfares, was the standard fare in science-fiction. Majority opinion, led by Fritz Lang's *Metropolis*, saw this as the recipe for dystopia. Made for Ufa Films (Berlin) in 1926 and inspired by Expressionism and the prototype of New York, *Metropolis* contained a sombre vision of a city stratified by class and function. In contrast to the stark workers' city buried far underground, the models of the upper city of Metropolis in the year 2000 (Figure 2.5) showed a vertical city devoted to business, consumption and the exercise of power.

Against this, a minority of film-makers used the same ingredients to convey a different message. David Butler's science-fiction musical *Just Imagine* (Fox Films, 1930), for example, depicted the New York of 1980 as a romantic and awe-inspiring place. The sets of the future city showed 200-storey skyscrapers and chasm-like motorways spanned by high-level bridges. The skies were dotted with flying machines of all descriptions (Figure 2.6). Intended as the background to a musical comedy, the luminous, almost ethereal quality of the lighting complemented the frivolous tone of the script. The result was a set that conveyed a sense of wonder rather than the claustrophobia and dystopia of Lang's vision.

Figure 2.5
The vertical city as dystopia: the upper city from Fritz Lang's *Metropolis* (Ufa films, 1926).

The highway

In the same way that the coming of the skyscraper encouraged the vertical growth of cities and increased centralisation, developments in transport technology promoted tendencies towards urban decentralisation. The growth of the streetcar and the electrified railway from the 1880s onwards created centrifugal forces that saw the middle-classes drifting away from the city. The spread of car ownership in the early years of the twentieth century dramatically reinforced these tendencies and presented prospects of radical change in urban form and society (Figure 2.7). The resulting visions comprised two main types.

One type consisted of linear city schemes, the earliest of which was 'Roadtown', a scheme proposed by a New York architect and patent investigator Edgar Chambless. Roadtown was a radical decentralist answer to the problems of the American metropolis. Chambless envisaged 'skyscrapers – laid on their sides rather than extending vertically – spanning the entire American countryside'.[13] The idea was for development in continuous narrow strips containing housing, industry and

Figure 2.6
The vertical city as romantic fantasy: New York from David Butler's *Just Imagine* (Fox, 1930).

Figure 2.7
The potential of mass car ownership in inter-war America.

services. There were integral transport systems, including a monorail system at basement level. By its very nature the scheme integrated town and country: not only was the 'town' resident's house situated near open countryside but the farmer would also live in Roadtown.[14]

Chambless based his linear city scheme around systems of public transport, but growing rates of private car ownership opened further prospects for urban form. Richard Neutra, for example, developed 'Rush City Reformed' to consider the potential impact of increased personal mobility. Although Viennese-trained, Neutra had entered practice in California in 1925. Neutra's scheme had a high-rise and high-intensity central business district, from which radiated belts of land that would comprise the linear city. Super-highways bounded each belt, permitting rapid access to the centre and comprising a grid within which lay rectangular neighbourhood units. Residential areas were divided into districts of similar housing designed to shelter families of a similar structure. Each unit would have an area of light industry to reduce commuting and traffic between and within neighbourhoods.[15]

The second type of new city prototypes were low-density decentralist schemes. Although most lie outside the remit of this study,[16] Frank Lloyd Wright's Broadacre City is well worth considering further. Wright began work on this project in 1924 and continued working throughout the 1930s.[17] Rooted in firm rejection of the big city, Broadacre City was an ultra-low density dispersed settlement. Its rationale rested on three innovations – the car, electrical intercommunication and standardised machine shop production. Families would have a basic housing plot of one acre on which to build homes to their choosing from prefabricated components. Wright allowed 'country seats', small towns possessing banks and public buildings, but large institutions, such as universities and factories, would be broken up and located among the houses. Most offices would be home-based. High-speed, gridded road networks would provide efficient movement for travellers by car and regular public transport. Petrol stations, positioned at strategic points in the communication networks, would have restaurants, leisure facilities and roadside markets – nodes of interaction for a mobile population.

Superficially, Wright's model anticipates elements of contemporary American urban growth, with decentralisation around shopping malls and low-density suburban housing. Some have also argued that Wright had no serious futurological agenda, because his scheme replicated the society of 1930s America.[18] Yet while the tendency to dress today's society in the clothing of tomorrow is a recurrent problem of utopianism, Wright was not attempting to replicate suburban society. Drawing on Thoreau's transcendentalist individualism, Jefferson's concept of self-government and Henry George's ideas about the right to land ownership, he sketched an ideal society intended to recover fundamental values and open possibilities for a new way of life.

Ciudad Lineal

If the Americans found an imagery of the urban future almost without looking, the European Modern Movement spent much time and effort consciously searching for it.[19] Although the first true modernist initiatives did not appear until the decade before World War I, there were a limited number of non-modernist schemes from the late nineteenth century that exerted considerable influence over the early Modern Movement. Of these, the most significant was Arturo Soria y Mata's *Ciudad Lineal*. Devised during the 1880s and developed on a limited scale in north-east Madrid from 1894 onwards, this linear city scheme was intended to tackle two problems. In specific terms it was designed to channel growth in the Spanish capital, combining the development of the urban fabric with an adequate transport system. More generally, it

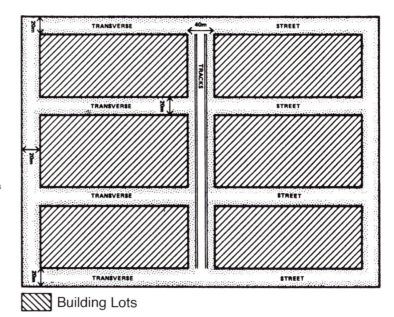

Figure 2.8
The basic format of Soria y Mata's linear city. Centred on its main spinal road with its tramway tracks, the development of the linear city offered rapid access to the existing city and close proximity to woodland and open country.

sought to answer the key problem facing Spanish society: how to modernise economically without creating severe social stresses.[20]

Soria's scheme is illustrated in Figure 2.8. The metropolis would be reorganised around a central spinal road that, for its entire length, also carried rail and trolley lines. Housing would take the form of separate family dwellings constructed on individual plots of land parallel to the main street; the individual plots reducing the danger of fast-spreading fires and epidemics. Soria placed houses, offices, shops, schools, factories and municipal buildings on geometrically regular plots that would form a lattice around the central corridor. By the very nature of the linear development, the city would be surrounded by open countryside and would seek a union between town and country. The city potentially could extend over great distances, with its central transport arteries maintaining efficient communications.

For Soria, the linear city embodied the very essence of progress and, as such, its form-giving feature – the central transport spine – became the symbol of modernity. Its significance transcended mere questions of access for it was argued that the development of the linear city form could bear the seed of profound social transformation. As Velez noted:

Soria thought that an environment constructed in harmony with the dominant 'form' of an era could mould the very nature of human relations and institutions. Thus, he contended that the 'progressive' spirit revealed in the linear city's form could affect the social system. Furthermore, since he believed that changes in the form reflected major changes in the development of civilisation, the growing dominance of the line signified not just the beginning of a new era, but also the end of an older form of human culture – namely, traditionalism.[21]

There was little discussion of social conditions in Soria's writings as he believed that the fundamental problem was not the socioeconomic system but the inability of traditional forms of urban organisation to meet the special requirements of the new industrial-commercial age. Quite simply, Soria worked on the assumption that people are totally products of their environment and, if there was a perfected urban habitat, all human relations would fall into their proper place. He scarcely broached the issue of social change, which perhaps explains why Soria could place his city within the framework of existing Spanish society without apparent contradiction. The linear city was conceived as the perfect environment capable of nurturing the development of a perfect social system.[22]

Cité Industrielle

Soria's new conception harnessed ideas about urban form and society to the decentralising tendencies of rapid transportation. His work was not directly part of the antecedents of modernism, but it nevertheless served as a prototype from which a long stream of related schemes derived. Similar thoughts apply to Tony Garnier's Cité Industrielle (industrial city). The son of Charles Garnier, the architect of the Paris Opéra, Tony Garnier formulated the main ideas for the Cité Industrielle between 1901 and 1904 while holding a Prix de Rome scholarship at the Ecole des Beaux-Arts. Given that a condition of the scholarship was to study in Rome at the Villa Medici, it is not surprising that the Cité Industrielle drew on classical as well as modern principles of design. From the former, he absorbed the use of axes and a gridiron pattern for street layout. From the latter, he absorbed faith in technology and new materials, notably reinforced concrete.

Garnier's Cité was a settlement intended for 35 000 people, a similar figure to that favoured by Ebenezer Howard for

Garden Cities. City development would proceed on the basis of a master plan. Residential districts were laid out in blocks without internal courts and set in park-like surroundings in affinity with the English tradition and with Camillo Sitte. Housing areas were separated from industrial zones but connected to the workplace by tramways. The houses themselves were far from the aesthetics of the Arts and Crafts Movement in their use of flat roofs, simple cubic geometries and their use of concrete and standardisation, yet retained elements of the picturesque in layout. Garnier explored the possibilities presented by new constructional materials and energy sources, particularly in portraying the potential uses of reinforced concrete for dwellings and public buildings.

The significance of this scheme perhaps rests on its influence on Le Corbusier, who met Garnier in 1907 and acknowledged a debt to him in *Vers une Architecture*.[23] Taken as a whole, Garnier's scheme supplied a convincing imagery for the functions of a modern town. It gave credence to the idea that rectangular cubic forms were the most suitable for reinforced concrete construction and for standardisation. Moreover, its design suggested that machine-age values of clear geometric repetition were the appropriate ones for modern society.

Città Nuova

If there remained a suspicion that Garnier took the Garden City and transferred it to a new setting, Italian Futurism opened a notable new source of urban imagery.[24] Founded in 1909 by the poet Filippo Tommaso Marinetti, the group included the painters Carrà, Russolo, Balla and Severini, the painter and sculptor Boccioni, the painter and architect Chiattone, and, latterly, the architect Sant'Elia. Futurists idolised the machine and its power to transform everyday life. The modern city, with its bustle and noise, was viewed as the setting for a glorious transformation in human affairs. The Futurist City itself would be 'like a gigantic machine', 'an immense, tumultuous, lively, noble work site, dynamic in all its parts'.[25] The past (the 'museum city') was a millstone round the neck of the present.

The Futurists never produced a full plan of their New City (*Città Nuova*) and the movement dwindled as an active force after World War I, with Sant'Elia killed in action in 1916 and

Figure 2.9
Apartment blocks in
Antonio Sant'Elia's vision
of the Città Nuova. The
illustration is notable not
only for its structural
forms, but also for its
multi-level circulation
systems.

Marinetti steadily drawn into the dystopia of Italian Fascism.
Nevertheless, the sketches left by Mario Chiattone and, in
particular, Antonio Sant'Elia provided powerful vignettes of
the urban future (Figure 2.9). They reveal the values that
Futurists felt would characterise the new age – speed, novelty,
dynamism, modernity and enormous scale. Avidly absorbing
ideas of verticality from American cities but rejecting their
historic adornments of skyscrapers, Sant'Elia's sketches portrayed a city made of reinforced concrete, steel and glass. The
centrepieces in the Città Nuova were not churches or civic
monuments, but railway termini, airports and power stations.
As the accompanying *Manifesto* noted:

> We no longer feel ourselves to be the men of the cathedrals, the
> palaces and the podiums. We are the men of the great hotels, the
> railway stations, the immense streets, colossal ports, covered
> markets, luminous arcades, straight roads and beneficial demoli-
> tions.[26]

Buildings themselves were grouped into high-rise clusters, with the impression of a new urban landscape of colossal buildings with stepped-back profiles towering above huge traffic arteries. There was suggestion of a multi-level street arrangement, with Sant'Elia envisaging that the street 'will no longer lie like a doormat at the level of the thresholds, but plunge storeys into the earth, gathering up the traffic of the metropolis connected for necessary transfers to metal cat-walks and high-speed conveyor belts.'[27]

Modern Man

After 1918, the most powerful centre for visionary ideas about the urban future switched to Weimar Germany. The war brought ruin to the wealthy classes of Germany, removing for some years the availability of significant numbers of private clients. In these circumstances, architects turned to commissions from the only clients available – the state and municipalities – to become involved in schemes for mass social housing (see Chapter 3). More generally, the external environment fostered an intellectual climate for new thinking about urban life. The 1920s saw the New Living (*die Neue Wohnung*), the New Architecture (*die Neues Bauen*), the New Objectivity (*die Neue Sachlichkeit*) and the New Man (*die Neue Mensch*) to whom the 'New' thinking would appeal.

The New Man – also known as 'Modern Man' – became a key notion in modernist thought. Distilled in equal measures from Social Darwinism, Friedrich Nietzsche's idea of the *Übermensch*[28] and plain utopianism, this normative model of human aspirations and behaviour was introduced into architectural circles in 1917 through the work of Henry van de Velde. An ardent admirer of Nietzsche, van de Velde wrote that Modern Man was: 'a product of the era of machine invention. He eats, sleeps, works and amuses himself efficiently, sweeping aside irrelevant objects despite their apparent glamour.'[29]

'Modern Man', then, was a thoroughly integrated member of the emerging industrialised society. Rational and progressive, he – and it was always a 'he' – had grasped the potential of technology to transform his and his family's life-style. Moreover, he favoured precisely those spartan values that were then in vogue with architects, such as hygiene and calisthenics, abstention, sacrifice, self-denial and re-birth.[30]

The desire for unadorned buildings and contentment with 'minimum habitations' (*Existenzminimum*) for dwellings were natural concomitants of these values and outlooks.

That the phantasm of 'Modern Man' emerged at a time of desperate shortages of resources should come as no surprise. It allowed necessity to masquerade as virtue. Armed with this idea, architectural theorists could justify almost any built forms, no matter how initially unpopular. They might not appeal to the 'bourgeois' society of the day, but would certainly meet the needs of the society to come; needs which architects themselves were specifying. Architectural ideology rarely wove a more self-insulating cocoon.

Weimar Visions

The Weimar period produced contrasting visions of future cities, ranging from the mystic to the ultra-rational. At one end of the scale lay the crystal visions of Expressionism. A pan-European movement that developed in the years before World War I, Expressionism emphasised the distortion and dislocation of modern life. Essentially hostile to the industrial metropolis, Expressionists turned to nature to generate visions of prospective cities. Particular emphasis was laid on structures based on the crystal, a symbol of natural and *social* perfection that had Biblical connections. The most powerful visions came from the work of Bruno Taut who between 1918 and 1921 developed the crystalline metaphor in a series of architectural fantasies designed to encourage the social and cultural redemption of a Europe emerging from war and revolution. These included projects for naturalistic settlements in the Alps; small and medium-sized star-shaped towns with houses shaped like crystals; and monumental civic buildings (*Stadtkronen*) intended for city centres.[31] These projects did not address practical planning but exercised an influence over the urban imagination of other architects, particularly through their advocacy of glass, the closest substitute for crystal, as a constructional material.

At the opposite pole of Weimar thinking came Ludwig Hilberseimer's *Hochhausstadt* (Skyscraper City). Hilberseimer taught at the Bauhaus and conducted research into town planning and its theoretical application. Like other Neue Sachlichkeit architects in Weimar Germany, he was interested in the relationship between the city, construed as a molar machine, and its component parts. Devised in the early 1920s, the Hochhausstadt envisaged a world in which types of dwelling unit and amounts of living space were unrelated to class. It contained huge slab blocks of flats placed on a grid, with shops and workplaces in five-storey podia beneath them. Pedestrian decks and bridges at sixth-floor level would link the blocks. In response to the growth of car-ownership, through-traffic was handled by cavernous roadways that separated the blocks, with residual movement by underground railway. The key variable was reduction of movement. Journeys to work or shops simply meant taking the lift. This brought the inherent problem that people would have to move every time they changed jobs, but Hilberseimer did not regard this as a significant drawback. In his view, future urban inhabitants would be happy with a more nomadic existence, satisfied with living in flats equipped as conveniently as hotel rooms and not feeling the need for private furniture.[32]

Hilberseimer's scheme was mostly received with enthusiasm as supplying a prototype that returned to first principles to address the problems of modern life. His subsequent observation that the exclusion of nature and greenery made his scheme 'more a necropolis than a metropolis' was not generally shared at the time. Even Hugo Häring, who criticised the scheme for resembling 'the swarming of an ant heap', attributed the error to an idea of the city already partly realised in North America. He concluded that 'it is not Hilberseimer's fault that we are a little appalled by his results'.[33]

The Soviet contribution

The Soviet Union generally held a deep fascination for intellectuals in the inter-war period. Until Stalin's suppression of the avant-garde ended the brief flowering of ideal city planning, there was a continual stream of ideas about urban form and the reconstitution of society emanating from the USSR. These, in turn, were widely reported in sympathetic publications in Western Europe.

In many respects, the material conditions resembled Weimar Germany. After recovery from war, revolution and civil war, Soviet architects found themselves faced with two challenges. First, they had responsibility for designing new settlements on virgin land in line with the nation's need for industrial development. Secondly, architecture was now an essential ingredient of social progress. Few architects believed that merely putting people in new buildings was enough to generate the new society, given their belief in the decisive importance of a transformation in the economic base of society. Yet settlements could act as 'social condensers'. Like electrical condensers transforming current, settlements could act as the scene for the transformation of society. Architects and city planners, therefore, had their parts to play in creating an appropriate environment for the future socialist society.[34]

These responsibilities, coupled with mistrust of Western concepts of the town, prompted profound debate on almost every aspect of town planning. There was sharp divergence in the strategies advocated. Traditionalists wanted to improve past practices rather than abandon them. Against them stood two groups of radical architects: rationalists who wanted new building forms based on 'objective' laws; and 'constructivists' committed to the reconstruction of the way of life. These disagreements spilled over into the design syntheses that were offered. At local level, options ranged from large blocks of flats to dispersed smaller groups of dwellings. At the urban level, opinion was divided between 'urbanists' and 'de-urbanists'. The 'urbanists', whose chief theoretician was Leonid Sabsovich, favoured large agglomerations of communal housing blocks clustered around the plants where the workers were employed. The 'de-urbanists' sought a new fusion of town and country. At one extreme, M. Okhitovitch recommended extreme dispersal. He recommended covering the whole country with a rectangular pattern of settlement based on a vast electricity power grid, neither favouring nor neglecting any area and countering the pull of existing large cities. Others, such as M.A. Miliutin and Lavrov, chose linear cities clustered along transport routes as their ideal city form.

In practice, limited versions of linear cities were built at the new industrial towns of Volgograd (Stalingrad) and Magnitogorsk. Early Soviet planners considered that the non-hierarchical character of this city form was considered 'particularly appropriate to the egalitarian aspirations of the inhabitants'.[35] The days of experimentation, however, were nearly passed. The strengthening of Communist Party control over planning matters ended both discussion of alternative forms and the avant-garde movements that supported them.

La Ville-Tour

The French contribution to thinking on the future shape of the modern city, initiated by Garnier, was continued by his colleague at the Ecole des Beaux-Arts, Auguste Perret. A notable innovator with reinforced concrete forms, he also coined the term *la ville-tour* ('the city of towers'). From 1920 onwards, Perret worked on schemes that combined verticality with effective movement systems and saw Fordism as holding a key to sociological transformation. None of Perret's designs survive, but an interview in the journal *L'Illustration* with Jean Labadié (1922) gave some impression of his thinking.

After noting the type of changes occurring in the central districts of American cities, Labadié described Perret's idea for a 15-mile avenue of 100 cruciform skyscrapers (*maisons-tours*) spread around the outer boulevards of Paris. The towers were built on ten-storey plinths, connected at their tops by walkways that allowed pedestrian movement. The towers that rose forty storeys above the plinth level would each house 3000 people. An artist's impression by Jacques Lambert indicated the aesthetic influence of New York's skyscrapers on the illustrator's thinking. The likely future city would contain Gothic-style tall buildings, wide avenues dotted with speeding cars and sweeping open spaces (although it is unclear whether Perret himself ever authenticated Lambert's drawing as truly representing his ideas).[36]

The scheme itself was not inherently practical; for example, the bridges between the buildings would have measured around 250 metres. Nor was it well received by his contemporaries, with Le Corbusier accusing Perret of throwing 'a veil of dangerous futurism over what was a sound idea'.[37] In particular, its replication of the Gothic trimmings of American skyscrapers drew scorn from modern architects who had rather different notions of the appropriate appearance of buildings. Nevertheless, Perret's ideas broadly captured the spirit of the early Modern Movement's thinking about the future city. As Le Corbusier himself noted, la ville-tour was 'a glittering epithet that aroused the poet in us. A word which struck the note of the moment. . .'.[38]

The urban visions of Le Corbusier

The true extent of Le Corbusier's influence over the Modern Movement's urban imagination remains contentious (see

Chapter 1), but there is no doubting that he successfully articulated holistic visions rather than a series of tactical exercises to solve isolated problems.[39] These coupled drawings with powerful rhetoric delivered in short staccato bursts, with the key expressions already italicised to serve as rallying slogans. Accompanied by powerfully evocative line drawings and photographs, they were always intended for promotional purposes; ideologically charged source material for the international group of architects that adhered to modernism. Yet they were not blueprints. As Ernö Goldfinger noted:

> Le Corbusier did these drawings and you could put them on the wall and admire them. But they did not tell you how to build the houses and streets or where to dig the drains. Not for a real city anyway . . .[40]

Moreover, while possessing considerable originality, Le Corbusier's plans were also remarkable for the dexterity with which he drew on the work of others. Design influences included Baron Haussmann, Eugène Hénard, Garnier, the Futurists, Bruno Taut, the formalism of the Ecole des Beaux-Arts, Auguste Perret and the gridded layout of the North American city. His ideas on society absorbed a similarly catholic range of influences. These included French regional-syndicalism, Utopian Socialism, Nietzsche, Saint-Simon, Taylorism, quasi-Fascist health and hygiene cults, and medieval monasticism. While these varying influences led him in different directions over time, no other modern architect synthesised ideas from so many sources or combined design and sociological ideas with the same facility.

Ville Contemporaine

Le Corbusier's published work on the future city began with fragmentary ideas for 'A City of Towers' (1920–3). This soon matured into his 'Contemporary City for Three Million' and culminated in the Ville Radieuse, which he continued to embellish for the rest of his life. The first attempts at devising imagery of the urban future are found in *Vers une Architecture*, which contains ground plans and impressionistic drawings of a City of Towers. These indicated 60-storey blocks of flats rising to over 230 metres and spaced 230–80 metres apart. The original caption stated that the towers would be placed among gardens and playing fields and that the main arteries, with motor tracks built over them, would allow rapid circulation of traffic.

When this book eventually appeared, these ideas had
already been incorporated into a full city plan for 'A Contemporary City of Three Million People', which Le Corbusier
exhibited at the Salon d'Automne in Paris in 1922. This, in
turn, was published in Le Corbusier's next major book *Urbanisme*.[41] The Ville Contemporaine (Figure 2.10) consisted of
three zones: the central city, a protected green belt (although
also the location for the airport), and the periphery containing
factories and the satellite towns where their workers lived.

The central city featured a rectangle containing two cross-
axial super-highways. At its heart was a six-level transport
interchange, a meeting place of underground and main-line
railways, road networks and, at the top, a landing-platform
for 'aero-taxis'. Around that point were 24 cruciform skyscrapers made from steel and glass, serving the city's civic and
commercial needs. Each was 60 storeys high and located in its
own parkland – its open aspect fulfilling the principle that Le
Corbusier termed *la grandeur de l'espace*. These buildings,
covering less than 15 per cent of the central area's ground-
space, would be raised on stilts (pilotis) so as to leave pan-
oramas of unbroken greenery at ground level. The general
impression was less that of parkland in the city than of a city
in a park.[42]

The Ville Contemporaine generated considerable interest as
a holistic conception of the future city, but equally attracted

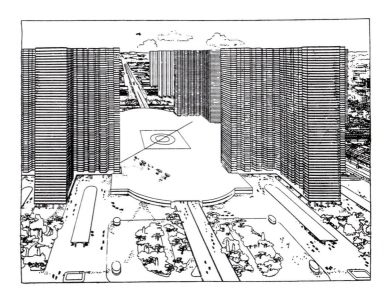

Figure 2.10
The central office towers
of Le Corbusier's Ville
Contemporaine with its
transport interchange.

critical comment. Fierce criticisms were directed at the class-based conception of life that it embodied, since Le Corbusier envisaged different classes being separately housed. Doubts were expressed about the Ville Contemporaine's scale and degree of centralisation. The city espoused space, speed, mass production and efficient organisation, but also offered a potentially sterile combination of natural and urban environments. Part of the reason lay 'in the Olympian formality of the designer's presentation which embodied a god's-eye view of the large-scale visual aspects, but neglected to deal convincingly with small-scale function'.[43]

Voisin Plan

If the Ville Contemporaine established Le Corbusier's reputation as an ideal city planner, the Voisin Plan established his claims to the mantle of Baron Haussmann. Named after the company who met printing and exhibition expenses, the Voisin Plan proposed the clearance and reconstruction of the Marais, the area of almost two square miles on the Right Bank of the Seine that contained Paris's business district (Figure 2.11). It reworked certain elements of the Ville Contemporaine. Le Corbusier proposed the construction of 18 double-cruciform 60-storey skyscrapers, surrounded by green open spaces. These buildings were intended to attract international corporations so that a modern Paris could act as a world centre for administration. There would be three clusters of luxury apartments, intended to keep the cultural elite in the city.

Particular attention centred on the road network. Le Corbusier wanted to destroy the street in order to save it. He was fully aware of the significance of the street in the drama of urban life, but believed that the traditional *rue corridor* ('corridor street'), with its rigid line of buildings and intermingling of traffic and pedestrians, was an impossible setting for that drama. Le Corbusier argued that the street had become: '*a machine for traffic, an apparatus for its circulation*, a new organ, a construction in itself and of the utmost importance, a sort of extended workshop'. Continuing this theme: 'it is in reality a sort of factory for producing speed traffic . . . We must create a type of street which shall be as well equipped in its way as a factory.'[44]

The new street system would have each functionally distinct traffic type occupying its own dedicated channel placed at different levels. Heavy traffic would proceed at basement level, lighter at ground level, and fast traffic would flow along

Figure 2.11
The Voisin Plan for Paris.

Figure 2.12
Pavillon de l'Esprit
Nouveau.

limited-access arterial roads that supplied rapid and unob-
structed cross-city movement. There would also be pedes-
trianised streets, wholly separate from vehicular traffic and
placed at a raised level.[45] The number of existing streets would
be diminished by two-thirds due to the new arrangements of
housing, leisure facilities and workplaces, with same-level
crossing points eliminated wherever possible.

A model of the Voisin Plan was first exhibited in the Pavillon de l'Esprit Nouveau at the Paris Exposition Internationale des Arts Décoratifs et Industriels Modernes in 1925 (Figure 2.12). Predictably, it caused outrage. Critics attacked its focus on the central city, where land values were highest and dislocations most difficult; the creation of vast empty spaces in place of close-knit streets with their varied civic life; and the proposed obliteration of much of the city's architectural heritage.[46] Although intended seriously, the Plan had immediate shock value, particularly for its determined approach to reshaping the central districts – the areas most resistant to change. Yet there was recent historic precedent for such action. Haussmann's far-reaching 'regularisation' of Paris was still within living memory. Whatever the admired virtues of the tree-lined boulevards, these were cut through the knotted entrails of the medieval city. In their day, they had aroused similar accusations of authoritarianism and philistinism. To some extent, therefore, Le Corbusier was merely following an established metaphor of planning as painful but necessary surgery designed to improve the health of the body.[47]

Linear cities and the Ville Radieuse

These criticisms of the Voisin Plan, coupled with reservations expressed about the social and political underpinnings of the Ville Contemporaine, led Le Corbusier in various directions. One was experimentation with linear city plans. Influenced by Chambless, Miliutin's linear city schemes in the USSR and the design of the Fiat Factory in Turin (with its roof-top car test-track), he completed a series of schemes with strips of urban development condensed into elongated megastructural forms. During a South American trip in 1929, he sketched plans for Rio de Janeiro, Sao Paulo, Buenos Aires and Montevideo featuring sinuous viaduct structures with residential accommodation stacked beneath the motorway on its roof. A later rendition of these ideas in the Algiers plan (1931–2) contained a continuous building, 15 kilometres long, 26 metres wide and 14 stories high. The sinuous nature of the viaducts, snaking their way from these ports to their mountainous hinterlands, dramatically revised the insistence on the straight line (Figure 2.13).

The other direction was development of the Ville Radieuse. The Ville Radieuse contained a sociological imagery intended to address criticisms directed against Le Corbusier's earlier work, while continuing to refine the design imagery of the

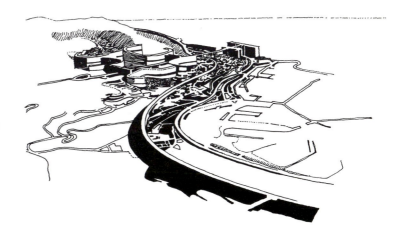

Figure 2.13
The Algiers Plan (1930).
The main commercial
buildings are down by
the harbour and are
connected by a great
viaduct with a vast
curving group of
interconnected blocks
of flats.

Ville Contemporaine. The plan for the Radiant City was first displayed at the Brussels meeting of CIAM in 1930 (see Chapter 3) although it was not available in published form until 1935.[48] It retained, but rearranged, the key features of the Ville Contemporaine. The basic ideas of free circulation and greenery were still present, but the juxtaposition of different land-uses had changed. For example, the central area was now residential instead of a skyscraper office core. The plan:

> was no longer a mandala of centralized power. Instead it spliced together an extendible linear city with the abstract image of a man: head, spine, arms and body. The skyscrapers of the Ville Contemporaine were rearranged away from the city centre at the 'head' . . . [The] 'body' was made up of acres of *à redent* housing strips laid out in a stepping plan to generate semi-courts and harbours of greenery containing tennis courts, playing fields and paths. These all faced south . . . [and] were raised on *pilotis* so that the entire surface of the city was a co-extensive, fully public space.[49]

Perhaps the most interesting feature of the Ville Radieuse was its conscious reworking of the design of housing. The idea of segregation of housing by social class was abandoned, replacing the different types of housing by high-rise dwelling units for 2700 people. These would have services that included communal kitchens, creches, shops and gymnasia supplied. Family size was now the guiding rule for housing allocation, without regard to the worker's place in the industrial hierarchy. These housing units were envisaged as an essential ingredient in constructing a 'classless society'.

In addition, there was conscious effort to sketch the life-style of inhabitants of the future city. Unlike Soviet architects, Le Corbusier believed in the power of architecture to bring social change without necessarily requiring the transformation in the economic base of society. The original name for the book *Vers une Architecture* was *Architecture ou Révolution*, signifying his belief in the power of architecture to alleviate the causes of social strife.[50] Yet he realised that envisaged benefits would come about only if individuals were willing to embrace the living patterns of the new urban utopia.

His arguments in support of that case replayed German discussion of the New Man. Taking leisure as an example, Le Corbusier asserted that the length of the working week would soon fall dramatically. As a result, leisure was potentially 'the menace of modern times', with the people potentially finding large amounts of free time on their hands.[51] Yet filling leisure time required a planned balance of activities that suited the needs of his vision. What were wanted were pastimes that worked to improve social cohesion and generated land-use demands that did not conflict with the general city schema. The pastime of gardening, for example, failed on both counts. It was primarily organised individually and generated demands for small plots of land that were antithetic to the desired creation of sweeping public open space. Rather different arguments, however, were used. In Le Corbusier's words:

> Growing carrots and turnips is not a means of entertainment. It is a job. *Modern man* [my italics], tired from his work in an office or factory, is not going to rest himself by turning to backbreaking agricultural work.[52]

Whether this had any known basis in real-world user preferences was immaterial. Le Corbusier had strong personal empathy with the idea of the New Man; indeed to some observers he was 'the very figure of the new man' himself.[53] Yet however personally appealing the notion, its strategic advantage was that the architect was free to specify precisely which activities, like gardening, individuals were happy to abandon and which they were keen to pursue. According to Le Corbusier, the latter comprised socially productive pursuits. They could consist of communal, disinterested projects 'achieved by the harmonious grouping of creative impulses directed toward the public good'. Alternatively, they might be participant sporting activities in which each person, young or old, 'would join his comrades in the races, the watersports, the walks that, given the immense amount of space available, will revivify their lungs, improve their circulation, strengthen their muscles, and fill them with joy and optimism'.[54] Either way, leisure activities took their place in the general scheme of things; a world in which enlightened and comprehensive policies of urban design would lay the foundations for a healthy society.

3   STAKING A CLAIM

Only in the architectural avant-garde were the ideal world of
art and the real world of empirical fact conflated without the
presumptive need for political revolution. Architecture
founded its promise largely on the belief that technology
could solve the practical and artistic problems of modern
social existence.

Alan Colquhoun[1]

Municipal housing schemes might seem modest undertakings
when measured against the lofty ambitions of ideal city plans,
but they represented valuable opportunities to make a statement when the only other commissions available were for
private villas or showpiece exhibition buildings. Housing
schemes allowed modern architects to present the public with
unfamiliar ideas about the design of built forms. They were a
proving ground for experiments in layout and construction.
They hinted at the new lifestyles on offer to the urban
proletariat. They provided architects with a chance to collaborate with one another and with industry. Above all, they
provided a valuable pretext for architects to stake an ideologically inspired claim for extension of their involvement in
the wider realm of town planning.

The initial sections of this chapter interweave these themes
when briefly discussing social housing in the Netherlands,
Belgium, Austria and, especially, the workers' estates (*Siedlungen*) of Weimar Germany. One such development, the Weissenhof Siedlung at Stuttgart in 1927, is identified as a key
event in delineating modern architects' shared interests in
town planning matters and in building the mythology of the
Modern Movement. The second half of the chapter deals with
the formation of CIAM. It discusses its founding ideals and the
progress of its first three Congresses, showing how initial
preoccupation with housing soon broadened into debate
about the shape of the future city. It then examines an episode
that provides important insight into the propagation of modernism, namely, whether or not the fourth Congress of CIAM
produced a statement of general principles of town planning
latterly known as the Athens Charter.

Social housing

The first significant opportunities for modern architects to participate in programmes for social housing occurred in the Netherlands when the city authorities in Amsterdam and Rotterdam commissioned schemes from their municipal architects. Hendrik Berlage, city architect of Amsterdam, designed estates in south Amsterdam (1902–20), using perimeter blocks of flats with interior courts devoted to gardens. These were intended to be units of collective dwelling, integrating model worker housing into a broader concept of urban living. Other members of the Amsterdam School adopted different strategies. Michel de Klerk, for example, designed five-storey blocks of flats at Spaarndammerplantsoen (1915–16) and Zaanstraat/Oostzaanstraat (1917–20) with Expressionistic façades. The intention was to lend dignity to workers' dwellings by means of monumentality, although, ironically, they were condemned as decadent and 'façade architecture' by critics.[2]

One of these critics was J.J.P. Oud, Municipal Architect for Rotterdam from 1918 to 1933 and a founder member of the De Stijl group.[3] Oud designed a series of housing complexes at Spangen, Tusschendijken, Oud Mathenesse and Kiefhoek (all in Rotterdam) and terrace-houses at Hook of Holland that expressed ideological commitment to technology and a sense of the power of architecture to achieve social transformation. In one of the later developments, Kiefhoek (1925–30), he produced a plan for 300 two-storey, single-family houses with associated social services (Figure 3.1). Oud believed that architecture should serve moral purposes, encouraging good behaviour and discouraging bad. The kitchens, for example, were designed on a narrow ground plan to make it difficult to use them as living rooms. Separate bedrooms were supplied for parents and children, with the possibility of separating children of opposite sexes. Apart from corner sites, the vast majority of the houses had a standard ground plan, so that it would have been possible to conduct experimental production of industrialised housing on similar lines to car production. Oud even talked about creating a 'Ford House' at Kiefhoek.[4] Lack of funds to cover the initial costs of establishing a production line, however, meant that the machine aesthetic of the development was in fact produced by traditional methods.

Figure 3.1
J.J.P. Oud, The Siedlung Kiefhoek, Rotterdam. Built 1928–1930, this view shows the way in which the wall-surface above the shops curves around the corner.

In neighbouring Belgium, work commenced on the Cité Moderne at Berchem-Sainte-Agathe near Brussels in 1921. Designed by the Flemish architect Victor Bourgeois, this development comprised rows of two-storey houses and maisonettes and three-storey walk-up flats laid out in a manner reminiscent of Garnier's *Cité Industrielle*. With their flat roofs, large windows and unornamented façades, the dwellings represent one of the first manifestations of the style that lay close to the heart of inter-war modernism.[5]

Superficial similarities were seen in France in a development of prefabricated housing that Le Corbusier designed for the industrialist Henri Frugès at Pessac, near Bordeaux. Although at first only asked to build some show-houses for Frugès's workers, Le Corbusier was able to build on his longstanding interest in prefabrication and develop this commission into a more ambitious 'Quartier Moderne'. He designed 130 houses between 1925 and 1928, using reinforced concrete frames with semi-industrialised building techniques on site. The difficulties experienced when using unfamiliar constructional methods and the delays arising from the protests of hostile local authorities foreshadowed the

problems repeatedly encountered by experiments in industrialised prefabrication.

Rather different developments were seen in Austria, where
the socialist Viennese city authorities resisted pressure to
develop garden estates on the city fringes in favour of estates
with large perimeter housing blocks enclosing sizable communal courtyards. Built between 1926 and 1933 and designed
by Karl Ehn, the Strassenhof, Bekelhof, Rakenhof and, particularly, the Karl Marxhof superblocks became some of the
most visited and iconographically influential housing developments in Europe.[6] From inception, they were designed with
integral social and communal facilities. The Karl Marxhof, for
example, contained public baths, offices, a youth hostel,
dental clinic, pharmacy, library, laundry, hospital and other
social facilities for the 5000–6000 people that lived in its 1382
flats.[7] Once again, they were a recipe for urban living rather
than simply dwelling units.

Siedlungen

Notwithstanding this broad scattering of examples, the most
significant involvement of modern architects in social housing
occurred in Weimar Germany. Economic revival and stabilisa-
tion of the mark brought an emergency programme of school,
hospital and, especially, house-building programmes. Germany faced acute housing problems after 1918. War damage
in East Prussia and elsewhere had left a shortage of two
million dwellings, causing severe overcrowding in Berlin and
other German cities. Although economic problems limited
activity before 1924,[8] the rate of construction rose from
124 000 dwelling units in 1924 to 320 000 in 1929 before the
Wall Street Crash and the persistent burden of reparations
effectively ended the housing drive.[9]

The key innovation in designing the new estates was *Zeilenbau* (row) housing. Under the Zeilenbau system, rows of
flatted housing were laid out at right angles to an east–west
road rather than the conventional system of constructing flats
around an interior courtyard. The north–south alignment of
the buildings ensured that rooms would face either east or
west to receive the maximum benefits of sun and light. The
layout was originally the idea of Theodor Fischer, who developed a Garden City-style development in this manner in the
Siedlung Alte Heide at Munich in 1919, but was brought

within the ambit of the Modern Movement by Otto Haesler. Haesler designed two Siedlungen, the Italienische Garten and Georgsgarten, at Celle, near Hanover in 1923–4. Their rows of identically aligned blocks of flats were roundly condemned for repetitious regularity by Bruno Taut and other members of the 'humanistic' wing of the German Modern Movement, but many subsequent schemes followed the basic ideas about layout.

The most significant were those developed by Ernst May, the city architect of Frankfurt. May, in collaboration with Martin Elsaesser and others, designed eight major housing developments for the city between 1925 and 1929. Collectively, these provided 15 174 living units – roughly 11 per cent of Frankfurt's total housing stock – primarily in peripheral estates of row housing. May's work was notable both for innovations in prefabricated concrete slab construction and for use of 'minimum habitation' (*Existenzminimum*) space standards to maximise the number of dwelling units created. Achieving these standards was dependent on extensive use of ingenious built-in storage, foldaway beds and kitchen design. Around 10 000 of the dwellings, for example, were equipped with the industrialised and ergonomic 'Frankfurt kitchen' which was intended to modernise and simplify household chores.[10]

Despite novelty of construction and interior furnishings, externally May's Siedlungen were remarkably conventional in all but their absence of period architectural detail. May had worked with Theodor Fischer in Munich and with Raymond Unwin in London, regarding his time spent at Unwin's office as 'the foundation on which the whole of my work is based'.[11] Hence despite using modernist forms, May always tempered his rationalism with a feeling for tradition. Even when housing schemes involved the grouping of very large blocks, they remained in touch with the Garden City tradition and even reached back to the quasi-picturesque plans recommended by Camillo Sitte.[12]

Walter Gropius attempted a different approach. Like Le Corbusier, he had a long-standing interest in prefabrication, starting with designs for standardised houses that he produced with his partner, Adolf Meyer, as early as 1910. Besides designing residential buildings specifically linked to the Bauhaus, of which he was Director between 1919 and 1928, his private practice also undertook housing schemes for municipalities and industrial combines. In 1926, for example, Gropius

Figure 3.2
Walter Gropius,
Working-Class Housing
at Törten-Dessau,
1926–8. The Siedlung's
Co-operative Stores are
in the foreground.

was commissioned by the city of Dessau to design a group of prefabricated one-family workers' houses at Törten (Figure 3.2). The reinforced concrete, cinder blocks, cross walls, beams and other major parts for the buildings were standardised, manufactured on site, and placed in position by crane. Altogether, 316 houses were completed by 1928, with some partly furnished by the Bauhaus workshops.

Weissenhof and after

No Siedlung, however, has a more important place in the history of the Modern Movement than the Weissenhof. It was built on the initiative of the Deutsche Werkbund, a body formed in 1907 that actively promoted synthesis between creative design and productive industry. It previously organised an exhibition at Cologne in 1914 that brought together artists, architects, craftsmen, scientists, engineers and industrialists to produce model office and factory buildings as well as a pavilion displaying machine technology.[13] In 1925, true to its maxim that the scope of modern design extended 'from the sofa-cushion to the city', the Werkbund's board proposed a new exhibition to deal with industrialised domestic architecture on the theme of *Die Wohnung* (the Dwelling). The site chosen for the exhibition was the slopes of a small wooded hill known as the Weissenhof, overlooking Stuttgart. A Werkbund Congress would also be held in Stuttgart, with its start coinciding with the start of the exhibition in 1927.

The general director of the exhibition, Mies van der Rohe, originally envisaged the exhibition Siedlung as a continuous urban form that sinuously followed the line of the hill, combining the intimate variety of a Mediterranean village with the fluid space of modern architecture.[14] The need to sell the houses after the close of the exhibition meant that the plan was revised to make each element more independent. This change made it possible for Mies to invite leading architects of the day to take charge of the design of buildings for discrete portions of the site. In all, 17 architects from five European countries participated in designing the 31 permanent dwelling units. These included Werkbund members such as Walter Gropius, Hans Scharoun and Peter Behrens, alongside foreign architects like Le Corbusier, Pierre Jeanneret, Bourgeois, Oud and Mart Stam.

The final site plan placed a small block of flats and short terraces of houses on the higher, western side of the site, with separate villas on the lower eastern edge. Although designed by separate individuals, Mies requested that the buildings should have flat roofs and walls of 'the lightest shade of colour possible' to give the settlement a unified appearance. Off-white was adopted as the colour for exteriors at a subsequent meeting, although discrete parts could be painted in different colours. The result was an unprecedented convergence in built forms. Exteriors were characterised by a simple regular geometry of defined planes, with general proscription of applied decoration and coatings of stucco over rough-cast concrete. Interiors displayed an austere spartanism that aimed to cut not only at the heart of consumer culture, but also at the way that bourgeois families used domestic space to construct identity and memory.[15]

When analysed dispassionately, there are many reasons for saying that the apparent unity displayed at the Weissenhof was either myth or a product of the tactics of representation. The constraint of having to produce designs for saleable one-family dwellings limited opportunities to create housing that hinted at new forms of urban living. The unified image of white-walled, flat-roofed buildings was partly produced through black-and-white photographic representation, although even at the Weissenhof modern architecture was never simply white. Only about one-third were painted in the approved off-white. Most had light-coloured walls, with dwellings by Stam, Le Corbusier and Pierre Jeanneret, and Bruno Taut decked out in bright colours.[16] Moreover, the style was more permissive than is commonly recognised. Some designs were clearly intended as prototypes for repetition elsewhere, others were site-specific. Beneath the commonly applied rendering lurked a variety of construction methods.[17]

Yet differences recognised with hindsight do not erode the fact that the Weissenhof was a promotional masterpiece. It showed the potential of mass-produced housing and presented an instant embodiment of the universal architectural style that Walter Curt Behrendt had recently described in his book *Der Sieg des Neuen Baustils* ('The Victory of the New Building Style').[18] The extensive coverage of events at Stuttgart in both professional and popular media made the Weissenhof a cause célèbre for detractors and proponents of modernism alike. Detractors criticised its 'cosmopolitan' character and machine aesthetic with a nationalist zeal tinged with xenophobia.[19] By contrast, enthusiasts saw it as a place of pilgrimage. A total of more than 500 000 visitors came while the exhibition was open and many others visited the site subsequently. They were presented with a spectacle that implied not only the collective vision of the international Modern Movement, but that here was a universal architecture, produced by rational application of technology, that transcended cultural context.

That theme was further emphasised five years later when the Museum of Modern Art in New York held its first architectural exhibition. Held between 9 February and 23 March 1932, the 'Modern Architecture – International Exhibition' presented developments in modern architecture to the American public.[20] Strongly shaped by the aesthetic and moral sensitivities of the historian Henry-Russell Hitchcock,[21] the exhibits were grouped into three sections. The first celebrated the work of leading European exponents, Le Corbusier, Oud, Gropius and Mies; Richard Neutra, by then was already practising in America; and comparable American architects, Frank Lloyd Wright, the subsequently obscure Bowman brothers, Raymond Hood and the practice of George Howe and William Lescaze. The second section, called 'The Extent of Modern Architecture', surveyed 40 projects by 37 architects from 15 countries – each represented by a single photograph. A late addition to the exhibition, this section was intended to beef up the notion that modern architecture was a global and not just a Euro-American phenomenon. The third section focused on large housing projects from America (e.g. Clarence Stein and Henry Wright's Radburn and Sunnyside Gardens schemes) and Europe (including the work of Oud, Haesler and May). While expressing no great enthusiasm for the design of

existing Siedlungen,[22] the exhibition organisers shared the
Weissenhof's intent of drawing together different expressions
of the same themes. Exhibits were linked through a cohesive
modern style that grew from a functionalist theory of design.
It was termed the 'International Style'.

The International Style was supposedly defined by three
principles: emphasis on volume as opposed to mass; regularity
as opposed to symmetry; and dependence on the intrinsic
elegance of materials rather than applied decoration. As the
eclectic group of exhibits showed, the International Style
seemed equally applicable for domestic, office, retail, industrial or commercial buildings. Moreover, given that there was
no single set of political beliefs or industrial production
involved, it was possible to replicate the International Style
endlessly as an expression of modern design. Partial though
the evidence may have been, no other contemporary architectural movement could appropriate a promotional message
that was anything like as powerful.

Besides its stylistic significance, the Weissenhof was also
important as a point of convergence, bringing the individual
leaders of the Modern Movement together in one location
and making possible direct comparisons between their work.
Those comparisons were not always to the advantage of the
architects concerned. Whatever the public displays of camaraderie, fierce rivalries existed just below the surface. At an
initial conclave in Stuttgart in June 1927, for example, Mies
reportedly argued that 'the movement must now be cleaned
up'. The group notionally identified to carry out the vetting
process was Mies, Gropius, Oud, Stam, Le Corbusier, Hans
Schmidt, Cornelis van Eesteren and Sigfried Giedion. Immediate attempts to do so produced little, but the idea surfaced of
generating an alliance of modern architects motivated by the
correct spirit. Even though there were no direct links, this
broad intention became important in 1928 with the establishment of CIAM.[23]

CIAM

If housing projects supplied the main practical outlet for
efforts to make statements about the city in the mid-1920s,
the foundation of the *Congrès Internationaux d'Architecture Moderne* clearly indicated the nature and scale of the Modern
Movement's ambitions. From inception its Congresses and

meetings of its organising council, the imposingly named *Comité International pour la Réalisation des Problèmes de l'Architecture Contemporaine* (CIRPAC), explicitly addressed urban problems and their solution. CIAM possessed little authority outside its own circle and, at best, displayed members' ideas rather than created schemata to guide their work, but its symbolic importance was immense. CIAM gave modern architects a platform that they would not have received in existing professional bodies. It fostered collective feelings of shared purpose and helped to codify the ideological mission of the Modern Movement. Capturing something of the heroic mystique woven around CIAM, for example, Auke van der Woud[24] remarked that:

> Architects who tried to adapt to the structural changes in society and prepare themselves to meet the demands made in respect of industrialization, housing and town planning in a world subject to a population explosion banded together in CIAM. . . . In the face of these gigantic tasks, they saw rationalization and standardization as the prime requisites for being able to solve the building problem in a humane manner.

In doing so, the new organisation freely appropriated the idea of camaraderie central to the rhetoric of the avant-garde. For public consumption at least, CIAM was a 'round table of architectural knights embarking on a collective crusade to ameliorate the modern city through large-scale rationalized planning'.[25]

Reality was more prosaic. The underlying power struggles seen at the Weissenhof and elsewhere belie the image of committed fraternity conveyed by these statements. Maxwell Fry, who participated in CIAM meetings from 1933 onwards, argued that frictions were endemic to CIAM:

> There was always a little friction in CIAM between the French, in the person of Corb, and the German/Dutch. This started in the 1930s. Gropius stood for another method in achieving the ambitions of CIAM and his method in some respects was wider.[26]

During the early years, these tensions proved mostly creative, providing a lively forum for ideas about housing and town planning when steady deterioration in the external environment made pan-national contacts difficult. In later years tensions between different factions proved increasingly corrosive, eventually splitting CIAM on ideological and generational grounds.

La Sarraz

The origin of CIAM illustrates the role played by perceived threat, real or otherwise, in encouraging avant-garde groups to work together. Le Corbusier and his cousin Pierre Jeanneret had submitted an entry in January 1927 for the competition to design the League of Nations building in Geneva. The rumour circulated that their entry was the jury's original choice as outright winner, but that the French juror Lemaresquier had argued for its exclusion because the drawings were mechanically reproduced rather than in ink.[27] This rejection was compounded by the local press's denunciation of the design as 'cultural Bolshevism' and by Le Corbusier's belief that the eventual winning entry plagiarised his ideas. Taken together, they produced a deep sense of injustice and of being under attack.

Contacts developed from the League of Nations controversy prompted a local dignitary, Hélène de Mandrot, to offer to host a meeting of modern architects at La Sarraz, her château near Lausanne. Le Corbusier supported the idea, insisting that Karl Moser, Professor at Zurich's Technical College and elder statesman of the Swiss Neues Bauen group, should preside over the meeting. The Swiss influence was later augmented further when Giedion, an art-historian at the University of Zurich, was chosen as Secretary-General of the new organisation.[28]

Le Corbusier then wrote the agenda for the Preparatory International Congress on Modern Architecture (later known as CIAM I). Arguing that the meeting needed concrete objectives, he framed six questions as the basis for its proceedings. These included the virtues of standardisation and rationalisation in the production of built forms, the links between architecture and the wider economic order, and town planning.[29] At a stroke Le Corbusier's schedule prescribed rationality, standardisation, geometric form and functionalist architecture as the starting points for the discussions of the three-day meeting in June 1928. It also left a lasting impression on the outlook of the new association.

The Declaration issued after CIAM I located architecture 'in its true sphere which is economic, sociological, and altogether at the service of humanity'. The Declaration comprised 23 statements grouped into four main headings. The statements on 'Architecture and Public Opinion' and 'Architecture and its

Relations with the State' presented the modern architect's credentials for an enhanced role in the future. The statements on 'General Economy' argued that the most efficient methods of production arose from rationalisation and standardisation. The five statements on 'Town Planning' affirmed the commitment to a functionalist perspective:

> Town planning is the organisation of the functions of collective life; it embraces the countryside as well as the cities . . . Town planning cannot be determined by the claims of a pre-existing aestheticism; its essence is functional order.

Subsequent clauses mapped out three key functions of the city – *habiter, produire, se délasser* (shelter, work and relaxation) – that were bound together by a fourth function, *circulation*, (transport and communications).[30]

The key mechanisms for carrying out town planning were identified as control over land-use, legislation and regulation of traffic. Another clause committed CIAM to approving land redistribution, but did so in a way that smacked of Le Corbusier's hope to escape from conventional politics (see Chapter 2). The chaotic partition of land through sale, speculation and inheritance should be abolished through 'just division between owners and the community of the unearned increment resulting from works of joint interest'.[31] Redistribution, therefore, still left private owners to share the fruits of development work with the community. Not surprisingly, the failure to address the political implications of this strategy left Le Corbusier and CIAM open to attacks from the left and right of the political spectrum.[32]

Superficially, unanimity reigned. The Declaration was signed by all 24 architectural participants. The emerging rhetoric saw CIAM as a 'congress of collaboration, not a congress in which each would report on his own specific field'.[33] Certainly its selection of specific foci for research and development of common formats for presentation of findings at Congresses testified to a willingness to focus on shared problems and tasks, but outward appearances concealed major disagreements.[34] Hugo Häring, for example, argued in vain at La Sarraz for an organic conception of building rather than the rationalist and functional approach adopted. The Austrian delegate Josef Frank also found the latter approach unpalatable, soon withdrawing to pursue a design strategy that stressed the importance of tradition and history.

Differences were also apparent in the names chosen for the new organisation (a matter not covered by the Declaration of La Sarraz). The German version of the organisation's title, *Internationale Kongresse für Neues Bauen*, had different connotations from the French *Congrès Internationaux d'Architecture Moderne*. This involved:

> a difference of opinion regarding the profession. *Neues Bauen* signified a repudiation of *Architektur*, of the art of fine building, and the espousal of the completely rational building technique. *L' Architecture Moderne* wanted to remain the fine art of building, but with the application of modern means. The attitudes of Gropius, May and Meyer towards the profession illustrate the one standpoint, the ideas of Le Corbusier, which he made particularly clear in *Vers une Architecture* (1923), the other.[35]

While seemingly subtle, this distinction translated into sharp divergences of approach when applied to an issue like social housing. The Czech and German Neues Bauen architects demanded more practicality than the conceptual approach favoured by Le Corbusier and his supporters.

Housing issues

In the short term, the former approach prevailed, despite the initial influence that Le Corbusier had exerted over CIAM I through creating its agenda. The German group alone had the focus and organisation to sustain the new association. Its belief that dwelling had primacy over the other functional elements ensured that the early Congresses and meetings of CIRPAC were dominated by housing issues. The focus only changed significantly when, first, economic recession put paid to the German public housing drive and, secondly, the rise of National Socialism put paid to the German Modern Movement itself.

CIAM II was held in Frankfurt in October 1929 at the invitation of Ernst May, whose housing schemes for the city were then nearing completion. Not surprisingly, CIAM II's theme was housing for lower income groups and the notion of the minimum dwelling (*Die Wohnung fur das Existenzminimum*). Extensive questionnaires, amounting to 38 pages, were sent to the 16 national delegations for completion before the Congress. These sought extensive statistical data on minimum incomes, building costs, space standards and a host of other details to act as a basis for discussion. As very few delegations completed the task, the focus of proceedings switched to an exhibition of around 100 ground plans of dwellings. These were supplied by members and redrawn by May's housing department to standardise their scale and cartographic conventions.[36]

The lack of firm conclusions emerging from CIAM II, due to lack of time and poor preparation, saw CIAM III return to the theme of low-cost housing and rational site planning (*Rationelle Bebauungsweisen*). It met in November 1930 in Brussels, another city actively engaged in constructing social housing. During its formal proceedings, the Congress discussed the relative merits of laying out areas with different styles of housing. The 56 examples considered covered the spectrum from freely grouped low buildings, through regularly aligned low-rise, medium-height and high-rise buildings. Displays of site plans plus associated statistics provided the basis for comparisons.

CIAM III was no more successful than its predecessor in generating positive results. It failed to establish any general guidelines for the dimensions, layout and management of low-cost housing other than recommending experimental use of high-rise buildings. Ironically, its most enduring result lay in highlighting an area of disagreement. While most exhibitors addressed the neighbourhood scale, Le Corbusier argued for the need to see housing schemes in their wider urban context. His early version of the Ville Radieuse, first shown at this Congress, proposed standardised dwellings in elongated blocks with major roads constructed on piles at first-floor level in order to allow free layout of footpaths. This scheme contrasted markedly with the Zeilenbau-influenced contributions of the German contributors, especially Walter Gropius. Each represented 'a concept for a modern city: a healthy, green city amenable to traffic',[37] but illustrated their divergent views about the future city.

The Functional City

The stage was set for further discussion of town planning. Delegates at Brussels chose the 'Functional City' as the theme for CIAM IV.[38] This Congress, initially seen as the first in a series, would ask member groups to prepare analyses that highlighted the problems of large cities in their home coun-

tries. Later Congresses – which, as events transpired, were
never held – would then deal with the programme for the
new city. Not all supported this strategy. Czech delegates and
the 'proletarian' wing of the German delegation, led by
Arthur Korn, argued that CIAM should move directly to
working on models for the new city rather than waste time
analysing the problems of anachronisms. Perhaps fearing that
any such move would produce little, given the range of
opinions represented, the majority view favoured examining
existing cities as a first step. The Dutch Group, led by van
Eesteren, agreed to supply a set of Guidelines for CIAM IV to
ensure that member groups prepared their exhibits to a
common remit.

These were presented to a meeting of CIRPAC in Berlin
(June 1931) and contained three main stipulations. The first
required participants to gather written information about the
local circumstances in their chosen cities. Secondly, they
would produce three sets of functionally based plans to show:
residential, work and recreational areas; the traffic network;
and the relationship between the city and its surrounding
region.[39] Thirdly, all participants would employ the same scale
as well as a standard set of symbols that was originally devised
for the Plan for Greater Amsterdam. It was hoped that the
Congress would then have a meaningful basis for cross-
national comparisons of the plans and, in turn, synthesis of
broader ideas for improved city design.

The Guidelines effectively committed members to a specific
form of plan-making. In some respects it drew on the
sequence of survey-analysis-plan first enunciated by Patrick
Geddes, but each stage of the process was constrained by the
predetermined functional approach. Reliance on extensive
survey work, especially concerning data collection on social
and economic conditions, was retained but the type of
information gathered was prescribed by the needs of the
exercise. Other data of potential interest to plan-making, such
as information relating to civic and cultural life, were largely
omitted. The analysis stage was also predicated on the functional approach, mapping data into the four categories and
reporting general features of needs and wants accordingly.
This perforce influenced the shape of any broader principles
that might emerge in the plan.

Perhaps inevitably in view of the mounting political difficulties in Europe, CIAM IV had a long gestation period. The

leadership of CIAM initially intended to hold the Congress in Moscow in 1932. It already had a standing invitation from the Central Council of Housing Cooperatives (*Tsentroshilsoyuz*) and a number of distinguished architects such as May, Hans Schmidt and Mart Stam had recently moved east to participate in the town-building programme (see Chapter 2). Initial delays, due to uncertainty about responsibility for organising the Congress, led to postponement until June 1933. In March 1933 Weinschenker, who had taken charge of promoting the Moscow Congress, contacted the leadership of CIAM requesting further postponement until 1934. An emergency meeting of CIRPAC in Paris resolved to decline the Russian invitation on the grounds that 'organisational difficulties' made it impossible to hold this meeting.

Whether or not this was a pretext is unclear. Giedion saw this occurrence in ideological terms: 'We immediately understood the reason for this measure: the Avantgarde had no place in Stalin's Russia.'[40] Certainly, the political situation in Russia had swung decisively against modernism. Soviet theorists argued that Western ideas of modern architecture were an outgrowth of contemporary capitalism; that its aesthetics were a symptom of the decline of bourgeois culture; and that its idealistic-utopian direction was a counter-revolutionary attempt to bypass the natural stages leading to Socialism.[41] Debates over the revolutionary credentials of modern art and architecture, however, had been commonplace in the USSR since 1920. The extent to which this was a permanent change in official policy is clearer in retrospect than at the time. That point gives credence to the opposing view expressed by Ernö Goldfinger, then Secretary of the French group of CIAM, that: 'There was never any question of political reasons, simply difficulties of communication.'[42]

CIAM IV

Another venue was quickly sought. Acting on Marcel Breuer's suggestion, the leadership chartered a cruise liner, the SS *Patris II* owned by the Neptos company of Paris, for a round-trip between Marseilles and Athens. Literally as well as figuratively cast adrift by events, CIAM IV was held between 29 July and 14 August 1933. A schedule of the Congress's day-to-day business is shown in Table 3.1.

Table 3.1 Programme for CIAM IV

29 July 1933	Formal opening; speeches by van Eesteren (CIAM president) and Le Corbusier
30 July–1 August	*Appointment of Committees*
	Athens Exhibition, Protocol, Press, Resolutions, Publications, Statistics
	Meetings
	Explanation of maps by group members
1 August	15.00 arrival in Athens. Social visits.
2 August	Official opening of Athens meeting
3 August	Exhibition of maps and works of members in Hall of École Polytechnique
4 August	Continuation of explanation of maps
5–9 August	Free time for visits to Greek islands
10 August	15.00 departure for Marseilles
10–13 August	Remaining maps explained
	Meetings of Committees, preparation of reports and resolutions
13 August	17.00 arrival in Marseilles
	Delegates meeting
14 August	Delegates and Resolutions Committee meetings

Source: compiled from MARS Circular Letter II, file SaG/90/2, British Architectural Library, pp. 2–3.

The Congress blended symposia with vacation. It was divided into three segments. The main working sessions were held on the outward and return sea voyages, with official receptions, excursions and an exhibition during the week's stay in Athens. The sessions held on the promenade deck of the ship (Figure 3.3) primarily involved presentation and discussion of each of the 33 city plans produced by the 17 national groups.[43] While in Athens, the plans – many of which were of considerable size[44] – were displayed alongside one another in the Hall of the École Polytechnique, along with other works that individual members wished to display (e.g. see Figure 3.4). Lectures by major participants were interspersed during the proceedings, including Le Corbusier on 'Air, Sound, Light', van Eesteren on the Greater Amsterdam Plan, and the Austrian statistician Otto Neurath on his graphical system of representing social statistics.

An Athens Charter?

The contentious aspect of CIAM IV concerns its outcome. Conventional wisdom holds that its deliberations directly led to a document known as the 'Athens Charter' that definitively

Figure 3.3
CIAM IV meeting on the
promenade deck of the
SS *Patris II*.

stated CIAM's view of town planning. That view became part
of the 'official' history of CIAM and was widely endorsed by
those with only secondhand knowledge.[45] Other observers,
including participants in CIAM IV, cast doubts on these interpretations. Ernö Goldfinger denied that any statement of
principles was ever produced. He suggested that the sheer
bulk of exhibits had meant there had been very little time for
such principles to emerge and that retrospective attempts to
produce an Athens Charter did not do justice to the proceedings of CIAM IV:

Seven or eight years later, Le Corbusier in Paris and Sert, who had already gone to the United States, wrote this *Charte d'Athènes*. There was never any question of any such document when we were in Athens. There was a large exhibition, but that is all.[46]

E 7   PERSPECTIVE CAVALIERE

Figure 3.4
Architectural project shown by Ernö Goldfinger in the exhibition at Athens for CIAM IV. The diagram shows a self-contained 27-storey housing scheme with services and a nursery school on the roof.

Maxwell Fry supported this position. He stressed that membership of CIAM brought 'a very serious responsibility' and that there was a genuine intention to produce a statement of principles of town planning, but that there was insufficient time to do so.[47]

That view is substantiated by available documentation. It was difficult to get real consensus at CIAM IV. Although subsequently given an image of camaraderie and successful dialogue by commentators, the Congress took place against a maelstrom of uncertainty and dissent. The rise to power of the Nazis in March 1933 and their sustained attack on modern architecture had already decimated the German Modern Movement and removed the intellectual drive of the group that had sustained CIAM during its early years. CIAM IV was beset by rumours of schism, most notably the potential formation of an alliance of left-wing architects by André Lurçat, a founding member of CIAM. This did not happen, but the rumours were persistent enough for Giedion to threaten darkly that:

> CIAM does not, of course, include all modern architects, but only those who are willing to work both actively and altruistically with us. It is a question of self-preservation for us to eliminate all groups or individual members who are unable or unwilling to cooperate in this spirit, irrespective of their particular qualifications. A purge of CIAM is imminent, and this may have to include some of our most prominent members.[48]

Added to these difficulties were the organisational and procedural problems of a hastily rearranged Congress. Wells Coates, a founding member of the newly formed MARS Group and an accredited English delegate to CIAM IV, summarised the range of problems encountered:

> The Congress was hampered (a) by lack of organisation and precise procedure (b) difficulty of combining work with holiday (c) absence of strong German delegation (Gropius being unable to attend) and also adequate French delegation (d) Le Corbusier's airy superfoetations (e) delays due to language difficulties (f) expressions of national and political temperaments.[49]

Indeed the poor record of inter-group cooperation prompted suggestions to reorganise CIAM into three 'temperamentally similar' geographical groups – Anglo-Scandinavian, central European and Mediterranean – rather than retain the existing pattern of unified international gatherings.[50]

This background underlines the likely difficulties faced in
any attempt to produce written reports or communiqués that
conveyed the collective will of the meeting. Following the
precedent set by earlier Congresses,[51] it was always intended
to publish a volume that gave wider circulation to ideas
generated at CIAM IV. The format of the Congress was established with this in mind, since the common brief provided a
basis for comparative analysis and statement of general principles. A Committee on Resolutions was elected at the start of
the Congress to coordinate this task and to provide collective
findings for a final report. It comprised ten delegates: van
Eesteren, José Luis Sert, Werner Moser, Rudolf Steiger, Ernst
Weissmann, Szymon Syrkus, Coates, Gino Pollini, Piero Bot-
toni and Giedion.

They found it difficult to make the desired progress. Most of
the meeting was occupied by lengthy discussion of individual
exhibits. Despite the standard format, the quantity and diversity of the exhibited materials meant that there was very little
time to delve into the exhibits in any depth. At the end of the
Congress, there were three options on publication:

> 1. 'Say something' (not necessarily connected with work pre-
> sented to Congress – Le Corbusier) 2. 'Do nothing' (with work
> presented, except to publish it as quickly as possible without
> further analytical research – van Eesteren, Giedion and most of
> the Swiss Group, with other adherents) 3. 'Do this' (with work
> presented, and lead to further work – MARS, Spaniards, Yugo-
> Slavs, and others).

The sub-group responsible for drafting the final communiqué,
consisting of Coates, Sert and Weissmann, took the third
option. Their draft report was concerned less with summaris-
ing agreed precepts than with creating an agenda for the
future. They suggested three *lignes generales* for further
programmes of work by member groups. These were: continuation of analytical work on maps, using supplementary
standardised questionnaires; preparation of schema for
replanning the different cities together with regional plans;
and preparation of projects by which groups addressed the
most urgent problems in their chosen cities.

By contrast, it took several months for any definitive draft
of general principles to emerge. These were termed *Feststellun-
gen* (Statements) in German, but were perhaps more accurately rendered by the French term *Constatations*
(Conclusions), with its sense of the findings of an inquiry. As

originally devised these comprised just nine pages of typed transcript. Besides an introduction and closing resumé, the main findings grouped under the four functional headings with an additional section on the special problems of historic areas of cities.[52]

'Dwelling' brought together observations on the deficiencies of sanitation, pollution, crowding and open space availability in different areas of the city and the failure of existing zoning laws. Suggested improvements included siting residential areas where they could enjoy better sanitation, light and air, in particular avoiding locations near heavily used streets due to the noise, dust and pollution created by traffic. It was observed – and no more than that – that modern technology made possible high buildings which, spaced at considerable distances, left open space and green areas for parks.

With regard to 'leisure', the authors analysed the deficiencies in existing provision, especially for the poorest areas of the city. Residential areas needed access to green space with all necessary leisure facilities. The green areas required protection but were appropriate sites for kindergartens, elementary schools and community facilities. Planned land reclamation might increase the supply of leisure space, although there were few substantive suggestions as to how to achieve this desired goal.

The findings on 'work' noted the ill-coordinated locational patterns of housing and workplace, with journeys-to-work of one hour in Berlin and $1\frac{1}{2}$ hours in London. The document highlighted problems of rush hour congestion and of business districts having no room to expand without destroying residential areas. Recommendations included reducing the distance between home and workplace while retaining a barrier of open space between residential and industrial areas; allowing only small-scale industrial activities (e.g. repair workshops) in residential areas; and locating industrial areas close to major road and rail transport routes.

On 'circulation', the document recognised how the legacy of the past impeded the efficient running of the city. Rigorous statistical analysis was needed to regulate and organise the transport network. Road provision should recognise the different speeds of movement and varying functions of traffic within networks. Recommendations for improving flows included creation of multi-level crossing points and separation of pedestrian routes from roads used by cars. Green space should separate housing areas from major routeways.

The penultimate part of the document comprised a short section on the need to conserve historic buildings, a subject close to the heart of the Italian group at CIAM IV. Conservation of buildings was approriate if they truly represented the past, did not constitute a health hazard and neither stood in the way of developing the transport system nor affected the organic growth of the city. The closing resumé consisted of brief observations about cities being unplanned and failing to meet the demands of their inhabitants. The 'functional city' – a phrase sparingly used in the document – was a recipe for blending spiritual with material values, liberty with collective action. Planning for the various urban functions must refer to the human scale, to the daily rhythm of work, recuperation and leisure. The resumé repeated the small number of tangible proposals for change to the circulation system and again emphasised the need to view city planning in its regional context.

Taken as a whole, the first draft of the Constatations constituted a remarkably un-Olympian document. The product of a small Committee rather than the assembly as a whole, its contents were fragmentary and contained no specific political view other than a gentle reformism. The tone throughout was far from aggressive or doctrinaire; outlining a commitment to a functional analysis but propounding few general principles. With the possible exception of the statements on street patterns, the Constatations mostly stated ideas that were common currency for groups interested in social improvement through redesigning the built environment. Moreover, the drafted clauses were just recommendations. The final decisions about the concluding acts of CIAM IV and any programmes for the future were delegated to the Secretariat who had responsibility for advancing CIAM's activities in the period between meetings.

Transformations

From this point, the findings of CIAM IV would undergo a series of transformations before emerging as the Athens Charter. The initial role in devising general principles was played by the Swiss group, indeed as Ernö Goldfinger remarked: 'If you wanted to know more about where any general principles came from, you would have needed to ask Giedion and his friends.'[53] The Swiss easily comprised the largest group at

CIAM IV with 31 delegates – as against 16 for France, 9 for Greece and 6 each for Germany, Spain, Poland and England. They also supplied CIAM's Secretariat, based at Zurich and led by Giedion. The definitive version of the Constatations was prepared by the Zurich group in the Autumn of 1933 in collaboration with the French group led by Le Corbusier. Comparison between the preliminary drafts produced by the Zurich and Paris groups' correspondence shows subtle, sometimes pronounced, textual differences.[54] Terminology was changed and the document became considerably longer, especially with regard to the final resumé of principles. New clauses were added on the role of the architect and the relationship of private to public interest.

The definitive version, published in Greek and French translations in November 1933, revealed further amendment.[55] In many places, the text lengthened by incorporating elements of both texts. Other sections of the text omitted items that indicated the disagreement of the parties involved. When discussing the implementation of town planning – a subject on which the original draft was mute – the Zurich version referred to the 'expropriation' of land and the French to its 'mobilisation'. Significantly the definitive version dropped the clause and thereby circumvented the differing political connotations of the rival terms.[56]

Further changes came about in the course of preparing material for publication, a process that would last a decade.[57] The Swiss group, led by Rudolf Steiger and assisted by Wilhelm Hess, initially led efforts to publish the proceedings of CIAM IV in book form. This began as a collation exercise, with Steiger vainly trying to assemble material from the national groups. A CIRPAC meeting at La Sarraz in September 1936 provided an opportunity to advance matters. Steiger invited other members of the Publications Committee[58] to meet several days in advance of the meeting in order to discuss progress. They now decided to produce two publications from the proceedings of CIAM IV rather than one. This decision was presented as providing a means for better dissemination of material, although it was partly motivated by trying to address the different 'conceptions' alleged to have held up the publication of the Congress's results.[59] The material collected by Steiger was handed over to the French and Catalonian groups, led by Charlotte Perriand, Le Corbusier, Weissmann and Sert. They would edit a brief popular edition for early publication under the working title 'Town Building in Creation', containing the original maps exhibited at CIAM IV. The Dutch group, led by van Eesteren and Stam, took responsibility for a longer, scientific edition called 'The Functional City', which would contain revised versions of the maps accompanied by reflective commentary.

Initially, the project made headway. By October 1936, Perriand reported that the French group had completed a dummy of the popular edition. The book would appear in three languages (English, German and French), with members' plans each receiving some four pages of text.[60] More than a year later, minutes of a meeting in London revealed that both books remained stalled, held up by the inability to find a publisher, the perennial problem of gathering material from members, and lack of funds.[61]

Meanwhile, changes appeared in the official terminology applied to CIAM IV that implied subtle shifts in thinking. Discussions at CIAM V in July 1937 saw two significant departures. First, during his Presidential address, van Eesteren referred to the 'Charter of Town Planning' formulated at the previous Congress.[62] A display screen exhibited in the Pavillon de Temps Nouveau purported to encapsulate the main features of the Charter, although in reality it was a freely adapted summary by Le Corbusier that included reference to ideas that simply were not part of the conclusions of CIAM IV.[63] Secondly, Sert introduced another term when acting as a rapporteur, referring to the possibility of CIAM working towards implementation of the conclusions of *La Charte d'Athènes* (the Athens Charter).[64]

CIAM V itself led to a low-budget volume entitled *Logis et Loisirs* (Housing and Recreation),[65] but it remained the aim to publish the results of the 1933 Congress as a defining moment in architectural thinking about town planning. Sert retained responsibility for the popular edition, despite his personal problems of having to leave Spain for exile, as a result of the Civil War. After moving to New York in June 1939, he continued to look for a publisher, now purely for an English-language volume. Although rejected by numerous American publishers, his growing links with Harvard eventually enabled him to secure a contract with its University Press in October 1941 for a book provisionally entitled *Should Cities Survive?*.[66] At the request of the publisher,[67] that was changed to *Can Our Cities Survive?* when eventually published in 1942.

From the outset, efforts were made to stress that the book was not the verbatim account of CIAM IV. Its subtitle states that it was *'based on* [author's emphasis] the proposals formulated by the CIAM' and an introduction by Giedion noted that:

> Circumstances in Europe making the work more difficult, J.L. Sert was finally asked by the Congress to complete the layout and write the entire text of the book. Complete freedom was given him, and his later experiences, particularly in America, enlarged its material in many respects. The accompanying text is exclusively the work of Mr Sert.[68]

Sert tried to retain continuity with the CIAM project by using direct quotations from a lightly amended version of the 'Constatations', now termed CIAM's 'Town-Planning Chart', as a frame for the book. The 15 chapters move from a contextual discussion of the Chart, through discussion of the four urban functions, to an appeal for a holistic view to overcome barriers to large-scale planning and implement planned action to 'save our cities'.

Yet architectural thought and practice had moved on since 1933. *Can Our Cities Survive?* was now as much a sourcebook of current planning practice as a retrospective glance at CIAM IV. In addition, it was now a commercial book aimed at the American market. Black-and-white photographs, procured from the *New York Times* and other archives, added images of American scenes to exemplify ideas for the reader. In the process these illustrations also showed recent developments in American planning practices – neighbourhood units, parkways, clover-leaf crossings and the rest – that simply were not part of the deliberations on the *Patris II*.

The new circumstances surrounding publication brought other changes to the text besides new visual materials. In addition to trivial changes brought by switching to non-metric systems of measurement, there were more substantive changes of approach. *Can Our Cities Survive?* hints at a biological and organic conception of planning that is absent from the original Constatations. Moreover, the Congress theme of 'La Ville Fonctionelle' does not appear in the Town-Planning Chart and, when introduced into the main body of the text, Sert took care to avoid the purely mechanistic interpretation of the term. Sensitive, perhaps, to comments made by Lewis Mumford when the manuscript was in preparation, Sert stressed that no city could be truly functional unless it satisfied and and stimulated the nobler aspirations of its people for a 'better life . . . which have always impelled men to seek a community existence'.[69]

Sert's book freely adapted the Constatations into a source-book of architectural perspectives on town planning, but did so in a manner that clung to the spirit of CIAM IV. By contrast, Le Corbusier's monograph *The Athens Charter* was an altogether different document. At once insistent, focused and crusading, its aim was to recast the spirit as well as the letter of the Constatations by converting them into a manifesto. After a potted history of CIAM told from Le Corbusier's standpoint, the reader was informed that after the 'two weeks of fervent work' of the Congress came 'a precious result: *The Athens Charter*'. It unlocked:

> all doors to the urbanism of modern times. It is a reply to the present chaos of the cities. In the hands of the authorities, itemized, annotated, clarified with an adequate explanation, the Athens Charter is the implement by which the destiny of cities will be set right.[70]

As presented by Le Corbusier, the Charter appears as a 62-page document divided into 95 numbered clauses, each of which carried an explanatory note. Although retaining the original structure, the text diverges sharply from earlier versions in both content and rhetoric; discrepancies partly justified by stating that the terminology needed 'some adjustments' since it was 'the result of debates among the assembled representatives speaking ten different languages'.[71]

Comments on the use of high buildings illustrate this point.[72] It was noted above that the Constatations stated that modern technology made possible construction of high buildings that, when widely spaced, could create large amounts of green open space and parks. Sert elaborated on this sentiment but retained its broad spirit:

> *Modern building technics* should be employed in constructing high, widely spaced apartment blocks whenever the necessity of housing high densities of population exists. Only such treatment of dwellings will liberate the necessary land surface for recreation purposes, community services, and parking places, and provide dwellings with light, sun, air and view.

For his part Le Corbusier, seeking endorsement for the Ville Radieuse, rendered it as:

> The resources offered by modern techniques must be taken into
> account. . . . High buildings, set far apart from one another, must
> free the ground for broad verdant areas.

Many changes went well beyond substituting Le Corbusier's
rhetorical style for more consensual statements. New elements were added. Previous versions, for example, made brief
reference to the problem of unplanned suburban growth and
its aesthetic consequences. Le Corbusier, a renown purveyor
of vitriol about suburbia, sharpened the invective considerably
in three clauses devoted to the subject. His commentary
lambasts the suburb as 'the degenerate progeny of the *fau-
bourgs*, or "bastard boroughs". . . the symbol for waste . . . an
urbanistic folly . . . one of the greatest evils of the century'. A
phrase interpreted by Sert as:

> frequently these suburbs take on the shape of shack-towns –
> disorderly groups of hovels constructed of all imaginable kinds of
> discarded material

is given a sharper sociological focus when rendered by Le
Corbusier as:

> The suburbs are often mere aggregations of shacks hardly worth
> the trouble of maintaining. Flimsily constructed little houses,
> boarded houses, sheds thrown together out of the most incon-
> gruous materials, the domain of poor creatures tossed about in an
> undisciplined way of life – that is the suburb.[73]

Perhaps the greatest changes concern the freewheeling
approach adopted towards the 'Conclusions', now subtitled
'main points of doctrine'. Besides resorting clauses into an
order that he found more palatable and adding further polem-
ics, Le Corbusier added new clauses about the traffic and the
street. The new speeds of road vehicles brought problems of
congestion, safety and hygiene. The solution was to recognise
the differences between urban and suburban traffic and clas-
sify them according to vehicle speed. On that basis, he argued
for major functional transformations that would equip city
and region with a road network:

> that incorporates modern traffic techniques and is directly propor-
> tionate to its purposes and usage. The means of transportation
> must be differentiated and classified for each of them, and a
> channel must be provided appropriate to the exact nature of the
> vehicles employed. Traffic thus regulated becomes a steady func-

tion, which puts no constraint on the structure of either habitation or places of work.[74]

Application of multilevel solutions to bring about efficient
flow was highlighted by noting: 'Urbanism (town planning) is
a three-dimensional, not two-dimensional science.' Adding
the element of height would not only solve the problem of
modern traffic, it would also assist provision of leisure by
allowing use of the open spaces created.

These final revisions completed the transformation of the
Constatations into the Athens Charter. What had started as
little more than quickly assembled and obscurely published
notes and precepts were made known to the wider world
through a lengthy sourcebook and a hard-hitting manifesto.
In its original draft, the Constatations was a permissive document. It left gaps that others, acting from variety of motives,
would later fill. To some extent, the addition of material
represented little more than necessary updating. CIAM, like
the Modern Movement in general, had an evangelistic commitment to the new. A decade had elapsed since CIAM IV in
which new ideas and prototypes had emerged. By embracing
these within the ambit of the publication project, *Can Our
Cities Survive?* and *The Athens Charter* stressed the relevance of
CIAM's thought to contemporary debate.

The production and embellishment of different versions of
the conference proceedings were symptomatic of wider issues.
At one level, the rewriting process reflected the personalities
involved in long-running conflicts about the leadership of
CIAM. The repeated 'jockeying for position'[75] was temporarily
resolved by the dispersal of the German and central European
groups, but old scores remained that, in all probability, would
resurface after the War. Seen in this light, the reworking of
the Constatations were linked, in part at least, to Sert, Le
Corbusier and their associates using the writing of history to
further their claims to leadership of the international Modern
Movement.

Yet this interpretation suffers from the limitation of arguing
from knowledge of the subsequent careers of the leading
players. In 1942–3 Sert was an emigré, branded as unfit to
follow his calling in his native Spain, who was attempting to
rebuild his life in the USA. Le Corbusier lived in isolation in
Vichy France, reasonably safe due to his Swiss origins but
with few opportunities to practise as an architect (see also
Chapter 7). Few then could have predicted their subsequent

significance in professional architecture. Viewed in that context, the positive tones of their books were a rallying cry for a generation of disenfranchised architects as well as for themselves. Sert and Le Corbusier were reasserting the claims of modern architecture at a black moment in world history. In wanting to present matters in the best possible light, they may well have exaggerated the importance of elements that signified consensus and common purpose within the Modern Movement rather than its diversity and conflict.

More crucially perhaps, the creation of the crusading Athens Charter from the mild-mannered Constatations symbolised ideologically-motivated efforts to advance the claims of modern architects to a role in the post-war reconstruction of Europe's cities. This is a theme to which we return later (e.g. see Chapter 7), but in the interim it is worth noting that even during the early years of the war, it was recognised that peace would require not just the repair of war-damaged cities but also major projects for social and physical reconstruction. These would scarcely have involved architecture as traditionally conceived but would intimately concern the new 'profession of architecture coming slowly together under the impulse of new social purpose, and extending its influence into fields of town planning'.[76] Here was a historic opportunity for a group of architects to build a new future for themselves. *Can Our Cities Survive?* and *The Athens Charter* presented their credentials for claiming a role in planning new neighbourhoods, city-building and the design of highway systems. There could be few more compelling reasons to bring the long gestation period of the Athens Charter to a conclusion.

4 FINDING ONE ANOTHER

In an electric train moving south I see a blue aeroplane; between a ploughed field and a green field, pylons in lovely juxtaposition with springy turf and trees of every stature. It is the relationship of these things that makes such loveliness.

Barbara Hepworth[1]

Barbara Hepworth's words captured perfectly the self-conscious strivings of those wanting to think and be 'modern' in mid-1930s Britain. To proclaim yourself modern meant mastering new vocabularies and enthusiasms. Modernists hailed the potential contribution of the 'indeterminate class of skilled workers, technical experts, airmen, scientists, architects and journalists, the people who feel at home in the radio and ferro-concrete age'.[2] They professed their fascination with aviation, electricity and modern design. They stated their eagerness to exploit new technologies and their impatience with traditional methods and solutions, which seemed to be irrelevant to the enormous social and economic problems of the age. They considered new aesthetics to be outward manifestations of profound changes in artistic and social consciousness. They supported new forms of architecture, at least in concept.[3] The pylon, the airman and the white-walled building quickly became powerful emblems of modernity for 'forward-thinking' individuals.

Modernism also implied subscribing to a package of progressive views, particularly belief in rational philosophy and the socially-redeeming virtues of science and technology. At this point, the views of modernists in the arts and humanities converged with a small, if vociferous, group of socialist or 'humanist' scientists and philosophers. These were mostly Cambridge-trained and included C.H. Waddington, J.D. Bernal, J.B.S. Haldane, and Lancelot Hogben. Their modernising project saw science, in Haldane's words, as 'the answer of the few to the demands of the many for wealth, comfort and victory'.[4] Both groups extolled the potential of new materials and processes for transforming architecture and town planning. Equally both advocated, with varying degrees of insistence, a comprehensive and scientifically based system of planning that would penetrate all major spheres of human activity.

This type of consensus, however, emerged only slowly. As late as 1930, with the possible exception of literature, there were no significant Modern Movements in Great Britain. The first parts of this chapter examine why architectural modernism took longer to materialise in Britain than in Continental Europe and then consider the early stages of its emergence, surveying isolated precursors from the 1920s and before. The next sections look at the background, profile and beliefs of those architects who identified themselves with the Modern Movement. The final sections deal with their urge to associate, as shown by the formation of pressure groups.

Noises from the margins

Modernism in Great Britain can claim many different points of origin. In 1910 and 1912, Roger Fry organised two exhibitions of Post-Impressionist painting that achieved the twin aims of acquainting English audiences with the latest in European art and alarming the artistic Establishment. The Camden Town Group (founded in 1911) and the London Group (1914) held exhibitions that briefly brought together works by English Futurists, such as Charles Nevinson, and the small pan-artistic Vorticist movement, led by Percy Wyndham Lewis. Yet there was no Sant'Elia to add to their number. Wyndham Lewis himself complained about the architect's apparent lack of interest in modernism, asking the question: 'Architects! Where is your Vortex?'[5]

Two new groups, founded in 1919, tried to revive the spirit of modernism after the hiatus of war. One, Group X, was an attempt by Wyndham Lewis to rekindle the Vorticist movement. It proved short-lived, producing one exhibition at Heal's Gallery in March–April 1920 and a magazine, *The Tyro*, of which just two issues appeared (1921–2). The other group, the Seven and Five Society, lasted until 1935. Formed by seven painters and five sculptors, its initial ambitions were limited. The catalogue of its first exhibition in 1920 cautiously noted that:

> The 'SEVEN & FIVE' are grateful to the pioneers, but feel that there has been of late too much pioneering along too many lines in altogether too much of a hurry, and themselves desire the

pursuit of their own calling rather than the confusion of conflict.[6]

The Group latterly gained more radical credentials through
the influence of Ben Nicholson, Hepworth, Henry Moore and
Ivon Hitchens, but for the 1920s distanced itself from the
more radical outlook of its Continental counterparts.

Architectural participation in these movements was minimal. Aesthetically, the outlook of the profession was dominated by the work of Lutyens, the Neo-Classicists and the
Neo-Georgians. Despite some involvement in the design of
large housing estates for the London County Council and
other municipalities dating back to the turn of the century,
schemes for mass housing remained largely in the hands of
the speculative builder and commercial developer. Few British
architects looked to, or identified themselves with, developments occurring in Europe; indeed senior figures in the profession radiated hostility towards Continental European
modernism. Gilbert Jenkins, the principal of the Architectural
Association – later regarded as one of Britain's most progressive schools – castigated Le Corbusier's houses at the
Weissenhof Siedlung as plate-glass boxes unfit 'as a home for
anyone save a vegetarian bacteriologist'.[7] Shortly afterwards
Sir Reginald Blomfield, a former President of the Royal Institute of British Architects and a leading neo-Georgian architect
of the day, mounted a campaign of denunciation of modernism. His book *Modernismus* considered modernism an 'epi-
demic' of 'cosmopolitan' extraction that had deliberately
abandoned 'all recognised standards of beauty'.[8]

Yet this did not mean that British architecture was entirely
conservative. Early assessments that Britain was 'temperamentally unsuited to make the sharp break with the past'[9]
belong to the promotional rhetoric of modernism. Quite simply, there were other niches for those interested in a radical
alternative. The Arts and Crafts Movement and the intellectual and practical legacy of architects such as Voysey, Charles
Rennie Mackintosh, Webb and Lethaby attracted those deeply
concerned about the orientation of contemporary architecture. The Garden City Movement, the dominant school of
thought on the future city in pre-1950 Britain, acted as a
natural home for progressive, but non-modernist, exercises in
housing or city design. There was a strong relationship, for
example, between the social architecture of that movement,

especially as illustrated by the work of Raymond Unwin, and the theory and practice of the 'new architecture'.[10]

Early prototypes

As elsewhere in Europe, the earliest applications of modern architecture were found in housing. Work started in 1919 on semi-detached and terraced cottages for workers of the Crittall Manufacturing Company at Braintree in Essex. Designed by W.F. Crittall and C.H.B. Quennell and based on a metric grid with concrete floors and flat roofs, the houses incorporated the metal windows and door frames that the company produced. In 1926, Crittall commissioned Thomas S. Tait to design housing for his new settlement at Silver End, Braintree. Influenced by Frank Lloyd Wright, Dudok and the De Stijl movement, the houses at Silver End were for sale to middle- to upper-income professional clients. Extensive coverage of these houses in the architectural press and the company's advertising contributed in no small measure to the 'horizontal' metal window's becoming a powerful symbol of

Figure 4.1
W. Sadler, 'Sylvan Hill'. An International Style house using Crittall metal windows depicted in a promotional magazine produced for homeowners by the Halifax Building Society.

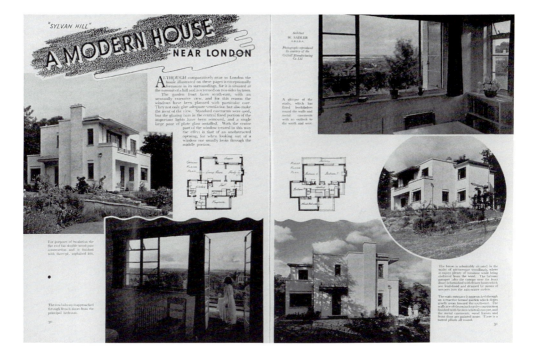

modernity, replicated in estates throughout southern England (Figure 4.1).

Another influence on the aesthetics of the Silver End houses was 'New Ways', a house at Northampton that the model manufacturer W.J. Bassett-Lowke commissioned from the Deutsche Werkbund architect Peter Behrens in 1925. With its flat roof and white-rendered brickwork, 'New Ways' was the first of a wave of scattered commissions for villas in the International Style built for upper-middle class clients, principally in the Home Counties. Building such houses relied on considerable commitment from clients, who might face the wrath of irate neighbours or local committees, but it also provided early opportunities for young architects like Serge Chermayeff, Berthold Lubetkin or the future members of the Connell, Ward and Lucas partnership to design in consciously Modern style (Figure 4.2).

Figure 4.2
Serge Chermayeff, garden front of 'Bentley Wood', Halland, East Sussex, 1935–8. Photograph by Richard Bryant.

The switch to these aesthetics was not immediate even among those sympathetic to modernism. British modern architects often retained their eclecticism, either through choice or to give themselves the maximum chance of gaining commissions. Maxwell Fry, for instance, was still designing

neo-Georgian houses in 1931, only attempting concrete houses in 1933 and International Style in 1935. William Holford designed a pair of identifiably modernist houses at Icklesham in East Sussex in 1937, but elsewhere adopted other styles. Many architects experimented with rendered façades, flat roofs, steel frames or prefabrication without being actively committed to the philosophy and values of modernism. The Glaswegian builder J.R.H. McDonald, for example, strongly argued that the flat roof was both structurally superior to conventional pitched roofs and provided creative opportunities for making use of an additional floor (Figures 4.3–4.4).

As the 1930s progressed, the number of overtly modernist buildings steadily increased. Owners of up-market stores in London saw the possibilities that modern styling provided for presenting a distinctive façade to the passers-by. Owen Williams's factory for Boots at Nottingham (1930–2) developed the aesthetic of curtain-walling. London and Dudley Zoos commissioned animal enclosures from the Tecton practice, with sculptural use of concrete. Cinema façades sometimes edged away from Art Deco to more consciously modernist

Figure 4.3
John McDonald's workforce demonstrates the strength of flat-roofs at one of the company's developments in Glasgow.

Figure 4.4
Putting a flat roof to
good use.

styling. Private developers of hotels in South coast seaside
resorts like Brighton and St Leonards consciously appropriated Le Corbusier's analogy of the decks of an ocean-liner
to devise an imagery apposite to the marine environment
(Figure 4.5). Along the coast at Bexhill, Chermayeff and
Mendelsohn designed the De La Warr Pavilion (1935) as a
public entertainment and leisure centre.

Blocks of flats in approved style were developed in affluent
areas of London, such as Wells Coates's Lawn Road development in Hampstead (1932–4), Frederick Gibberd's Pullman
Court at Streatham Hill (1935), and Lubetkin and Tecton's
Highpoint I (1933–5) and II (1936–8). There was also a
handful of municipal developments that hinted at the
wider possibilities offered by flats. These included isolated
schemes which had drawn inspiration from Continental
European prototypes. Such projects included the work of
Lancelot Keay at Liverpool (Figure 4.6), with its echoes
of Viennese public housing, and R.A.H. Livett's Quarry
Hill estate in Leeds which combined modernistic styling
with the Mopin industrialised building system devised in
France.

Support from the media

Despite these examples and the settlement at Silver End, very little was essayed at the urban scale. Knowledge of the wider dimensions of the Modern Movement's urban imagination, therefore, came less from direct acquaintance with important prototypes than from writers who had seen modernist designs on their travels and, in some cases, knew members of the European Modern Movement. The writer and photographer F.R. Yerbury, for example, spread awareness of contemporary European architecture through his articles for the *Architect and Building News*. These were later consolidated into a series of finely-illustrated books that presented a glowing image of new architecture in France, Denmark and other West European nations.[11]

Translations also played their part. Le Corbusier's early works were translated into English by Frederick Etchells, an artist-member of the Vorticist movement who turned to architecture after the collapse of Group X. *Vers une Architecture* appeared as *Towards a New Architecture* in 1927; *Urbanisme* as *The City of Tomorrow and its Planning* in 1929.[12] Similarly, the writer P. Morton Shand translated Walter Gropius's *The New Architecture and the Bauhaus* in 1935, presenting British readers with an image of an architecture that ranged in scope from

Figure 4.5
The aesthetic of the ocean liner in publicity material for a development by R. Dalgliesh and R.K. Pullen, Marine Court, St Leonards on Sea (1935–7).

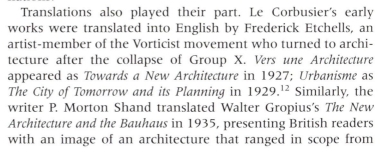

Figure 4.6
Gerard Gardens,
Liverpool.

the design of domestic artefacts, through standardised housing, to the layouts of residential estates.[13]

By this stage modern architecture had gained important
support from several, sometimes surprising, sections of the
media. For instance, the magazine *Country Life*, frequently
regarded as a bastion of tradition and Establishment, briefly
flirted with modernism in interior design and domestic architecture. Editorial commentary, for instance, lambasted the
poor quality of the manufactured products seen at the 1931
British Industries Fair, calling for a revolution in training
along the lines of the Werkbund, perhaps with the establishment of a British Bauhaus. Sympathetic coverage was
extended to modern houses deemed to harmonise with the
surrounding landscape. Praise was lavished on the clean lines
of exhibits shown at the Exhibition of 'British Industrial
Design in the Home' at London's Dorland Hall in June 1933,
especially a modern bungalow at Rugby designed by Chermayeff and a mock-up of one of the 'minimum flats' from
Coates's Lawn Road development. This phase passed by 1934.
Its influential editor, Christopher Hussey became increasingly
disillusioned with the 'false functionalism' and erosion of
rural architectural tradition considered inherent in modernism. Thereafter modernism was considered hostile, even antithetic to the values of the countryside.[14]

Rather more typical of the genre was *Circle: International Survey of Constructive Art*. *Circle* was intended as the first of an annual series of publications. Although these never materialised, *Circle* itself recorded a broad cross-section of modernist endeavour in abstract art which it linked to kindred developments in other fields of endeavour. United by 'an attitude to life',[15] these contributions were gathered together under the deliberately neutral banner of 'constructive art', a term intended to emphasise its positive quality rather than link it to the ideological purpose of Constructivist Art. It contained articles by Jan Tschichold on typography, the crystologist J.D. Bernal on art, Léonide Massine on choreography, Moholy-Nagy on photography, and Henry Moore on sculpture. The planning and architectural contributions included essays by Maxwell Fry and Giedion on concepts of the city, Lewis Mumford on monumentality, Le Corbusier and Jeanneret's plan for Nemours in North Africa, Paul Nelson's proposal for a Hospital City at Lille, and a model of part of a 'Garden City of the Future' by F.R.S. Yorke and Marcel Breuer (see Chapter 5).

Further patronage for modernism came from the British Broadcasting Corporation (BBC), then under the chairmanship of Sir John Reith (later Lord Reith). The BBC supported modernism in three ways: commissioning modern architects to undertake interior and exterior work; exploring modernist themes in radio broadcasts; and publishing transcripts of relevant talks in its periodical *The Listener*. A series of radio debates explored the basis, pros and cons of modern architecture alongside other issues involving contemporary design.[16]

The most significant source of patronage, however, came from the London-based Architectural Press. Owned by Hubert de Cronin Hastings, the Press actively propagated architectural modernism after 1930 through its monographs and periodicals. The weekly *Architects' Journal*, monthly *Architectural Review* and annual publication *Specification* offered openings in architectural journalism for an editorial staff that included Nikolaus Pevsner, F.R.S. Yorke, John Betjeman and J.M. Richards. The *Review*, in particular, was the mouthpiece of British modernism. Its supportive editorial line gave prominence to buildings and artefacts that seemingly embraced the correct spirit. Much of the force of its presentation stemmed from the authority of its authors and illustrators, attracting a rare collection of the talents of the architectural and artistic avant-garde to its columns. Shand, Raymond McGrath, Robert Byron, Herbert Read and Hugh Casson all wrote regularly for the magazine, with illustrations supplied by artists as gifted as John Piper, Osbert Lancaster, Paul Nash and Gordon Cullen.

Its influence was assisted by innovative typography and illustrations. Photography was particularly important, with staff photographers like M.O. Dell and H.L. Wainwright turning the black-and-white photograph into a powerful weapon in the armoury of modernism. Roughcut concrete walls were rendered gleaming white and made to stand out against deep-toned, cloud-strewn skies by heavy use of red and yellow filters and by hand re-touching of photographs. Camera angles heroically accentuated the geometry and angularity of modern houses. The result was a much imitated form of representation that provided valuable propaganda for modern architects.[17]

Profile

Like Modern Movements elsewhere, the core group converged on a metropolitan city, in this case London. The capital alone offered the environment for a critical mass of modern architects to form and develop their own supportive infra-structure of associations, pressure groups, periodicals, exhibitions and informal meeting places. The importance of the community of sculptors, designers, academics and architects that developed in Hampstead in North London, for instance, was recalled by Maxwell Fry:

> You have to imagine too that the (architects were) part of a much wider movement amongst high intellectuals – which included philosophers like Collingwood of Oxford, scientists like Wadding-ton. All these people were quite naturally part of the same community, and very often met, for example, at places like Henry Moore's studio in Hampstead. We all knew each other.[18]

The earliest advocates and practitioners of modern architecture in Britain – those who received their training before 1930 – were socially homogeneous but came from geographically disparate backgrounds (Table 4.1). Socially, they mostly came from upper-middle or upper class families, with parents capable of meeting the costs of their lengthy training. Unusually at a time when most architects entered architectural

Table 4.1 Biographical details of significant figures in the inter-war British Modern Movement

Name	Date of birth	Birthplace	Country of education and training
Ove Arup	1895	Newcastle-upon-Tyne	Denmark
Serge Chermayeff	1900	Grozny, Russia	England, Germany, France, Netherlands
Wells Coates	1895	Tokyo	Canada, England
Amyas Connell	1900	Taranaki, New Zealand	New Zealand, England
Jane Drew	1911	Thornton Heath, Surrey	England
Maxwell Fry	1899	Wallasey	England
Frederick Gibberd	1908	Coventry	England
Ernö Goldfinger	1902	Budapest	Switzerland, France
Berthold Lubetkin	1901	Tiflis, Georgia	Russia
Colin Lucas	1902	London	England
Raymond McGrath	1903	Sydney	Australia, England
Leslie Martin	1908	England	England
Peter Moro	1911	Heidelberg	Germany, Switzerland
Nikolaus Pevsner	1902	Leipzig	Germany
P. Morton Shand	1888	London	England, France, Germany
William Tatton Brown	1910	London	England, France
Basil Ward	1902	Wellington, New Zealand	New Zealand, England
F.R.S. Yorke	1906	Stratford-upon-Avon	England

practice through a period of apprenticeship supplemented by part-time study, many of the emerging group of modern architects had been full-time students: Fry at Liverpool University; Gibberd and Yorke at Birmingham University; Wells Coates and the New Zealanders Amyas Connell and Basil Ward at London; Leslie Martin at Manchester; Colin Lucas, McGrath and Shand at Cambridge; William Tatton Brown at the Architectural Association and Cambridge.[19]

Several won academic prizes or undertook privately financed trips that allowed them to study art and architecture in Western and Central Europe before entering practice. Others gained opportunities to obtain working experience abroad. Fry, for example, worked in New York while a partner in Thomas Adams's planning firm, serving as a consultant on the First Regional Plan for New York (1929–31). William Tatton Brown unsuccessfully applied for work in Le Corbusier's office and finished up working in the Parisian *atelier* of the ardent Communist André Lurçat, albeit without 'any clear idea of who he was or what he stood for'. Pilgrimages to

France or Germany to inspect buildings identified as important by Yerbury, Yorke or other cataloguers of modern buildings were common.

Many of the British Modern Movement's pioneers were migrants or had far-flung family connections. Although educated in Britain, Chermayeff was Russian-born and subsequently studied at various West European art schools and universities. Coates, born in Tokyo of missionary parents and educated in Canada, came to Britain initially to undertake doctoral studies in engineering. McGrath, born and educated in Sydney, eventually undertook graduate studies at Cambridge. Ove Arup, born in Newcastle-upon-Tyne but trained as an engineer in Copenhagen, moved to Britain in 1924 to work for the engineering firm of Christiani and Nielsen. The Georgian Lubetkin came to Britain in connection with an ultimately abortive commission for a house in 1930, settled in 1931 and helped form the Tecton practice in 1932. The Hungarian-born Ernö Goldfinger was educated at the Ecole Nationale Supérieure des Beaux Arts in Paris and was one of the first students at the Atelier Auguste Perret. He finally settled in London in 1934, although he first came to Britain in 1925 in connection with a commission to build a beauty salon in Grafton Street for Helena Rubenstein.

Besides the availability of work, the reasons for moving to Britain varied. For Lubetkin, the main attraction was the 'progressive intellectual milieu in the sciences and humanities', particularly at Cambridge: 'Looking at events in the world at that time, this seemed to be the spearhead of advance . . . that is why I decided to come here.' By contrast, he felt that the architectural environment offered him much less. Architects might talk about 'improvements' but rarely functioned at the level of 'general ideas' or were able to articulate a coherent conceptual grounding for their work.[20] Goldfinger found the artistic and living environments attractive, while echoing the gist of Lubetkin's appraisal of the architectural scene. Evaluating the commitment of British architects to modernism, he noted that:

> Individually some of them were quite good, but many were not that serious. They were full of loose ideas about people and how they acted. . . They might talk about the avant garde and serving the people, but these were not the proletariate.[21]

Yet provided they had the right connections, Britain was at least somewhere that modern architects might continue to work. From 1933 onwards, a wave of refugee architects arrived from Continental Europe. To come to Britain in the first place, they needed to enter partnerships with British or British-naturalised architects: hence Gropius and Fry, Yorke and Breuer, Chermayeff and Mendelsohn. Collectively, the refugees were too vulnerable and marginal to shape the emerging British Modern Movement. The new partnerships were often brittle, short-lived collaborations and were responsible for only a handful of significant projects, but the arrival of the refugees had an important psychological impact. Their presence helped to 'decrease the feeling of isolation' among British modernists and boosted their self-confidence at a difficult time.[22]

The more distinguished of the refugees moved to appointments in the USA after a few years. Walter Gropius, for example, left in 1937 to take up the chair of Architecture at Harvard University. Marcel Breuer joined him at Harvard in 1937, also sharing an architectural practice that lasted until 1941. Laszlo Moholy-Nagy moved to Chicago in 1937 as Director of the New Bauhaus and later the Institute of Design. By contrast, a much larger group of refugees remained in Britain, often enduring a somewhat precarious existence. They included Erwin Gutkind, Eugen Kaufmann, Arthur Korn, Peter Moro, Nikolaus Pevsner, Eugene Rosenberg, Felix Samuely and Walter Segal.

Peter Moro described the type of predicament in which the refugees could find themselves. Moro had trained in architecture at Heidelberg and Zurich. He had come to Britain on a visitor's permit in 1936, hoping to find a job with Gropius:

I came to get out of Germany, because I had a Jewish grandmother on my mother's side. My father was a Professor in Heidelberg and remained there; he had no such problems. I wanted to come to England, but you couldn't take any money out of Germany other than 10 marks – which did not get you very far. You had to have someone here to look after you. Apart from a fellow ex-student, an American, who was over here and said he would meet me, I had absolutely no prospects at all. A former assistant to my father, (who was a paediatrician), was over here and met Gropius at a party at Dr (Jack) Donaldson's house (which Gropius and Fry had designed). She told Gropius about my desire to come here and said I was the son of her former boss. Gropius said 'sure, that will be alright, he can work for me'. She wrote to me and I was absolutely over the moon, because Gropius was a famous name whose work meant a lot to me then. Dr Donaldson

wrote the necessary letter of invitation, which let me in and stated
that I wouldn't be a burden to the taxpayer. I arrived here and on
the first morning I went to see Gropius who denied the whole
thing and said that he had never heard of me . . . And that was my
first day in England. I was completely penniless.

Moro was saved from having to return through contacts with
'another Zurich man', Fred Lassere. Lassere, a Canadian, was
working for Tecton in London. He successfully introduced him
to the practice, where Moro then worked for two years before
forming a partnership with Richard Llewelyn Davies to build a
house at Birdham in Sussex. While this project was under
way, Moro was again confronted with deportation when the
Home Office refused to extend his work permit. A one year's
extension to complete the house project was overtaken by the
outbreak of war whereupon Moro was interned at Huyton.
Having narrowly missed transportation, he was reinterned at
Douglas on the Isle of Man (see Chapter 7).

By the late 1930s, a new cohort of modern architects had
come through the British higher education system. These
included Denys Lasdun, Arthur Ling, Percy Johnson-
Marshall, Peter Shepheard and Ralph Tubbs. Most ascribed
their initial interests in modern architecture to the inspiration
of individual tutors or contacts with fellow students rather
than to the curriculum or attitudes of the departments in
which they studied. Arthur Ling, for example, recalled that
the Professor at his university:

> adored everything that was Georgian – he even on occasions
> dressed up in Georgian costume and travelled by coach and
> horses. He looked with disfavour on the Modern Movement. On
> the other hand, quite different developments were taking place at
> the Architectural Association at that time, with a move away from
> tradition to the Modern Movement and we . . . were quite jealous
> of what the AA were doing. We reacted by producing quasi-
> modern designs for some of our projects; they didn't get, however,
> a very good mark. Indeed, one or two people left. . . and went to
> the AA.[23]

After 1935, several schools of architecture offered a supportive intellectual environment for students interested in modernism. The Department of Civic Design at the University of
Liverpool had taught town planning alongside architecture
since its foundation in 1909. Under Patrick Abercrombie and
especially Charles Reilly, it developed an openly eclectic
approach to new developments. The Department also sup-

ported the notion of public service in local government or state agency as an appropriate career for an architect. Keay, the city's Director of Housing, actively recruited students and graduates, with work on slum clearance and redevelopment providing opportunities for civic design on a large scale.[24] As Percy Johnson-Marshall observed:

> Reilly and Abercrombie fitted in civic design as an idea and concept of all architectural training and education. That ran through the whole school and the results were clear – Liverpool graduates after the war filled a large number of important planning jobs.[25]

There was, of course, an important difference between permitting students to complete projects in modernist style and teaching them within a distinctively modernist pedagogic framework. Most departments introduced change gradually. Hull University's School of Architecture under Leslie Martin, for example, offered a coverage of contemporary town planning issues without fundamental changes in the syllabus. A symptom of more dramatic changes was seen in the conflicts at the Architectural Association (AA) following the appointment of E.A.A. Rowse as Principal in 1935. Rowse founded a graduate school for planning, the School for Planning and Research for National Development, under the aegis of the AA, but also took steps to reform the AA's traditional five-year programme.[26] This was replaced by a unit system that focused students' attention on longitudinal projects, often with sociological and town-planning content (see Chapter 6). Conflict with the conservatively minded Director of Education, H.S. Goodhart-Rendel, led to Rowse's dismissal in early 1938 before fierce resistance from the staff subsequently led to Goodhart-Rendel's resignation in the summer. The incoming Director and Principal, Geoffrey Jellicoe, established a committee in 1939 to advise on matters. The weighting of avowed modernists on that committee effectively propelled the institution towards a modernist curriculum. It was an important harbinger of developments after the Second World War.

The urban challenge

By any standard, British cities were in crisis by 1930. The inefficiency, confusion and inequity of the Victorian industrial metropolis made a ready case for bold, comprehensive

Figure 4.7
Traffic congestion in
Regent's Street, London,
1932.

approaches rather than piecemeal policies cast within existing
parameters. City centres suffered severe land shortage and
traffic congestion (Figure 4.7). Working-class districts adjacent
to the core were overcrowded and decrepit (Figure 4.8);

Figure 4.8
Back-to-back housing in
Leeds in the 1930s.

Figure 4.9
'Live where you like'.
National Building Society
poster from the late
1930s.

conditions clearly recognised by the national slum clearance
campaign that followed the Labour Government's Housing
Act (1930). Beyond them lay the rapidly-expanding suburbs,
where growth of suburban housing was fuelled by the
upsurge in demand for home-ownership among the professional middle-classes. The London conurbation, in particular, doubled in area between 1919 and 1939 (Figure 4.9).
Speculatively-built estates, constructed by private developers,
mushroomed along the lines of the major roads and railways
and caused enormous affront to those concerned about the
accretion of seemingly formless suburbs at the urban
fringe.[27]

Yet despite the challenge posed by the state of the cities, it is
important not to overstate the degree of consensus among
British modern architects over town planning matters. Most
would certainly have shared Arup's view that:

> We were for the underdog. The centre of our concern was with
> housing, especially housing the working population. We were
> concerned with the basic standards that people ought to have in
> housing and wanted to break free of the constraints of the 1930s
> and build decently for people.[28]

Those interested in town planning would also have accepted the view that: 'it was through housing that we saw cities being rebuilt'.[29] Most liked the word 'planning' – 'you couldn't believe in new cities without it' – even if they had little agreement about what it meant aside from the 'most elementary ideas'.[30] Beyond these points, however, there were profound differences in orientation.

First, many architects were far more concerned with application of modernism to individual buildings or interior design than with wider issues. During the inter-war years, few architects had any wish for employment in the public sector, where relative anonymity and low status were often compounded by having work vetted by the borough engineer or district valuer.[31] Working in small practices relying on commissions from private clients for shops, offices or houses, their work rarely touched on wider matters of town planning. In Britain, the architectural concern for neighbourhood or city planning was restricted to a small group of individuals who were mainly, but not exclusively, centred on the MARS Group and linked to CIAM.

Secondly, there were sharp divisions in political orientation and in underlying views of social commitment. A few observers saw the Modern Movement as having an overt political mission:

> The whole Modern Movement in architecture was an attempt to follow the revolutionary movement in politics. It was no secret that after the revolution in the Soviet Union, architecture and planning went through a revolutionary movement, or so they thought at the time. The logic of this was inescapable: an attempt to bring technology that had been developed in other spheres into planning and architecture. The movement developed through certain key groups like the Bauhaus, the de Stijl group and so on, with the three key centres of Paris, Berlin and the Bauhaus, and figures like Le Corbusier, Gropius and Mies van der Rohe. The idea that animated us in the 1930s was the feeling that we had to make a revolution; we had to change the whole idea of what architecture and town planning were about. And for the first time, this was linked to a kind of social ideal – of planning for everybody, and an architecture for everyone. That, I would stress, was a social ideal; it was not the sort of aesthetic ideal which, say, the Art Nouveau movement had had before.[32]

Others were sceptical of such ideas. They saw matters less in revolutionary terms than as the social guilt of a privileged and educated minority who wanted to make amends to the working class. They argued that architects might espouse left-wing sympathies, subscribing notionally to radical politics, but that they largely adopted an apolitical stance when approaching their work. For example, neither Coates nor Chermayeff were strongly politically motivated, but both could be found writing about the broad notion of planning as a social ideal. Coates stated that 'as creative artists we are concerned with a future which must be planned';[33] Chermayeff that architects 'must participate in the reconstruction of society'. Yet in practical terms, many saw town planning more as an extension of reformist debate about health and sanitation, rather than in terms of bringing about greater social and spatial equality of resources. If, as J.M. Richards suggested, modern architects influenced the shape and the design of the cities of the post-war period, it was:

> purely in the sense that it was the pre-war Modern Movement that began to lead architects to regard the shape and development of cities at all . . . going back, say, to the 1920s – things like city development and, for that matter, housing were not matters that the architectural profession came into in the least. There was no planning profession and the growth of cities was not regarded as a problem on which action had to be taken – it was a laissez-faire matter – except purely for authorities controlling things like public services, and the architects did not come into that at all. So, it was very largely the result of influences from the growth of the Modern Movement that made architects think of enlarging their terms of responsibility and start thinking about matters like housing and city development as something they should be concerned with. Everything that went on in those fields before that was considered right outside the control of the architectural profession.'[34]

Sources of vision

'Have the right vision and the right action will follow', wrote Elizabeth Denby, a housing reformer who collaborated with Maxwell Fry and other modern architects in the inter-war period.[35] It was an opinion that many would have supported in principle, even if the sources of vision varied. Developing later than its Continental equivalents, the British Modern Movement had a reservoir of existing ideas on which it could draw.

Not surprisingly, many British modernists had absorbed influences from Le Corbusier. For Ling, the attraction of his thinking lay in scientific analysis and synthesis of the city: 'taking everything to bits and putting them back together again in a new form; starting from scratch with basic functional needs, (sun, air, work, recreation, traffic etc.), and building an architecture around them rather than starting with a style and then fitting the needs into the style, or accepting a city as it exists and adapting it to new requirements.'[36] For others, the attraction lay not in rationalism but in romanticism; in Le Corbusier's 'poetic vision', oratorical flair and compelling visual imagery.[37] Johnson-Marshall noted:

> In every age there is a need to know what tomorrow might look like – most people are terrified of it. But Corbusier and his group did set out very clearly as to how the new ideas of town planning and architecture could form a complete conception. It was only later that we found out that Garnier in his Industrial City (1902) had laid out the basic model that Corbusier developed. But Corbusier did a very important job in trying to put a dream forward.[38]

By contrast, despite later working extensively with Le Corbusier, Fry distanced himself from Le Corbusier's urban projects. Fry argued that modern architects drew their views of the urban future from a much wider source than simply the work of Le Corbusier:

> I was however much more concerned with the German version than by Corbusier. . . I personally recoiled from the Radiant City. I thought it was not for a free society. It couldn't be given the amount of organisation that it would have required, with all the tower-blocks and everything else. It sounded alright but socially I had strong suspicions about it . . . Corb talked a fair amount of nonsense in his time, although it wasn't seen to the same extent at the time. There were always those who were a little sceptical.[39]

For his part, Johnson-Marshall commented that as students 'our heroes were more Gropius and the Bauhaus, some of the Dutch leaders, and we were very attracted to Scandinavia and what was happening in Stockholm'.[40]

The influence of Swiss, Dutch and Scandinavian ideas is worth stressing here. Aileen Tatton Brown, for example, toured Scandinavia in 1935 having been advised by Leslie

Martin that it offered some of the best designed modern housing to be found.[41] The so-called 'Swedish Grace' was a lasting source of inspiration that surfaced again in the post-war period with the Festival of Britain and early public housing programmes (see Chapter 9). In Richards's words:

> Sweden, with her instinct for using materials well and her serious sense of social values, has set an example to all Europe of the way modern architecture can solve such problems as the housing of industrial workers and the mass production of elegant household furniture.[42]

Others observers cited a range of North American influences on early British modernism, notably applications of prefabrication[43] and the humanism of Frank Lloyd Wright and Neutra. By way of summary, Jane Drew characterised the dominant view of the time as 'roughly Bauhaus ideas with a great deal of Corb's rather different ideas tacked on, plus somewhat under-recognised ideas like those of J.D. Bernal, Gerald Barry and the philosophers', mentioning in particular the American writer Lewis Mumford.[44]

The importance attached to Mumford's views provide an excellent example of the way in which the imagery of the future city comprised a constellation of different elements. His writings were widely cited as an influence in their own right: to one observer they were 'at the time, the most profound influence on our lives'.[45] The attraction lay in two different elements. First, he clearly recognised the role of electricity in urban and regional transformation, as was taking place in the Tennessee Valley. Secondly, his approach interpreted the city's vital place in cultural history and looked beyond the city to the region. Despite being a strong supporter of the Garden City Movement, Mumford's thinking converged frequently with that of the Modern Movement: 'in a way they were working towards the same goal'.[46] To elaborate:

> The important thing about Mumford was that he developed the CIAM ideas but humanised them. The trouble with too many of the CIAM architects was that they weren't really interested in human beings and that is still characteristic of many of today's architects who are more interested in forms and shapes and plastic harmonies, but not in people. Mumford brought humanism into the job and indicated its enormously wide scope, leading right up to the Tennessee Valley Authority. That was the fundamental message that animated us. We wanted to see Britain with a

national plan, regional plan, city plans – these were the great dreams in which architecture was just a component.[47]

The common ground

At one level, the initial views that modern architects held with respect to the physical form and structure of the future city may justifiably be termed 'very broad and very vague'.[48] Yet at another level, there was a dynamic that favoured finding common ground. Reflecting on the varying views of the urban future held by those who came together in the early British Modern Movement, Johnson-Marshall commented that:

> Like all these movements, it included people with different approaches, which appear to be the same in the early days. Before the war, the differences were concealed because of the fact that the revolution had barely taken off – it was still nascent – and therefore the emphasis was on a common approach.[49]

As a result, areas in which beliefs and orientations converged were assiduously cultivated. Some of the more consistent among these shared viewpoints included preferences for the absence of applied ornamentation on buildings; use of

Figure 4.10
Modern industry. Factory chimneys at Ford plant, River Rouge, Detroit (1927).

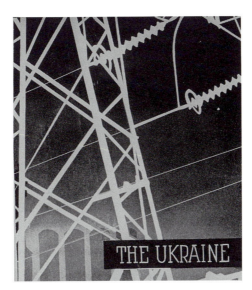
THE UKRAINE

Figure 4.11
The pylon as icon:
electricity and regional
transformation.

advanced constructional techniques and new building materials, such as steel, glass and reinforced concrete; and the assumption that the spirit of the times was tied to the development of scientific rationality and the evolution of mechanisation. Idealising the modern industrialisation process without necessarily understanding the structural implications of industrial change, modern architects expressed their beliefs in mass production, with a multiplication of standard patterns (Figure 4.10). New energy sources, especially electricity, were hailed as mechanisms for regional transformation. The examples of the Tennessee Valley Authority (see also Chapter 7) and the Ukraine, appealing respectively to liberal capitalist and Marxist interpretations of social and economic change, were prominently discussed (Figure 4.11).

In tackling urban problems, British modernists affirmed the need for the metropolis, 'the real city',[50] rather than smaller or decentralised urban units. To address that scale of city and rectify the mistakes of past urban environments, however, meant going beyond the traditional scale addressed by architects. For Arthur Ling, it was:

> this wider conception of architecture that led me to the Modern Movement in the first place. Architects could design individual buildings but if their clients didn't care for more than the profit that could be made out of a building then there would be a hotch-potch of buildings and not a city of quality . . . I saw the Modern

Movement as advocating a rational approach to the design of the urban environment as well as of individual buildings.[51]

The key to rational planning lay in the use of zoning to separate land-uses into different functions. Most British modernists accepted CIAM's division of urban functions into dwelling, work, leisure and circulation as a logical means of avoiding the conflict and tensions between different uses. They also believed in the value of master plans that extended from local to regional scale. As Ling added:

> I wanted architecture to have its chance. The only way that it could be appreciated to the full was if there was a rational base on which it could be constructed, namely logical design with form following function at all levels from the chair to the region and, if possible, extending even further.[52]

Advocacy of flats, especially for mass housing, was an important ingredient in the argument. That advocacy rested on the 'prima facie imaginative appeal, the vision of a tall block of flats with open space around it'[53] and the pivotal place that flats occupied in the Modern Movement's ideas for urban reconstruction. Flats were the testing-ground for new building techniques, allowing experiments in mass production and industrial prefabrication of building units (Figures 4.12–4.13). As professionals who could offer expertise in designing these complex residential structures by using unconventional construction techniques, architects had a route by which they could get involved in questions of working-class housing.

Flats, in turn, were interwoven into broader strategies of urban planning.[54] They were an answer to the perceived problems of urban sprawl, countering the cottage ideal of the Garden City Movement and 're-urbanising' housing in a more concentrated form. They were an important component in new thinking about planned 'neighbourhood units', in which residential areas were comprehensively replanned with provision of housing and services (see Chapter 6). Constructing blocks of flats on purpose-built estates allowed the creation of open space that could be used by the population as a whole:

> The great thing that we were concerned with was more open space. The street plans of the time, say, down in the East End, were of mile after mile of two-storey buildings with pretty narrow streets, and all the kids playing in the streets. We thought them

Figure 4.12
Kensal House flats in
Ladbroke Grove,
London, 1936–7. The
executive architect was
Maxwell Fry, with a
committee of Robert
Atkinson, C.H. James,
G. Grey Wornum and
Elizabeth Denby.

Figure 4.13
View from the roof of
Highpoint One, Lubetkin
and Tecton, 1933–5.

appalling and thought the great thing was to stack them, to up-end the terraced house and free all that amount of land. So the way to get open space was to think on a much larger scale and concentrate the buildings on the smallest fraction of the site leaving the rest of the area as open space.[55]

Entwined with this argument were beliefs about building a healthier society. The 1930s were a period in which health and fresh air were emphasised, with firm support for preventive medicine in order to get and keep the population healthy (Figure 4.14). The idea that people could live on green estates with free circulation of wind and air had a powerful impact when set against the counter-image of the densely packed city slum.

Flowing from the modernisation of the dwelling came ideas about the modernisation of life-style. Coates, the most ardent supporter of this notion, was influenced by his experience of Japanese dwellings and by German notions of *Existenzminimum*. The 'Isokon' flats at Lawn Road, Hampstead that he designed for the furniture manufacturer Jack Pritchard made an ingenious use of interior space after the Frankfurt model. When completed, the rents included bed-making, shoe-

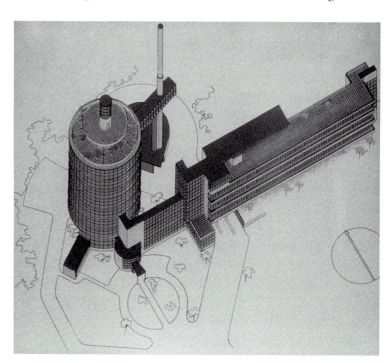

Figure 4.14
Individual Health Centre, unrealised project by Connell, Ward and Lucas.

cleaning, laundry and window-cleaning services, with the availability of hot meals from the staff canteen. Coates suggested that the rationale for the flats was the advent of 'new habits of life' that demanded a response from architects. He argued that people actually desired smaller dwellings. This meant that they could re-allocate money to the things that, allegedly, now mattered more to them – such as travel, leisure and new experiences:

> We don't possess our homes in the old, permanent, settled sense; we move from place to place, to find work or to find new surroundings . . . We don't want to spend as much as we used to on our homes. So the first thing is that our dwellings have got to be much smaller than they used to be. . . . we cannot burden ourselves with permanent tangible possessions, as well as our real new possessions of freedom, travel, new experience – in short, what we call life.[56]

Others gave support to this interweaving of arguments about ideal forms of housing and ideal society, albeit drawing more on Le Corbusier than the Neue Sachlichkeit. F.R.S. Yorke, for example, argued that:

> Modern innovations have transformed the problem of life within the house. We are oppressed by the old type of home and the old-fashioned interior . . . We demand a greater service from the things about us; they must serve a real purpose, without involving constant attention and work. We cannot afford rooms that have no other function than to be decorative interiors, to impress the visitor.[57]

Anthony Bertram, another writer under the spell of Le Corbusier's writing style, asserted: 'We do not want our rooms crowded with the useless and the sentimental. Our house is not a mausoleum nor a curio shop nor a tableau of the days when granddad [sic] was a boy: it is a machine for living in'. By contrast, the new architecture is described as 'logical, clear-sighted, unsentimental, creative'; characteristics that matched the new personalities of those who would dwell within.[58]

Views differed about the seriousness with which ideas about imminent social transformation through architecture were held by British modernists and about their grasp of the realities of working-class housing (e.g. Figure 4.15). Seminal blocks of flats of the day were often initiated as housing that would transform living conditions for the lower-middle or working-classes, but finished by attracting residents from the

local avant-garde. At Lawn Road, a combination of high rents plus the aura of social experimentation meant that the new residents were primarily recruited from progressive-minded members of the upper-middle class. Tecton's Highpoint I became luxury flats leavened with a few units let at low rents, even though the project started life as a scheme for workers' housing at a site in Camden Town for Zigmund Gestetner, the office machinery manufacturer:

> the original tenants of Highpoint were to have been the employ-ees of Gestetner. He approached us (Tecton) because he wanted to house all his employees there. It was designed as a working-class thing. . . There was to be a club where people would have had communal meals and other schemes of that type.[59]

Yet whatever happened when intention eventually confronted reality, ideas about social transformation through architecture were, as seen in Chapter 2, undoubtedly useful. Particular living environments, (the modern house or flat), and the life-styles associated with them were offered as the prototypes of the new urban future. The justification for saying so rested on the notion of 'Modern Man', the theoretical concept spun from the Modern Movement's interpretation of what they regarded as emerging patterns of urban life. Of course, it could not be proven at the time that such patterns would soon diffuse widely throughout urban society but nor, by the same token, could the assertion be refuted. Only experience could undermine these initial premises and it would be many years before those lessons were learned.

The urge to associate

Almost from the start, British modernists looked to find like-minded individuals with whom they could associate for mutual support. Lubetkin, for example, recalled a meeting with Coates at London's Café Royal in 1931 at which the two discussed the possibility of launching an architectural association to foster progressive architecture. Coates wanted to found a body that might oust power from the Royal Institute of British Architects, the established professional body:

> We were talking about how to achieve a breakthrough in view of the obstruction (to modernism) of the RIBA. It appeared to him that the whole delay was due to the RIBA which . . . would not let anyone new break in. He thought that only when these administrative heights of the profession were taken would it be possible to move forwards and that required people to band together into a new unit.[60]

Lubetkin replied unenthusiastically, pointing to the absence of criteria for deciding the basis upon which such a body would be founded. Such circumstances would mean that the organisation would be filled with friends and personal acquaintances rather than individuals prepared to work to a shared conception and commitment.

Coates's suggestion did not lead to any direct result at that stage, but the event encapsulates the Modern Movement's familiar complaints of being excluded from decision-making and beset by adversaries. Throughout the 1930s, individuals felt a powerful urge to associate into groups for mutual support and defence, as well as conveying a positive message about modernism and working to change prevailing opinion. Of the four most significant groups, two were pan-artistic groupings in which architects participated and two others were established by architects themselves.

Pan-artistic groups The first of the pan-artistic groups was established in July 1930 under the leadership of Mansfield Forbes, a Cambridge academic whose interests in the arts went far beyond his specialism of Romantic literature. Its founding members were Forbes, three architects – Coates, Chermayeff, and Howard Robertson – and Jack Pritchard. Other members who soon

joined the nascent group included McGrath, Shand and Noel
Carrington. Initial meetings discussed proposals for a specific
exhibition of 'Modern British Design' (see Chapter 5), and
sufficient common interest was found to suggest formation of
a definite group. Given the title 'The Twentieth Century
Group', its aims were:

> To define the principles to which contemporary design should
> conform.
>
> To make known these principles by writings, lectures, and discus-
> sions etc. and by contact with Government authorities, with
> manufacturers and other business enterprises, and with existing
> Societies interested in design.
>
> To co-ordinate the efforts of modern British designers, with a view
> to the achievement of architectural unity.
>
> To promote exhibitions of contemporary design in relation to
> architecture and interior equipment.[61]

The Group laid down strict criteria for balance among the
membership. It would be restricted to 150 members of whom
90 would be architects and related professionals ('practising
structural engineers and allied designers') and 60 other members. Anyone who contravened the rules of the Group or who
acted 'contrary to its purpose or spirit' would be excluded
from meetings.

Despite committing itself to a complete exhibition, including a full housing scheme and displays of mass-produced and
standardised equipment within three years (see Chapter 5),
the Group had faded away by 1933. Indeed problems had
revealed themselves rather earlier. Coates, for instance, had
written to Forbes in February 1932 about an evening's discussion that the Group intended to have with the Architecture
Club, noting:

> It seems to me that the inactivity which has followed our recent
> attempts to get things moving only confirms my view, which is
> that we are not organised as a public debating corps, not even
> having reached any kind of agreement in our private debates. I
> think it would be fatal to present an unco-ordinated front to a lot
> of old men feeling rather pleased with a good dinner and a brandy
> thereafter. However, it might be possible to do something without
> mentioning the 20th Century Group, and I am sure you and
> Robertson (who were anxious to accept Elder Duncan's sugges-
> tion) ought to put up a good show between you. I personally am
> not prepared to take a part.[62]

Forbes replied quickly by hand, stating that he was 'well sick' of the Group's fractiousness and inability to pull together, that he had 'wasted a d-d (damned) sight too much time *and money*' on the whole thing, and that he had told Elder Duncan of the Architecture Club that 'there's 0 (zero) doing'.[63] Not surprisingly, perhaps, the Group achieved little in any direct sense, but it did set a typical agenda of stridency and propaganda that others would seek to emulate. It also supplied an important meeting point for key members, who would go on to collaborate in similar groups.

The second group, Unit One, tried to do for the arts what the Twentieth Century Group had attempted for design. Formed as a collective in early 1933, the group consisted of 11 members, most of whom lived in or near Hampstead in North London. The initiative came from the painter Paul Nash, who took the nucleus of Unit One from contributors to the 'Recent Developments in British Painting' exhibition in 1931. Originally titled the English Contemporary Group, its character changed when Coates was invited to participate. By extending its scope to include architecture, the group briefly offered 'the glimmer of reflected Bauhaus ideas'. Quite apart from 'unit' being something of a buzz-word in the 1930s, the group apparently took the name 'Unit One' to denote a combination of individuality and unity.[64]

Its members comprised two architects (Coates and Lucas), two sculptors (Moore and Hepworth) and seven painters (Edward Wadsworth, Ben Nicholson, Paul Nash, Edward Burra, John Bigge, John Armstrong and Frances Hodgkins – who was later replaced by Tristram Hillier). It was described by its guru and leading sympathiser Herbert Read as 'a solid combination, standing by each other and defending their beliefs', with the aim of forming 'a point in the forward thrust of modernism in architecture, painting and sculpture, and (hardening) this point in the fires of criticism and controversy'. Read concluded that the formation of Unit One was the most important event 'to have happened in the history of English art for very many years'.[65]

Reality proved a disappointment. The group staged just one exhibition, held at the Mayor Gallery in April 1934 at which small selections of work by each member were shown. Coates showed photographs of the Lawn Road flats under construction, a shop front for Cresta Silks, a studio designed for the BBC and different models of his bakelite Ekco radios. Lucas showed illustrations of an International-Styled modern house

at Wrotham (Kent) and a combined music room and boat-
house at Bourne End on the Thames. The accompanying
volume allowed brief personal statements of the individual's
attitudes towards modern art, which remain a useful baro-
meter of mid-1930s thinking. Despite the talk of solidarity and
defiant rhetoric, Unit One then faded away. Whatever it
contributed to the general development of the arts, it contributed little to the development of the architectural Modern
Movement. Architects tended to talk to other architects rather
than seek involvement in pan-artistic groups, notwithstanding the high-profile activities of Unit One. Certainly it was
from primarily architectural circles that two other important
groups emerged, namely: the MARS Group and the Architects' and Technicians' Organisation.

The MARS Group

The MARS Group was a model of durability compared with
the short life-span of other modernist groups formed in the
1930s. Established in early 1933, it lasted until January 1957.
Throughout its existence, MARS remained the British organisation that sent delegates to CIAM and it played an important
role in the post-war Congresses at Bridgwater in 1947 (CIAM
VI) and Hoddesdon in 1951 (CIAM VIII). In fact, its longevity
can be partly attributed to the fact that participation in CIAM
activities provided MARS with a coherent focus around which
to organise its own activities.

Certainly CIAM contacts actively promoted the establishment of the MARS Group. From the surviving correspondence,[66] it is clear that the initiative for founding the Group
stemmed from contacts between Shand and Giedion. Shand
originally wrote in January 1929 to Giedion (with whom he
was already acquainted), to ask for details about CIAM I in
1928. Giedion, who was keen to promote full British participation in the newly formed international group, replied
shortly afterwards, asking Shand about an appropriate person
to approach. Shand suggested his cousin Howard Robertson,
then Principal of the Architectural Association, and Giedion
wrote enthusiastically seeking a direct British contribution to
the exhibition held at CIAM II (Frankfurt, 1929). Robertson
replied coolly, stating that it was impossible to arrange an
exhibit in the time available and, more generally, that: 'In the
first place we do not have a modern movement similar to that
in Europe. The average English view of what is modern in
housing does not correspond with that abroad . . . [and] in the

second place English architects are not very interested in sending their work abroad'.[67]

Robertson, along with several colleagues, attended both CIAM II and III, but clearly failed to establish any rapport with Giedion or the other leaders of CIAM.[68] Robertson called a meeting in late 1930 at the Architectural Association to explore the prospects of forming a British branch of CIAM, but informed Giedion there was little prospect of being successful. Having received further cool responses, Giedion contacted Shand in the autumn of 1932 to find an alternative person to approach. Shand suggested Coates, whom he had met through the Twentieth Century Group. Giedion wrote to Coates, alluding to his fruitless transactions with Robertson with regard to the formation of a British group and somewhat despairingly asking: 'Please let us know if interest in the new architecture is still so luke-warm in England'.[69]

Coates replied that such interest did exist and set about forming the British Group, calling a meeting on 28 February 1933 of a small number of colleagues to discuss the composition of the Group and its constitution.[70] The Minutes of the first meeting contained three important pointers to the future shape of the group.[71] First, they laid down the initial principles of association, derived from CIAM's own statutes, which convey the widest possible interpretation of the scope of architectural endeavour:

> To formulate contemporary architectural problems.
>
> To represent the modern architectural idea.
>
> To cause this idea to·penetrate technical, economic and social circles.
>
> To work towards the solution of the contemporary problems of architecture.

Second, they specified three categories of people who would be admitted to membership of the group, namely: professional architects, engineers, town planners and others able to 'present proofs' of their adherence to the group's principles; 'sympathetic laymen'; and professional or non-professional 'snob' names of the intellectual or 'international' type. Third, and significantly, they suggested exclusion of those who might design in modern styles but were insufficiently committed to modernism *per se*. The initial Minutes left the Group without an official name, although Coates, who wanted to find a pithy acronym reminiscent of the Soviet model, had suggested 'The

Group of British Modern Architecture' (GMBA). The name
'Modern Architectural Research (MARS) Group' was agreed
shortly before the press release announcing the formation of
the group on 25 April 1933.

From inception, then, MARS consciously associated its
activities with CIAM and the international Modern Movement. The press release referred to MARS as being 'officially
linked with the research programme of the International
Congresses', but the 'research' element was always controversial. Fry suggested that Coates's main intention in adding
the word 'Research' was primarily concerned with supplying a
memorable acronym.[72] Richards maintained that what Coates
actually had in mind was 're-search' in the sense of searching
back to architecture's roots to find fundamental principles.[73]
Lubetkin argued that the Group did harbour a dream of
collaborating in the programme of the Government research
establishment, the Building Research Station, based at Gar-
ston.[74] Certainly in April 1934, the Group's Minutes still
emphasised a responsibility to undertake research, pledging
that: 'To carry out its aims effectively, MARS organisation has
been designed on a basis of effective work for every participant, its technique of procedure being at every point of the
programme linked with specific research subjects and activities'.[75]

To maintain this dedicated focus, everything possible was
done to create a small and committed group on the notional
model of the European avant garde. Conferment of membership by invitation only would ensure the adherence of the
faithful and exclusion of those with lukewarm commitment.
This strategy foundered when it was discovered that there
were no criteria by which to judge commitment to the
Group's ideals.[76] As Sir John Summerson commented: 'It was
always hard to know what the criteria were that made people
suitable or not. One is tempted to say that it was safer never to
have built anything than to have built something that was not
quite up to the mark.'[77]

Group membership grew steadily from an initial core of 13
in 1933 to 70–80 in the late 1930s. This altered the style of
Group meetings, even though the number of active members
remained relatively small.[78] The commitment to serious
research was quietly dropped. The Group effectively became a
discussion forum, undertaking occasional activities for exhibitions or in connection with CIAM Congresses. Personal invitation remained the key to membership, a point that effectively

maintained the Group's social homogeneity. The new members matched the profile given earlier: dominantly young, upper-middle class, university-educated architects, holding mildly left-of-centre views, and working in independent, if normally struggling, private practices in the London area. The last point should be stressed. Despite efforts to achieve a wider national basis,[79] the Group remained confined primarily to London, albeit with the CIAM connection contributing broader horizons.

Looking back, former members evaluate the Group's significance in various ways. To some, the value of such a grouping was mainly confined to needs of personal identity and of the defensive needs to belong to a wider collectivity. Richards, for example, observed: 'Its value at home was simply that it existed; that it gave a small minority of architects, who felt virtually excluded from their own profession, a sense of safety in numbers and strength in numbers.'[80] Other participants placed a stronger interpretation on the value that they placed on MARS activities *per se*. To Ling, it supplied 'a club where people of kindred spirit met to analyse what architecture meant to themselves and to society'.[81] The Group was not 'a dedicated . . . Pre-Raphaelite brotherhood',[82] but there were collectively held values and shared 'aesthetic, social and intellectual views. It was not the case that people were exactly all the same, but they were in parallel'.[83] Furthermore, the fact that there were underlying differences in philosophy, politics and aesthetics among Group members did not place the strains on group harmony that occurred in the post-war period.

Judging the significance and extent of shared ideals, Susan Digby Firth, who acted as secretary to MARS meetings in the mid-1930s, remarked: 'Even if they acted as individuals rather than out of any group consensus, there clearly were ideals that they shared. In a way they were almost brought together to find themselves; to try and define what they should be doing and how they should move forward'.[84]

Architects' and Technicians' Organisation

The Architects' and Technicians' Organisation (ATO) was established at a meeting at London's Conway Hall in February 1935 by Francis Skinner, Lubetkin and other Tecton members. Although its foundation was prompted by the general decay of the international situation, one of its four founding aims was 'to form research and study groups on housing and town-planning questions, with a view to the formulation of a

definite line of action in these spheres'. A defining characteristic of that 'definite line' lay in its commitment to socialism
and to 'support working class organisations fighting for better
housing conditions'.[85] To some extent, this was a response to
the lack of political commitment exhibited by MARS,
although it must be emphasised that many architects
belonged to both organisations. Indeed Lubetkin suggested
that it credited too much historical importance to the MARS
Group – then scarcely two years old – to see the ATO as
primarily a response to its activities:

> The left-wing didn't think seriously about MARS at that time. But,
> we took the ATO very seriously. The main campaign for shelters
> and for community architecture (although not known by that
> name) came from this source. We went and talked to tenants and
> spoke with them about political matters – the Spanish Civil War
> and so on – as well as about a WC in the house.[86]

As Lubetkin suggested, the ATO made direct connection
between domestic issues and national and even international
politics. That stance was not entirely effortless, as shown by
the response by members as well as outsiders to the contents
of the ATO's 'Working Class Housing' exhibition in April 1936
(see Chapter 5). The group did briefly direct its attention to
problems that were more directly concerned with architecture. A Town Planning Group, formed in 1936, was intended
to complement the efforts of the Housing Standards Group.
Their joint remit centred on analysis of the costs of speculative
building and to examine rehousing schemes. The latter
included: 'a careful critique of the standards of existing
rehousing schemes by various local authorities, together with
recommendations on the possibilities of higher standards,
better planning and the use of modern materials and construction, good equipment and social amenities.'[87]

Little resulted, however, other than for the ATO to support
housing and social welfare schemes with which Tecton were
involved, such as continuing involvement with the 'Working
Class' Flats Project (1935) and the Finsbury Health Centre.
Events in the external environment led the ATO to refocus its
attention on other issues. Its aim of opposing tendencies
towards 'Fascism and war . . . which (*inter alia*) prevent
architects and technicians from fully discharging their social
responsibilities',[88] prompted the ATO to give active support to
the Republican cause in the Spanish Civil War. Domestically, it
made common cause with the radical scientists to campaign

against the National Government's policy of population dispersal and small-scale personal shelters as protection against
air-raids, sensing that the policy was driven by tactical rather
than humanitarian considerations.[89]

By 1937 the impetus given to the ATO by a small group of
committed individuals was ebbing away. Its gradual dissolu-
tion coupled with its willingness to collaborate with like-
minded groups soon brought the ATO's independent life to an
end. In 1938 the ATO, whose peak membership was around
one hundred, became part of the much-larger Association of
Architects, Surveyors and Technical Assistants (AASTA).[90]
Originally established in 1919, the AASTA offered representation on various important professional committees and had
gained radical credentials since A.W. Cleeve Barr became
Secretary in 1937. To a limited extent, ex-ATO members
gained a stronger professional voice and access to greater
resources. For its report on the design, equipment and cost of
air-raid shelters, for example, it sent Skinner to Barcelona to
gain first-hand experience of aerial bombardment.[91] Nevertheless, the ATO had joined an organisation undergoing an
active membership drive in which architects were only one
section – indeed the AASTA, shortly afterwards to rename
itself the Association of Building Technicians, became a trades
union in 1941. With these changes came the loss of the
agenda of housing and town-planning reform that were part
of the ATO's rationale.

5   EXHIBITING THE FUTURE

Every so often, there are these attempts to jettison the
impedimenta of history, to do without that ever-frustrating
weight. And because history accumulates, because it gets
always heavier and the frustration greater, so the attempts to
throw it off (in order to go – which way was it?) become more
violent and drastic.

Graham Swift[1]

Exhibitions, festivals and fairs have played a key role in the
history of architecture. The 1889 Paris Exposition saw the
construction of the Eiffel Tower, one of the foremost symbols
of nineteenth-century engineering. The World's Columbian
Exposition, held in Chicago in 1893 to celebrate the 400th
anniversary of the discovery of America, promoted the aesthetics of the City Beautiful movement. The result materially
influenced American town planning, for good or ill, for more
than a generation.[2] The 1925 Exposition Internationale des
Arts Décoratifs et Industriels Modernes in Paris launched the
Art Deco movement. The 1927 Weissenhof Siedlung brought
together and codified the International Style. Each event had
a profound impact not only on the cultural heritage of the
host city, but also on the broader history of architecture and
design.

The use of architecture to create spectacle and visual excitement continued into the 1930s. The 1938 Empire Exhibition
in Glasgow, for example, created a striking spectacle at Bella-
houston Park in the depressed south-west of the city, with
modernist-styled temporary pavilions and the 300 foot 'Tower
of Empire' by Thomas S. Tait (Figure 5.1). Perhaps inevitably
for a decade of fierce political confrontation, exhibitions also
expressed ideological conflict. Most notably, the 1937 Paris
International Exposition saw architecture in the front-line of
the war of cultural politics, with Sert and Luis Lacasa's
curtain-walled Spanish Pavilion, housing Picasso's *Guernica*,
alongside the colonnaded monumentalism of the neo-classical
German and Soviet pavilions.

These international exhibitions, of course, were only the tip
of an iceberg. The 1930s yielded an endless stream of specialist
and popular exhibitions showing trends in art, architecture,
and industrial and interior design. The London galleries

Figure 5.1
The 300 foot 'Tower of
Empire' by Thomas
S. Tait.

around New Bond Street held numerous exhibitions of
abstract and surrealist art, some of which toured provincial
cities. The Design and Industry Association (founded 1915)
and the Society of Industrial Artists (1930) organised well-
attended exhibitions in London. There were also many exhibitions by the architectural establishment, offering an 'official'
view of developments in architecture (Figure 5.2). Individually and collectively, these exhibitions were key instruments
for information and propaganda, supplying an important
means of publicising causes and displaying materials in three-
dimensional form in this pre-televisual age. People visited
exhibitions 'as much to see the stands and the way that they
were laid out' as to see what they contained.[3]

By contrast, modern architects had few opportunities to put
their case across through exhibitions. Although keen to emulate other groups' achievements in this field, staging exhibitions required resources, time and a clarity of vision that they
often failed to muster. In this chapter, we examine their

Figure 5.2
The opening of the
Exhibition on the
'Architecture of Modern
Transport' by H.G. Wells,
Tuesday, 21 April 1931.
On the left of Wells is
Sir Bannister Fletcher.

varying success in attempting to organise exhibitions that
hinted at the Modern Movement's urban imagination. The
first part considers an abortive proposal for an exhibition by
the Twentieth Century Group that reveals something of
the forlornly grandiose scale of exhibition to which British
modernists sometimes aspired. The second section considers
exhibitions on 'New Homes for Old' (1934) and 'Working
Class Housing' (1936) that provided an opportunity for modern architects to express ideas about social housing. Finally,
we survey in detail the one event that gave the opportunity
for a full overview of the Modern Movement's thinking about
the wider urban scale, namely, the MARS Group's 'New
Architecture' Exhibition held at London's Burlington Galleries
in January 1938.

'The House of To-day'

The desire to promote exhibitions of contemporary design in
relation to architecture and interior equipment was, as noted
in the previous chapter, a founding aim of the Twentieth
Century Group. Chermayeff and Etchells, two of the Group's
early members, had tried unsuccessfully to float the idea of an
exhibition of British modern design as early as 1923. The

recent success of the 1930 Stockholm Exhibition of Modern Industrial and Decorative Art and, more specifically, a Swedish Industrial Arts and Crafts exhibition at the Dorland Hall (1931) provided the Group with models to emulate.

A meeting in February 1931 had committed the Twentieth Century Group to organising a comprehensive exhibition, including a complete housing scheme, within three years. The 'Proposal for Immediate Activity' urged members to refer to this Exhibition as 'actually projected'. In imitation of best Soviet fashion, it was the subject of a three-year plan, with the Group's Council trusting that all members of the Group would be willing to perform 'a definite function' in achieving its goals. Moreover, once detailed plans for the main exhibition were complete, the Council proposed holding a small private exhibition for potential patrons.[4]

Despite the Group's internal problems and the already ambitious nature of this project, it was soon scrapped for something grander. At a meeting held at the Arts Club in late November 1931, members of the Twentieth Century Group's Council decided to draw up plans to 'capture' the 1933 Daily Mail 'Ideal Home' exhibition. Coates, Chermayeff and Etchells met at Etchell's office on 2 December to discuss strategy. Coates then drafted plans of the proposed layout of the exhibition in the Hall at Olympia at 1:192 scale. These were considered the next day at a Group meeting at the Hampstead home of the Secretary, Gibbons Grinling.

A memorandum by Coates recorded the proposals put to that meeting.[5] The exhibition, to be organised by Etchells, would take a housing theme under the name 'The House of To-day. . . with no adjective like "modern" or "suntrap" or whatnot'. The ground plan centred on a full-scale 'Street of To-day' on which would be constructed four types of housing, each appropriate to a different income bracket. Types A and B were detached houses, type C a semi-detached house. Type D was a small tenement house 'with flats of single-rooms, double-rooms, and three or four rooms, with certain communal services such as heating, washing space, etc but not "service flats" in the usually accepted sense'. Other spaces would accommodate facsimiles of up to 12 different flats, with the possible grouping of some to form 'the ground floor social rooms of an ideal tenement house scheme'. Exhibits elsewhere would present the latest trends in appropriate fitments and fixtures, with display stands exhibiting drawings and other materials such as 'graphs of population, housing density, air-maps of congested areas'.

Coates stressed that absolute secrecy was necessary regarding the exhibition 'at this stage and. . . for some time to come' to allow the development of ideas to the point that proposals could be submitted to the *Daily Mail*. Work would cease on any smaller exhibition by the Group prior to the Olympia exhibition. Somewhat predictably, that stipulation was then contradicted by the accompanying suggestion of holding additional 'spearhead' exhibitions 'combined with the Daily Mail exhibition idea in some specific way' at building sites near London underground stations.

With hindsight, Coates and the Twentieth Century Group need not have worried about securing absolute secrecy for its plans. Disillusionment, disagreements over key issues, and lack of resources or personnel to carry out ambitious plans meant that 'The House of To-day' exhibition proposal never reached the *Daily Mail* for consideration. Indeed, the Group had faded away long before the 1933 Ideal Home Exhibition was held, though ambitions to hold an exhibition to promote modern architecture persisted.

Housing exhibitions

Another opportunity for modern architects to realise that ambition came in March 1934 in the shape of an invitation to the MARS Group to contribute to a housing exhibition. The invitation came from the Housing Centre, a pressure group for housing reform. It had been allocated space at the Building Trades Exhibition scheduled for Olympia (London) in September 1934 and it invited MARS to contribute to its exhibit on the problems of slum housing entitled 'New Homes for Old'.[6]

This offer precisely fitted the Group's own plans. They had previously developed a basis of material on the replanning of London for CIAM IV and by early 1934 had devised three areas of long-term research and one area of short-term research for future activity. The long-term areas were analytic in character: historical analysis 'of the growth of a new conception in architecture and its relations to the changing structure of society since the industrial revolution'; sociological analysis of 'the architectural demand from the various classes of the community'; and technical analysis of such issues as planning, construction techniques and the organisation of the building industry.[7] The short-term research programme was on slum clearance. Following on from work done for CIAM IV, the Group aimed to focus on one London borough and to move beyond the stage of analysis in order to produce a 'general replanning scheme'. The borough chosen was Bethnal Green in London's East End.[8]

The MARS Group, therefore, accepted the offer with alacrity. They were allocated one of the seven bays of the exhibition hall offered to the New Homes for Old Committee – a space measuring 10×13 metres – for a 'detailed scheme for the replanning of a built-up area'.[9] An Exhibition Sub-committee, consisting of Fry, Hazen Sise and Eugen Kaufmann, was given responsibility for initial planning. It, in turn, allocated the two tasks necessary for preparing the exhibit. One was to collect and present statistics on poverty, crowding, types of dwellings, size of families and industries. The other involved drawing plans and perspective diagrams for the proposed replanning scheme for Bethnal Green, as well as providing costings and making models of the proposed housing, schools and social facilities.

Only the former were undertaken, as the MARS Group gradually retreated from presenting a replanning scheme. This was partly due to problems of finding enough people to volunteer time to prepare the exhibit, but also reflected a fundamental debate within the Group. Lubetkin, in particular, argued that the Group had not produced any satisfactory theoretical basis on which it could design such a scheme. Attempting to save at least something of the design synthesis, the Exhibition Committee submitted an urgent memorandum which tried to shift the ground away from the specific case of Bethnal Green to a more general exhibit by which one could discover 'the general technique of replanning any urban area'. The memorandum stated that to do this, the Group needed to make:

> (1) An Analysis of Needs. . .to discover what accommodation and services could reasonably be demanded as the rights of *modern man* [author's italics], in consideration of the industrial means he now has at his disposal. (2) An Analysis of Means to display the technique of modern building, showing methods which could be universal if the industrial scheme were properly managed for mass production. And (3) a Model (or Models) to try to give the appearance of what might be described as a 'Metropolitan cell'. That is, the height and proper dispositions of a group of habitation

buildings with their satellite service buildings – schools, laundries, clinics etc. forming a nearly self-contained unit which could be repeated over and over again with local variations.

The memorandum ended with the earnest statement that this programme could be carried out in the time available if 'strictly limited to essentials'.[10]

Yet even though this proposal contained many ideas that were relatively uncontentious, it fell short of mapping out a coherent structure for the replanning scheme. The eventual exhibit was very different in both content and purpose. It consisted of a stand containing five large, but portable, screens that analysed social needs in the Bethnal Green district of London's East End. These identified the problem but completely avoided suggesting possible solutions. The stand was designed by a small core of members, many of whom would later play an important role in the ATO. These included Lubetkin, Skinner, Samuel and Lassere, assisted by several non-MARS Group members who were associates of Lubetkin. These, in turn, included Misha Black, a young graphic designer who provided the overall design for the panels; the writer Claude Cockburn, then employed by the *Daily Worker*, who advised on the political dimension of the display; and Arthur Korn, a German architect with experience in exhibition design, who had come to London in June 1934 as a delegate to the CIRPAC meeting.[11]

The panels dealt with overcrowding in London; the cumulative effect of poor planning; a comparison of the density of Bethnal Green with the more fortunate borough of Chelsea; an analysis of present conditions in Bethnal Green; and an exposition of 'the necessary readjustment of economic factors, which must form the basis of any plan for improving existing conditions'.[12] The screens emphasised the need for planning to avoid urban chaos and bring about greater equality, but dealt purely with the wider social dimension of architecture. They scarcely hint at the contribution the architect might make to alleviate the problem of the slums. Ironically, the New Homes for Old Committee's exhibits said more about the architectural dimension than did the MARS Group's presentation. These, for example, included a model of a nursery school and various designs for flats. Moreover the exhibition as a whole included a suite of a specimen flat, arranged by G.E.W. Crewe, 'with particular reference to economy of space and labour in the kitchen'.[13]

To Lubetkin, this was relatively unimportant. Talking about his collaboration with Cockburn, he remarked:

> For him [Cockburn] and for me, this exhibit was an instrument of propaganda. It showed clearly what the housing conditions were like in some areas and how badly they compared with other areas. This was itself a very important thing – the architecture is like mustard, it merely helps the thing to be appreciated . . . architecture was, I think, only a pretext.[14]

Yet in spite of the overt political commitment, its ideological function was scarcely different to other projects shown at the Exhibition. The organisers were propounding a basic analysis of housing deprivation; acceptance of that analysis would pave the way for appropriate remedial action. This point was forcefully confirmed by William Tatton Brown, when he observed that the prime purpose of the exhibit was:

> to expose the problem and to create a climate of opinion that would demand rebuilding London and this in itself would give us the opportunity to exercise our talents.[15]

The MARS Group was invited to contribute to subsequent 'New Homes for Old' exhibitions, but was primarily concerned with holding its own exhibition (see next section) and only offered its 1934 displays for reshowing in 1936. By that time, those members that had actively prepared the original exhibits were pursuing similar themes under the aegis of the ATO, notably for the 'Working Class Housing' exhibition. This opened at London's Housing Centre in April 1936 and then travelled to Liverpool, Birkenhead, Fulham, Manchester and Cambridge. It comprised four sections. The first, 'Housing Conditions' was a display of statistical material designed to show that: 'The housing conditions of the large mass of working-class families are as bad today as they have been at any time at least since the (Great) War.' In particular, those unable to afford new accommodation were forced to accept sub-standard housing and overcrowding. A summary of urgent needs led on to a section on 'Social Effects'. Again primarily statistical, it presented illustrations to show that: 'The social effects of bad housing are the terrible toll in death and disease among the working-class people, especially the children.' The third section levelled particular criticism at the treatment of housing as a private matter subject simply to the laws of supply and demand.

The 'Working Class Housing' exhibition met with criticism from within as well as outside the group's ranks as being too 'political'. In an initially unapologetic rebuttal, the Executive Committee hit back at its critics:

> The Exhibition was criticised as 'political' and in many quarters the ATO was dubbed a 'political' organisation. Apart from those who fix the label 'political' on to any technical body which occasionally speaks its mind about the private interests preventing it from fulfilling its work satisfactorily, some ATO members and others have seriously thought that the Organisation has concentrated on the social and political obstacles to good architecture to the neglect of the more technical, constructive problems of architecture itself.
>
> The Executive Committee, in reply to these criticisms, wishes to stress first that in dealing with housing it was inevitable that a thorough critique should be made both of the vested interests in building and the legislation which helped or retarded the pace and quality of building. The ATO need not therefore apologise for its vigorous excursion into the 'political' field. Secondly there was no other organisation at that time capable or prepared to undertake precisely that kind of survey which the ATO thought it necessary to make.

Having made these points, the authors then immediately softened the rhetoric:

> However, now that the complacency of certain sections of the community have been slightly punctured and public interest in good housing seems to be re-awakening, the ATO believes that it has, to a certain extent, fulfilled its function in that sphere.[16]

As a result, they announced that henceforth the group would use its limited resources to concentrate on problems that were more architectural in form and content. Even among 'progressive' architects, therefore, it was not always easy to maintain a radical stance.

New Architecture

The disappointments the MARS Group itself experienced over the New Homes for Old project did not diminish the enthusiasm for exhibition projects. Shortly after the New Homes for Old exhibition, the MARS Group decided to hold an exhibition of its own 'extending the analysis and synthesis'.[17] This was scheduled for the spring of 1935, with the empirical focus remaining Bethnal Green, but the process of organising an exhibition proved far more difficult and time-consuming than was ever envisaged.[18] The date of the exhibition was continually deferred and the task of organiser was allocated in turn to no less than four individuals – Hazen Sise, Godfrey Samuel, Laszlo Moholy-Nagy and finally Misha Black.

In February 1935, a programme of work circulated by the Central Executive Committee proposed that: 'an exhibition of international modern architecture on a well-thought out schedule be held in London in May–June if possible, in any case not later than October–November'.[19] In June 1935, the exhibition was scheduled for November 1935; in September it was rescheduled for April 1936; and in January 1936 it was again put back until the summer.[20] During the latter part of 1936 and early 1937, plans became firmer. In February 1937, the date for the exhibition was set for 14 June 1937, with the New Burlington Galleries in Burlington Gardens (off London's Bond Street) booked as the venue. This timing again proved to be too optimistic and the date was subsequently postponed, first until October 1937 and finally to January 1938.[21]

Part of the delay was due to limited resources. A full-blown exhibition was an ambitious undertaking for a group that had no full-time staff, no money and only met in the evenings.[22] Yet matters were not helped by dropping the case-study focus on Bethnal Green. Without that focus, there were continuing problems in defining the exhibition's objectives or potential target audience. As Fry recalled:

> Some of the group wanted a popular exhibition and thought in terms of the 'Daily Mail' (Ideal Homes Exhibition) and so on. I was violently opposed to that and so was Tolek (Lubetkin) . . . We argued that if you wanted to disseminate information, you had to disseminate it at the highest level and let it disseminate downwards and through the schools. To go direct to the public would have been a pure disaster . . . There was also a good deal of argument which went on about the actual contents of the exhibition.[23]

Symptomatic of the extent of the disagreement was a dispute over the very nature of modern architecture. An 'Intermediary Report' of the Exhibition Committee in April 1935 suggested a small initial undertaking 'to explain to Architects and the general public the general principles or Anatomy of the so-called "International Style"'.[24] This attempt to associate the Group's exhibition with the theme employed at New York's Museum of Modern Art three years previously was fiercely resisted by those who believed that modern architecture was most emphatically not a style but merely constituted non-aesthetic built forms driven by realisation of functional necessity and social needs.[25] At a subsequent meeting characterised by 'much disagreement on many points', the group decided to delete mention of the International Style without articulating an alternative definition of modernism.[26]

By March 1936, a circular letter to members referred to a 'fairly well-studied scenario' having been worked out for the 'MARS Propaganda-for-and-explanation-of-modern-architecture Exhibition'.[27] Shortly afterwards, the Minutes stated that Laszlo Moholy-Nagy had been approached to translate that scenario into 'an equivalent pictorial form', in order to discover the time needed to prepare the exhibition, the amount of space required and the likely costs.[28]

Over a protracted period, agreement slowly emerged. In February 1937, a pamphlet containing a draft prospectus was circulated to potential sponsors.[29] The pamphlet, largely written by Godfrey Samuel on behalf of the Exhibitions Committee, was circulated with a form requesting sponsorship from each to the sum of £100. The pamphlet's brief content sought to answer basic questions that such sponsors might have. The wider claims of modern architecture were stressed at the outset:

> [Modern architecture] is an architecture which attempts to solve contemporary problems directly, without preconceived ideas of what a building should look like. The growth of industrial England has accumulated on the one hand new problems in town-planning, housing and social services, and on the other hand new means of solving them, new materials, new methods of production and new forms of power. It is only recently however, that architects have woken up to these facts and appreciated the possibility of a revival of their art. Now that the experimental stage is over there are enough examples to show the practical advantages of such buildings and the enjoyment that is to be derived from them.[30]

It was suggested that the forthcoming exhibition would be divided into three main sections: analysis of 'the social needs which the modern architect is called upon to fulfil'; the techniques of modern building; and the aesthetic qualities of

modern architecture. The report ended with a layout plan.
This indicated that, after a screen indicating the 'architectural
problem', the first section would show the needs of the
individual, the family and the town; the second would contain an exposition on industrial prefabrication and standardisation in building techniques; and the third would contain
models and photographs of rooms and buildings.

The continuing vagueness of this scheme is readily apparent. Indeed it was only in the last few months of preparation
that the Group decided to return to an integrating theme
suggested by Godfrey Samuel in 1935. His idea, which retains
an air of intellectual contrivance, consisted of recasting these
three sections in terms of Sir Henry Wotton's aphorism that:

> In Architecture as in all other Operative Arts, the end must direct
> the Operation. The end is to build well. Well building hath three
> Conditions: Commoditie, Firmenes and Delight.[31]

'Commoditie' was interpreted as building needs, 'firmenes' as
qualities shown by 'the contributions of the scientist, the
engineer and the manufacturer', and 'delight' as the achievements of the modern architect.[32] This gave a measure of
progression to the exhibition's contents, although opinion was
sharply divided about whether they were intelligible to the
show's estimated 7000 visitors.

The Exhibition's title was left unresolved almost until
the end. An Executive Committee meeting just two months
before the show was still trawling through a wide range of
options without reaching any decision. Among the suggestions on offer were 'Sticks and Stones', 'Architecture Today',
'Birth of an Architecture', 'Live Architecture', Building for
Today', 'Human Architecture' and 'Architecture for
Humans'.[33] In the end the anodyne 'New Architecture' was
selected, partly for its echoes of the translated title of Le
Corbusier's *Towards a New Architecture*.

Plan and contents

The exhibition opened at the New Burlington Galleries on 11
January 1938 and ran until 29 January.[34] In due course, this
avowed piece of 'propaganda . . . to win the loyalty of those
who have not already made up their minds'[35] would leave the
MARS Group with considerable debts and acrimonious rela-

tionships with the firm of Beck and Pollitzer, their contractors for the exhibition.[36]

When designing the final displays, close attention was paid to visual appearance as a vital part of communicating the exhibition's message. As Richards noted, the ideas of the Modern Movement 'were almost completely unfamiliar to the British public. . . (MARS) were at great pains to try to depict modern architecture as something lively, enjoyable and providing the Good Life'.[37] Vivid and imaginative presentation was seen as an essential part of that process. To some extent, too, the appearance was a response to the small size of the gallery, making full use of partitions, raised levels and a variety of visual effects to make best use of limited space. Yet there is no doubt that, at times, visual novelty was employed for its own sake. Perhaps understandably for a project in which some 15 individuals had taken responsibility for separate tasks within the framework of a loose brief, the opportunity had been taken to indulge creative talents.[38]

Critical judgment in the London press and in professional journals was mixed. Several reviews argued that the visual presentation of material interfered with the exhibition's message. For example, a group of students from the Architectural Association – always likely to be well-disposed towards modern architecture – complained that the organisers at times 'were speaking in a visual language amongst themselves and seemed to have forgotten that what they were trying to say had to be made intelligible to the public'.[39] Even among MARS Group members not centrally involved in the exhibition, opinion was divided between those who considered the presentation to be 'inspiring to the eye' and those who felt it was spoiled by 'meretricious formalism'.[40]

The exhibition layout is shown in Figure 5.3, which depicts the gallery compartmentalised into the three requisite sections. Visitors followed a set route around the exhibits, as indicated by the arrows. The entrance hall contained exhibits that juxtaposed the problems of the existing city, with photographic illustrations of London's traffic congestion, lack of open space and overcrowding. The centre-piece was a large scale-model of a modern metropolitan city, entitled the 'Concrete City', which might have been taken to be a possible answer to those problems.

The visitor then passed into the first room, devoted to 'building needs'. A large screen, designed by Peter Moro with assistance from Gordon Cullen, illustrated Wotton's dictum, with 'commoditie' symbolised by a plan, 'firmenes' by a section and 'delight' by a perspective. The remaining screens tackled the needs arising from various aspects of everyday life, including dwelling, leisure, work, transport and services. Each screen laid out a brief analysis of the implications of these needs, accompanied by pictures illustrating relevant modern buildings. In the corner was a Town Planning display, which was intended to provide a demonstration of where the analysis of needs might lead.

The second section, laid out in the corridor connecting the two main rooms, dealt with structural technique. Devised by Ove Arup with assistance from William Tatton Brown, this consisted of nine show-cases that explained the nature and significance of methods of industrialised production and pre-fabrication. The corridor itself was unlit except for top-illumination in each of the show-cases, with the aim being to focus attention firmly on the exhibits.

The third section, occupying the second room, depicted the way forward in the shape of the finished products and achievements of modern architects. Stands dealt in turn with the 'textures' of material, 'equipment', and the 'universality of modern architecture'. An 'architecture in the landscape' exhibit included a garden pergola, complete with garden furniture, plants and shrubs, intended to give the impression that the scope of modern architecture did not end with buildings. As the caption on the stand stated: 'The architecture

Figure 5.3
Layout plan of the 'New Architecture' exhibition, 1938.

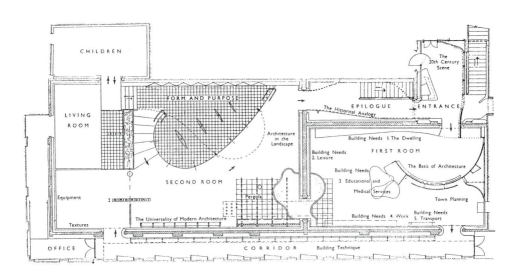

of the house embraces the garden. House and garden coalesce, a single unit in the landscape.'[41] This area also accommodated full-sized replicas of two interiors (a living room by Wells Coates and a child's bedroom by Ernö Goldfinger) and a selection of three-dimensional scale-models (Figure 5.4).

Figure 5.4
'Form and Purpose' exhibit, 'New Architecture' exhibition, 1938.

The final screens gave telling insight into the exhibition's true intent. One portrayed modern architecture as a continuation of the centuries-old tradition of English building rather than as a sharp break with the past. Against a sequence of photographs that started with Bamburgh Castle (Northumbria) and ended with the newly completed flats at Kensal House (Ladbroke Grove, London),[42] the caption proclaimed modern architecture as a style appropriate to its age in the same way that the Norman Castle, the Gothic Church, the Renaissance Palace and the Palladian terrace were to their generations. In other words, the argument over the true nature of modern architecture was implicitly resolved: what was presented here was a *Zeitstil*, instead of the non-stylistic product of rationally addressing social needs by means of modern technology. A final closing screen, placed over the stair-well at the exit, then recapped the propaganda theme: 'We claim your loyalty for an architecture that is worthy of this age and worthy of the future' (Figure 5.5).

In thematic terms, the most coherent scenario in the exhibition was that associated with the dwelling and domestic living

Figure 5.5
Closing screen, 'New
Architecture' exhibition,
1938.

patterns. This was scarcely surprising. By 1938, there were
now a small, but growing, number of modern housing
schemes completed by MARS members that could be pressed
into service as potential prototypes from which to generate
ideas about future living patterns. The subject was introduced
by a screen, which identified 'dwelling needs' at different
scales: individual, family and communal. The portions
devoted to the individual showed a figure striding into a
centrally heated bathroom, with the caption listing individual
needs as 'clean air, light and warmth proportioned to climate
and season . . . space to move . . . a setting that is humane:
sympathetic in scale and texture'.

The 'family' section contained a collage of modern room
interiors and noted that the dwelling 'must be modelled upon
the routine and variations of family life, harmonising the
needs of worker, housewife, child and guest'. At the wider,
community scale, the language became openly prescriptive,
putting forward the vision of a collective, scientifically progressive, orderly and, above all, planned society: 'the larger
unit is the product of collective needs, responsibility is shared
and delegated, public services are planned comprehensively,
eliminating waste, canalising the knowledge of the scientist
and engineer'. The graphics continued this theme, matching
symbolic representations of the various functions of everyday
life with perspective drawings of new urban landscapes,

reminiscent of Le Corbusier's Ville Radieuse. Commenting on this screen, Richards downplayed the significance of the particular prototype, stressing that no single urban vision commanded universal approval. Instead, the significance of the screen was that it underlined:

> a general feeling that planning, as compared to laissez-faire, did mean cooperation and a communal conception of how people were going to live and viewing towns as communities. It was effectively the opposite of the suburban villa where each man was for himself.[43]

Suburbia reappeared as *bête noire* in the corridor section. Alongside illustrations of good practice (the Quarry Hill flats in Leeds, modern school buildings, an American timber-framed house), appeared a showcase depicting a tile-hung, pitch-roofed suburban house overlain by a model of a flat roof, cut-away to reveal its constructional materials (Figure 5.6). The villa represented tradition, the flat roof the way ahead. The captions strongly suggested that adopting these construction techniques and materials was the only way to meet modern social needs: 'We cannot . . . continue with the traditional methods because they will not provide the form of shelter which present conditions demand and we cannot return to tradition, however much we may desire it.' The flat roof was advocated:

> because of its outstanding importance. Sociological and economic changes have necessitated the concentration of population in limited areas, and it is necessary to re-utilise the site area occupied by building if we are to provide an adequate area wherein the population may obtain some access to light and sun.

In doing so, the argument shifted from the constructional advantages of different forms of roof to the wider strategies of housing policy.

The third section, as noted above, contained exemplars of design held to be appropriate for the community's needs. At the level of interiors, the message was unambiguous. Modern architecture sought to make all space serve a definite function, designing for flexibility and convenience, building in features to economise on the total amount of space needed and incorporating labour-saving devices for an age in which domestic service was disappearing.[44] Strongly influenced by Coates's interiors at Lawn Road, the exhibits deliberately

Figure 5.6
Structural Technique:
'Exhibition, Testing,
Classification'. 'New
Architecture' exhibition,
1938.

embraced a spartan quality, a belief that the 'minimal was the desirable'.[45] Enlarging on this point, Summerson suggested that the attraction lay in:

> the clean edge, economy of style, simplicity, the clean white form penetrating chaos. We have lost that kind of pleasure. There was an invitation to fill these empty spaces with human activities – good food, intelligent conversation, intimacy – the sensuous qualities of life were to be enhanced by the simplicity of the environment. It was a sensual view of life, conducted with style and elegance against a very severe background.[46]

Turning to the types of housing shown in this section, one encounters the immediate paradox that the much-reviled detached villa featured more prominently than the much-admired flat. Six out of 15 of the scale models were of modern villas and bungalows, against two for flats. The reason for this, however, lay in the circumstances surrounding the exhibition. Lacking money and time, the MARS Group used models that members had left over from their commissions, many of which had been for villas. This tactical necessity, however, should not be confused with approval. As Fry commented, villas *per se* had 'no place in the MARS Group's view of the future city . . . there was a broad commitment to flats'.[47]

That commitment was expressed by a prominent display of photographs of many of Europe's best-known schemes for flatted housing, such as the 16-storey blocks of the Cité de la

Muette (Drancy, France), the Bergpolder flats (Rotterdam) and the Doldertal flats (Zurich), as well as schemes in which MARS members had participated (Figure 5.7). These schemes were given prominence partly because they showed 'the more dramatic kind of modern architecture', but also because they indicated 'the architect's concern for housing policy rather than houses individually'.[48] They also illustrated a new way of handling the relationship between housing and its surroundings. With the vistas of open space and greenery available from their large windows and balconies, modern flats were held to be a way of integrating the dwelling with its 'natural setting'.[49] Both in the sense of flexibility of interior layout and in their permeability to the external world, flats were considered to offer 'an open plan way of living and designs were full of these undertones'.[50]

The broad coherence of the general scenario for housing was not matched by the scenarios for the other urban functions, primarily because there was no consensus on anything but basic outlines on how these elements should be treated. This is amply illustrated by the subject of work and the workplace. Although idealising the industrial process and electricity as forces for beneficial economic and social transformation, the Group's ideas about either the ideal design of offices and factories or about the location and planning of work were rudimentary. An initial screen headed 'an architecture exactly disciplined to the needs of hand and eye' had divided work into four categories – agriculture, industry, commerce and administration. The most detailed was the case

Figure 5.7
The residential point blocks at Drancy in Paris, designed by Beaudoin and Lods were one of the best-known modern housing developments from the inter-war period, displayed on a screen at the 'New Architecture' exhibition, 1938.

for agriculture. Essentially borrowing Le Corbusier's notion of the Radiant Farm,[51] the exhibit appealed for the industrialisation and reorganisation of agriculture, for cooperative farming villages, and for the planning of agricultural activities within the wider context of urban-rural relations.

Statements concerning industry, commerce and administration were altogether vaguer. For industry, the captions supported planning factories with reference to broader landscape considerations. Though recognising that electricity and secondary energy sources loosened the locational ties of manufacturing industry, all that was proposed was placing light and well-ventilated factories on green-field sites with adequate room for expansion. There was no indication of the relationship of industry to the city as a whole besides what might be gleaned from the adjacent Town Planning exhibit (see next section).

With regard to commerce and administration, the focus was principally micro-scale and ergonomic. Offices at that stage were considered poorly sited and badly planned. Better design would eliminate 'needless fatigue' by improved lighting and ventilation and by providing for greater convenience and flexibility in usage. Apart from the accompanying photographs, which implied approval for the corporate slab or tower, there was little attempt to explain the implications for the city or working lives of its inhabitants.

Recreation was tackled by the 'leisure' screen in the first room. Devised by Fred Lassere, Kit Nicholson and Christopher Tunnard, the screen focused on two types of leisure activity – public entertainments and outdoor sporting pursuits. These were illustrated by photographs of sports stadia, the work of Tecton on animal enclosures at London and Dudley Zoos, swimming pools from Germany and Czechoslovakia, the Royal Corinthian Yacht Club building at Burnham-on-Crouch (Essex), cinemas and theatres.

Opinions differ sharply about how these were to be interpreted. For some,[52] they merely signified the extension of modern architecture into new areas of activity in which there were no traditions to be challenged and overthrown. For others, the emphasis on high culture entertainment and on 'healthy' outdoor sports was symptomatic of a wider intent like that seen in the work of Le Corbusier and others (see Chapter 2). William Tatton Brown, for example, suggested that the broad purpose underlying the choice of material derived from contemporary advocacy of sport and exercise as ways to promote physical health and, in turn, 'social health'.[53]

Treatment of transport was brief, but broadly followed the typical ideas of European modernists: namely, segregating distinct types of flow into separate channels and allowing efficient interchange between different media. In the words of the catalogue: 'Transport demands an architecture modelled on a planned flow of traffic, an architecture eliminating stress and confusion at terminal points, clarifying the transition from foot to wheel, from wheel to air or water.'[54] Eight media were identified: the pavement, the cycle track, the road, the railway, the underground railway, marine transport, the aeroplane and the dirigible. These were depicted on a revolving wheel construction, with pictures to illustrate the opportunities that each presented for modern architecture (Figure 5.8). No direct impression was given at this stage or, for that matter, later in the exhibition about how the broader questions of segregation of flows or system interchange were to be handled.

Towards a synthesis

This description of the contents of the New Architecture exhibition necessarily reveals the fragmentary approach of a project that lacked an overall integrating concept of the prospective city. At best, two quite different exhibits offered some explanation of how these component elements might be synthesised. The first, the Town Planning display, offered an interpretation that drew on strands of the MARS Group's previous work. Based on work originally prepared as the MARS Group's submission to CIAM V (see Chapter 6), the stand featured proposals for the reorganisation of London on linear city principles.

The display had three parts. The first surveyed the problems that occur when decentralisation is allowed to proceed without planning controls. The rapid spread of the metropolitan area of London during the inter-war years was creating problems for communications systems, dissolving the ties that bound communities together, and sterilising land through ribbon development. The second portion suggested replacing unplanned ribbon growth by planned linear development. A specimen plan for a mile-long residential or 'neighbourhood unit' arranged around the spine of a high-density through-

Figure 5.8
Transport Wheel, 'New Architecture' exhibition, 1938.

route was put forward (see Chapter 6). The third portion included maps contrasting likely development over the next 15 years: one showing what might be expected to happen if suburban expansion was allowed to continue unchecked; another illustrating the future for London if population growth was channelled along radial strips.

Yet despite being associated with the MARS Group's Town Planning Committee, the caption at the top of the display stand distanced the Group as a whole from endorsing this exhibit: 'The Town Planning needs of the community are here illustrated by a typical example. A preliminary survey of London by a *section* [author's emphasis] of the MARS Group.' Put another way, this scheme may have been accepted as the official MARS submission to CIAM V, but here was presented, without the official imprimatur, as simply the work of a sub-group.

This scheme was not the only conception of the prospective city presented. There were also various representations of the alternative notion of the 'city of towers', including facsimiles of Le Corbusier's Radiant City plans and the 'Concrete City' model found in the entrance hall. The latter was a 1:360 scale model designed by F.R.S. Yorke, a founder member of MARS, and his partner, Marcel Breuer. Built for the Cement and Concrete Association in 1936 and originally entitled 'A Garden City of the Future',[55] the model had previously been displayed at the Ideal Home exhibition in 1936. It was intended as a 'demonstration of principle' and was essentially a pastiche intended to cram as many different features as possible into a small space. There was no underlying prototype of urban form or any explicitly postulated relationship between the form of the street system and user needs.

The model measured 290 × 170 cm (Figure 5.9). It only showed a portion of the central area of a city bordering on to a lake, but this was considered large enough to show the interrelationship of land-uses as well as appropriate transport systems. Its purpose was to reveal the interrelationship of residential, retail, commercial, industrial and recreational land-uses as well as appropriate transport systems to a public unfamiliar with such ideas. It embraced three design principles: geometrically-regular layout, strict functional separa-

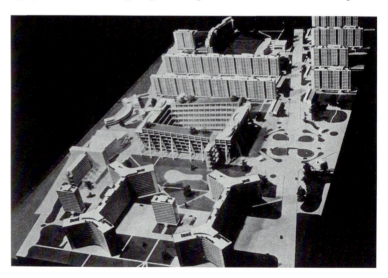

Figure 5.9
'The Concrete City', originally known as 'A Garden City of the Future'.

tion of land-uses, and segregation of traffic flows. The housing
consisted of 12-storey slabs of flats, raised on pilotis and laid
out according to the Zeilenbau north–south alignment, with
windows facing east and west to afford the maximum light.
The blocks themselves embraced Le Corbusier's concept of the
unité, with shops placed at the ends of blocks and schools
centrally grouped between the blocks. It was stressed, however, that the model only showed part of the city and that
lower-rise flats and even individual houses would be built
near the fringe.

The decisions on forms and locations of housing also
reflected the policy on movement within the city. As Yorke
and Breuer had noted in an earlier description of this model:

> The adoption of higher buildings ensures . . . the distances from
> point to point are reduced to a minimum. With this type of plan
> too, the simplification of traffic conditions becomes automatic,
> there are fewer house doors, fewer streets, and above all, fewer
> street intersections. . . . The private house in the centre of the city
> complicates immediately the traffic problem.[56]

Transport flows themselves would be channelled on to
purpose-built, high-capacity routeways of the type exemplified by the axial road that ran across the model. Through-
traffic could move unimpeded; traffic serving the megastructural retailing district, the waterfront entertainment district or
the office complexes could leave or join the axial road by a
modified clover-leaf intersection. Parking spaces or other indications of where vehicles were left when not in use are
virtually absent from this conception.

Looked at together, the presence of both centralist and
decentralist future city schemes can be explained in three
contrasting ways. The first is to suggest that MARS simply
lacked firm criteria on which to make judgments. There is
ample evidence to support this view. The repeated delays in
arranging the exhibition were partly attributable to the difficulty in defining the Group's common ground and integrating
it into a conspectus that might be understood by the wider
public. Moreover, the material appeared at various points to
be either vague and imprecise (as in the scenarios for work,
leisure and transport) or even downright contradictory to the
Group's objectives, (for instance, the weighting towards villas
as opposed to flats in the choice of the scale models).

Another interpretation would be to argue that the confusion was more apparent than real: a product of the tactical need to re-use materials, of varying suitability, that had been originally prepared for other purposes. Again, ample evidence could be marshalled to support this point. The available choice was constrained. Not many modern buildings had been constructed in Britain before 1938 and only a handful of appropriate town-planning schemes had been completed. Given the lack of resources to custom-build materials, it is not surprising that the exhibition should contain elements that might now seem incongruent.

A third interpretation, which is more helpful, is also possible. As Johnson-Marshall[57] observed, the two prototypes were not seen as being mutually exclusive. Despite reaching very different syntheses, they were considered 'broadly similar conceptions' that shared a common basis and heritage and that could be equally supported as valid bases for research and further development. Hence, just as Le Corbusier and others could work on both types of scheme when extending modernist notions to the city-scale, so too could the MARS Group without having to select and endorse one specific prototype. These ideas are of continuing relevance as we turn to look at urban projects and plans produced during the late inter-war period.

6   PROJECTS AND PLANS

Architects today are perfectly aware that the future of architecture is inseparably bound up with town planning. A single beautiful house or a single fine residential development accomplishes very little. Everything depends on the unified organization of life. The interrelations between house, town, and country, or residence, labour and leisure, can no longer be left to chance. Conscious planning is demanded.

In a single building something extraordinary may be sought and achieved. The whole body of a city, however, shows beyond dispute the state of the architectural knowledge of a period. It shows the extent to which the period was capable of organising its own life.

Sigfried Giedion[1]

Although not all modern architects would have accepted Giedion's assertions about the orientation of contemporary architecture, fascination with the future city led many to experiment with plan-making. Maxwell Fry, for example, provided illustrations for the First Regional Plan of New York in 1929 that moved away from conventional interpretations of verticality towards a more spacious and cubist conception of the future city.[2] William Holford and a group of colleagues from Liverpool produced a competition entry in 1933 that attempted to combine the environmental benefits of a garden city with a 'superdense' Corbusian scheme.[3] As the 1930s progressed, many similar experiments in form-making were undertaken by modern architects. By and large, they fell into one of two categories. One followed the Geddesian approach, relying on extensive survey work and subsequent analysis to generate the plan. The other was primarily conceptual, taking general ideas about urban form and the arrangement of functions and loosely applying them to existing settlements.

As a general rule, modern architects aspired to the first approach but usually ended up adopting the second. Extensive survey-work was beyond the time and resources available to individual architects and required a clarity about aims and methods that groups plainly lacked. In this chapter, we examine in some depth two sets of schemes which give insight into both contemporary thought and the problems encountered. The first part examines the growing interest in modernist ideas about urban form and function in the architectural schools, highlighting projects undertaken by students at the Architectural Association. The remaining sections provide a case-study of the evolution, contents and intent of the MARS Group's Master Plan for London. Although formally published in June 1942, it was effectively an outgrowth of the inter-war period rather than a specific response to the new conditions and challenges of wartime. We examine the various versions produced before arriving at the final published plan, the analyses employed, the interweaving of the social and design imageries of the projected metropolis and the response that the plan generated.

Student projects

The changing climate of ideas within the architectural profession started to influence the curriculum of the architectural schools after 1935 (see also Chapter 4). University departments at Liverpool, Hull and elsewhere permitted students to take a comprehensive approach to the built environment in their project work. The Architectural Association, however, was unique in the extent that it provided active encouragement to such initiatives through changes in its teaching structure. In 1936 the new Principal, E.A.A. Rowse, replaced the five progressive 'years' of study with a system of 15 'units'. Each contained about 17 students and was run by one instructor or Unit Master. The resulting semi-autonomous units were intended to inculcate teamwork rather than foster the supposed individualism and competitiveness of the Beaux-Arts approach.[4] Inspired by Geddes's advocacy of sociologically motivated surveys, students were encouraged to undertake lengthy project work. Two such projects stand out from this period: the Ocean Street Study (1939) and 'Tomorrow Town' (1937–8).

The former broke new ground by examining the real views and preferences of slum-dwellers; a cause recently canvassed by the documentary movement through films such as *Housing Problems*[5] and the work of Mass Observation. Ocean Street (Stepney) was a 'clearance area' where the London County Council (LCC) was to demolish 729 houses and replace them with 15 five-storey blocks of flats. Finding little correlation between the residents' preferences for 'houses' and the flats that the LCC were going to provide, the students formulated alternative plans. Working within the financial and legal constraints of the clearance legislation, they produced a scheme which combined duplex-units of two-storey flats into a low-rise flatted estate. The 'houses' in this arrangement therefore qualified as flats for funding. The existing conditions were photographed, a model of the proposals was made, and a scripted film made of the residents' case.[6] The scheme received considerable publicity with press briefings and public meetings. It had achieved little official support before the outbreak of war put an end to further discussions, but it pioneered techniques of public participation in planning.

'Tomorrow Town' was a study for a new town of 50 000 people carried out in 1937–8, under the direction of Rowse, by a group of students that included Anthony Cox and Elizabeth Chesterton. The scheme was originally produced as a rectilinear plan for a hypothetical flat site, but was subsequently applied to a site at Farringdon (Oxfordshire). The plan was influenced by Rowse's view that town planning should address two broad goals. In terms of physical planning, the planner should put into practice:

> the most all comprehending interpretation of the term 'preventive medicine'. That is to say that the task proposed is the removal from environment of all those conditions which make for susceptibility to disease. It is the natural extension of the work of Chadwick and Pasteur.[7]

In terms of catering 'for the mind and spirit', the planner must address the lack of any sense of community suffered by the 'amorphous, sprawling modern city'. These goals led, in turn, to a series of principles for designing 'Tomorrow Town'. Some were principles to guide the creation of the physical fabric of the new town, such as the need to create social facilities to allow the development of community and for economy of cost based on standardisation. Others hinted at the wider regional scale, including provision of an optimum diet and minimisation of journey-to-work distances.

The scheme for the new town drew on current interest in the concept of the 'neighbourhood unit'. Derived from the work of Clarence Perry on the First Regional Plan of New York, neighbourhood units had excited interest on both sides of the Atlantic.[8] The neighbourhood unit represented a seemingly logical building block for the construction of new settlements. They were essentially housing estates for 5000–10 000 people, built with integral social services: indeed the size was often predicated on the rule that no child should need to walk more than a half-mile to school. A related interest in the separation of pedestrian and vehicle movement systems, following the example of Radburn (New Jersey), supplied further ideas about urban structure and layout.

'Tomorrow Town' was envisaged as a system of urban villages coordinated into an urban region of approximately 30 square miles, of which the built environment occupied around 10 per cent of the total area. For the Farringdon site, a soil survey prepared by Reading University was used to suggest sites for development away from areas of fertile loam soils, thereby addressing the goal of an 'optimum diet'. The new town comprised five neighbourhood units, each containing 2000 families, located around the town centre. The dwellings, which would be factory-produced and assembled on-site, comprised both flats and terraced houses. Twelve-storey flats, suggesting the influence of both Gropius and the recently-completed Highpoint, were placed to the east and west of a town centre, set in a park. Further to the east and west were lower density areas of terrace housing that also contained the necessary social services for the community living there. A green belt separated the town from its industrial areas to the north and east, with the latter, being downwind, housing any noxious industries. The town centre contained the rail and bus stations. Perimeter roads surrounding the residential areas and town centres catered for motorised transport, with entirely separate circulation systems for pedestrians and cyclists.[9]

These two schemes had some importance other than being simply barometers of current thinking. 'Tomorrow Town', for instance, was one of a number of future city schemes shown in the 'Coventry of Tomorrow' exhibition during the war 'to persuade the leading citizens of the need for new ways of thinking in the building and rebuilding of cities.'[10] The Ocean Street study was pivotal in the career of Max Lock, since it developed participation techniques taken further in Lock's *Middlesbrough Survey* (1946) and, much later, elsewhere.[11] While these schemes may now seem commonplace, even naive, at the time they were revolutionary within a British school of architecture and had biographical significance for their participants.[12]

From Athens to Paris

The MARS Group's association with CIAM brought commitment to the CIAM's 'Functional City' project. This was initiated by the hurriedly prepared analytical survey of London produced to the standard brief of CIAM IV in 1933 (see Chapter 3). As displayed in Athens and on the SS *Patris II*, this exhibit comprised written material on the city's historical development and future growth patterns, along with nine transport maps and a large general map of London and its region.[13] It also initiated an empirical focus on the planning of London which was developed further with the approach of CIAM V.

The MARS representatives at CIAM IV agreed to lead an international study of housing and planning legislation, but when asked to contribute a section on 'Housing Legislation' to the CIRPAC meeting in Amsterdam (June 1935), they were only able to display again the London map produced for CIAM IV.[14] Reporting back after the CIRPAC meeting, Maxwell Fry noted ironically that 'delegates felt that the English group had put in very little actual work except the proposed work on legislation which had not yet been started'.[15] While the commitment remained to organise the contribution on 'Housing Legislation' at CIAM V, it was eventually realised that this would not be forthcoming.[16] The report of the Group's Annual General Meeting in February 1937, for instance, stated that Fry had informed CIAM's Executive Committee that 'all work from the English Group would be limited as all efforts were being concentrated on its (1938) Exhibition'.[17] With the absence of any alternative, Ernö Goldfinger suggested that the endeavours of the MARS Group's own Town Planning Committee could be adopted as its official contribution to CIAM V. This course of action was eventually ratified by the Group on 10 June 1937, when it was decided that a report would be submitted to the Congress entitled 'The Interpenetration of Town and Country, Example: London'.[18]

There is no record of when the 'Town Planning Committee' was originally formed, although such a Committee was mentioned as being 'active' and 'working on a definite programme' by March 1936.[19] It is clear, however, that the Committee then consisted of only three individuals: the chairman, Hubert de Cronin Hastings, and William and Aileen Tatton Brown. Hastings was deeply interested in the nature of

the city and of the significance of patterns of human interaction ('contacts') for urban form. Having examined previous
work on urban futures, he had become intrigued by the
recent revival of interest in the potential of linear city principles. Lacking the time to conduct the research himself, and
also perhaps wishing to remain in the background,[20] he
privately commissioned William Tatton Brown and his wife
Aileen to undertake research on the forms that a linear city
might take. William Tatton Brown was then working for the
Tecton practice in London; Aileen Tatton Brown (née Spar-
row) had also worked at Tecton but, by this time, was
employed by Hastings at the Architectural Press. William
Tatton Brown recalled undertaking this research:

> Hastings . . . commissioned us to do some research on his ideas on
> the *cité linéaire*. We came up with a scheme based around main
> arteries – like motorways. Hastings was very much against the
> radial city and everything coming out from the *Etiole*. He said that
> the future city would be linear . . . [and] said that he wanted us to
> investigate it for him. We used to have lunch with him once a
> week or . . . fortnight in Jermyn Street and tell him what we had
> found out. We did this as a spare-time activity . . . We showed
> how the unplanned growth of London would cause greater and
> greater congestion at the centre and access to the countryside
> would be more and more remote.'[21]

Their work supplied the basis of William Tatton Brown's
presentation to CIAM V in Paris (September 1937). His report,
now entitled *'The Theory of Contacts' and its application to the
Future of London*, consisted of three sections.[22] The opening
part analysed London's problems, including the deteriorating
physical fabric and the stresses caused by demographic
growth, suburbanisation and changes in the industrial structure. Emphasis was placed on the implications of a projected
doubling in car ownership from 1.5 to 3 million in the period
from 1935–50. The second section discussed the lack of comprehensive powers and direction in the contemporary planning system and the limitations of other initiatives to improve
matters – such as Garden Cities, Trystan Edwards's campaign
for 'A Hundred New Towns',[23] and the strangulation that
Green Belts imposed on metropolitan growth. The third section set out the alternative approach. This began with a
'theory of contacts'. It was argued that existing proposals for
planning the future city paid insufficient attention to the need

for contacts between people. Functionally, cities could be viewed as centres that facilitated human contacts (or trans-actions) of all types – whether intellectual, social or commer-cial, but this meant more than just efficient communication. Contacts were the root of social harmony, with the city's effectiveness depending on both the quality and quantity of the contacts that it provided.

Naturally, transport occupied prime position in considering how the ideal future city could maximise the potential for effective and harmonious contacts. For discussion purposes, the plan divided trips into four categories: pedestrian move-ment (below 10 km/hr), local traffic (up to 100 km/hr), rapid highway traffic (more than 100 km/hour), and air travel. Each form of movement placed different demands on the

Figure 6.1
Projected development
of the Linear Strips,
1935–50.

transport system, which in turn had implications for urban form.

Figure 6.1 applies linear city principles to planning for the future metropolis.[24] Growth for 15 years to 1950 would be channelled into 13 linear strips that would radiate into the surrounding countryside. Their purpose was to convert the dynamic that caused unplanned ribbon development into the precursors of a new urban form. Factories for growing industries or decentralising firms would be placed in planned cells of development along the designated strips, where the spinal high-speed road arteries would give them easy access to the metropolitan and national economies. That done, it would be possible to cope with the planned demographic growth of London by a linear city arrangement that would provide jobs in the locality. Residential developments would be sited near the central spinal roads, but would be screened from them by placing the through routes at sunken levels, with additional earth-works to screen them from the houses. There would be multi-level intersections at one-mile intervals, frequent enough to provide access for traffic destined for, or joining from, the 'neighbourhood units' that were placed along the

Figure 6.2
One Mile Unit
(Neighbourhood Unit).

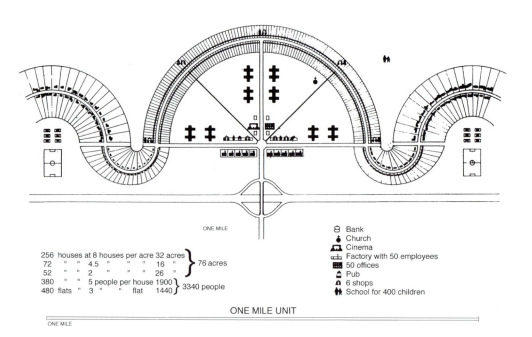

ONE MILE

256	houses	at	8	houses per acre	32 acres	} 76 acres
72	"	"	4.5	"	"	"	16	"
52	"	"	2	"	"	"	26	"
380	"	"	5	people per house	1900	} 3340 people
480	flats	"	3	"	"	flat	1440

⊟ Bank
⚲ Church
🎞 Cinema
⚒ Factory with 50 employees
▦ 50 offices
🍺 Pub
⌂ 6 shops
👫 School for 400 children

ONE MILE UNIT

ONE MILE

route of the road but not so frequent as to impede the flow of through traffic.

The adoption of the concept of the 'neighbourhood unit' as the basic building block of urban development was an important element in the plan. Figure 6.2 shows the extension of such ideas in the shape of the hypothetical layout of a one-mile long neighbourhood unit designed to supply homes, amenities and a substantial part of the employment for a population of 3340. Given that society was differentiated by dominant function into 'producers' (working class), 'distributors' (middle class) and 'consumers' (upper class), there was also a three-fold differentiation in the types of housing offered (flats, row housing and villas). The aim was to offer a range of dwellings that would satisfy the needs of everyone (although it was realised that many of the 'consumer' class would remain attracted to the exclusive residential districts of the city's core).

Residential accommodation comprised 480 flats and 380 conventional houses. As seen in Figure 6.2, the houses situated on the sinuous distribution road consisted of both larger villas and modern, continuous row housing, with an average density of five houses per acre. The flats, by contrast, were clustered around the neighbourhood centre. They comprised eight multi-storey blocks, each of 60 flats, with a double-cruciform plan reminiscent of Tecton's design for the newly opened Highpoint One. The neighbourhood centre would contain the necessary social and retail services for a community of this size, also providing premises for the factories and offices. In turn, the neighbourhood unit would contain sufficient children to justify two schools, (each to take 400 pupils), with the schools placed at half-mile intervals in the interstices between the loops of the distribution road. Everyone would have ready access to the wedges of protected open countryside left between the linear strips, also allowing playing fields to be located close to residential areas.

The neighbourhood units were joined together in the physical fabric of the linear strips. Figure 6.3 shows how ten units could be assembled to provide homes and employment for approximately 30 000 people. The units here are connected laterally along the line of the spinal road and form mirror-images of each other on either side of the road. Taken overall, the possibilities of contacts would be greatly enhanced by the linear city design, especially because different forms of move-

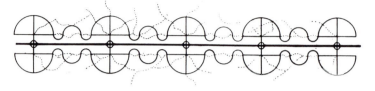

Figure 6.3
An example of a Linear
Strip formed from an
aggregation of
neighbourhood units.

Five one mile units. Population 30,000

ment (with their differing speeds), were now segregated into
purpose-built route-ways.

So far this scheme only offered a vision of how to build new
settlements on green-field sites beyond the urban fringe,
saying little about the existing metropolis apart from housing
part of its population and drawing in some of its new and
decentralising industry. In the longer term, however, the
linear strips were also intended to transform the entire city
region. Although the report was presented in terms of pre-
venting the further expansion of the built-up area of London
and planning for new growth, it was hinted that any redevelopment of the metropolitan area might extend the linear city
corridors *inwards* towards the core and, in turn, open up
wedges of green space. As William Tatton Brown explained:
'Development would have taken place naturally along these
axes, with people leaving the slums and moving out to these
new nodes. You could then drive green wedges of countryside
into the heart of London as opposed to the constriction
improved by a green belt'.[25]

Taken to its theoretical conclusion, one could envisage a
change in the nature of contemporary contacts. The contact
pattern in 1935 showed intense contacts in the metropolitan
area and new nodes growing in peripheral towns. By 1950,
the creation of linear strips would generate strong contact
patterns along the corridors and reduce levels of contacts
within the metropolitan area. Theoretically, with the establishment of suitable clearance policies, one could move to a
new axial pattern within another 15 years which would allow
rapid interconnection between the urban strips and the city's
core.

Seen in retrospect the 1937 plan was an innovative undertaking, projecting a future London based on linear city principles with efficient road transport arteries and new
relationships between housing and open space. In doing so, its

authors were trying both to channel urban growth and breed a new texture back into the existing metropolis with the opening up of wedges of green space. It was also a significant attempt to develop neighbourhood unit ideas in a British context. At the same time, various aspects of its demographic and social structure were at best tentatively formulated. There was no formal explanation of why such neighbourhoods would operate with a much lower population size (3340) than the norm of 5000–10 000 figure employed elsewhere, nor how the varying housing provisions would relate to the social structure. The provision of schools for 800 pupils would suggest the unlikely situation where almost 25 per cent of the population would be aged between 5 and 14 years. Moreover, its unusual mixture of flatted accommodation and conventional housing did not appeal to many other members of the MARS Group, for whom the plan smacked too much of compromise with the established order. As Fry noted: 'houses-with-gardens had no place then in our view of the future'.[26]

Social units

This sense of distance between the principles behind this plan and the general views of MARS members influenced further development of the London project. It may have been expedient to use the 1937 plan when there was no alternative, but within the MARS Group it was regarded as no more than a formative basis for future research. That research came from a reconvened Town Planning Committee, which met in December 1937 with a new and enlarged membership.[27] Writing to the MARS Group's Central Executive Committee in February 1938 the Town Planning Committeee's chairman, Arthur Korn, stated that his colleagues were working on a new plan for London.[28] The letter also mentioned many features that would appear in the final product – CIAM's four-fold typology of urban functions, a preference for flats, attention to mass transport, and allusion to the concept of the linear city. Nevertheless, the letter stressed that much research remained before arriving at a final synthesis.

Some indication of the problems encountered in arriving at that synthesis is indicated in a personal letter from the previous chairman, William Tatton Brown, to Sert in August 1938:

> Tomorrow I lunch with Quorn [sic] . . . I am having a big fight
> with the English group (of CIAM) on the scheme for London. It is
> very "woolly" at the moment and the arguments are a trifle
> fruitless – as each one makes a different set of assumptions such as
> the following:-
>
> 1. The Thames is diverted.
> 2. The existing railways do not exist and can be moved where we
>   like.
> 3. Everyone travels to work on the L.T.P.B. (Public Transport).
> 4. Everyone travels to work in his own car.
> 5. Everyone lives within direct communication with his work.
> 6. No private cars are allowed near the centre.
>
> According to one set of assumptions – the core of the town should
> be a park – according to another – a railway terminus. It just
> depends on the assumption! I think that the scheme should start
> from a little closer analysis of the existing conditions . . .[29]

Apparently the lunch did not go well. Later the same month,
Tatton Brown wrote again, reporting that he and his wife
were having 'tremendous battles' with Korn and Samuely,
trying to win them away from their particular conception of
linear city planning and its dependence on railways. He added
optimistically that it 'is a long and painful business but we will
succeed in the end. I think.'[30]

His optimism was misplaced. The Tatton Browns remained
part of the group that discussed the London Plan, but they
regarded the new emphasis on railways rather than roads as a
retrograde step and decided to develop their ideas about the
car and the street separately.[31] The emerging plan owed most
to Korn's ideas and enthusiasm. Korn had extensive connections with modernist groups in continental Europe[32] and had
previous involvement in town planning projects. In particular,
he had met Miliutin while on a visit to the USSR in 1929 and
had himself applied linear city ideas in work on the Greater
Berlin Plan.[33]

The key step in moving discussion forward came when he
persuaded Arthur Ling, a young architect then working in
Maxwell Fry's office, to supply a schematic plan of social
structure. Ling was just completing a Town Planning Diploma
thesis at the Bartlett School under the supervision of Patrick
Abercrombie.[34] The thesis surveyed current thinking on the
structure of neighbourhoods and cities and proposed a hierarchical arrangement of urban 'social units' that could be
fitted together in a coherent and orderly manner. His hierarchy contained five levels: residential units of 1000 people,

neighbourhood units (6000), town or borough units (50 000), city or regional units (500 000) and the capital city (5 million).

In the form contained in his thesis, Ling's scheme conceived housing as comprising a mix of flats and conventional houses-with-gardens. Korn, however, requested that Ling might supply a new version that could help the Town Planning Committee's deliberations by focusing on flats as the sole form of residential accommodation. Ling noted that while this change made the task of draughtsmanship easier, it eroded the plausibility of the resulting plan, taking 'the schemes still further away from the reality of London and the human needs of its people.'[35] Nevertheless, he agreed to the request in the interests of assisting the plan-making exercise.

Figure 6.4 depicts a specimen neighbourhood unit, with its component residential units. The design of the residential units reflected several aspects of contemporary thinking. The projected size of the neighbourhood units (6000) was rather larger than in the 1937 plan and much more in keeping with the norm of 5000 employed elsewhere. The design of the blocks of flats was influenced by Le Corbusier's concept of the *unité d'habitation*, with the layout of the flats reflecting the *Zeilenbau* pattern. The residential units themselves fitted together in a cellular structure arranged around a central corridor in which could be found the educational and community services for the neighbourhood. Traffic within the residential units would be solely for access; traffic within the neighbourhood units would be purely local, with through traffic kept to the outside margins.

Figure 6.5 shows how eight such neighbourhood units might be arranged into a borough unit, with four units being laid out north and south of a corridor which contained civic amenities, sports facilities and parkland. This would be bounded north and south by through-roads from which distribution arteries would connect at regular intervals. Ling, however, stressed that the exact disposition of these and the larger units in his hierarchy were a matter for adaptation to environmental and other circumstances. The idealised forms expressed in these diagrams were simply intended to demonstrate a set of principles.[36]

These drawings, accompanied by explanatory notes, were delivered to the Town Planning Committee in mid-1938. In many respects, they stemmed from a different tradition from

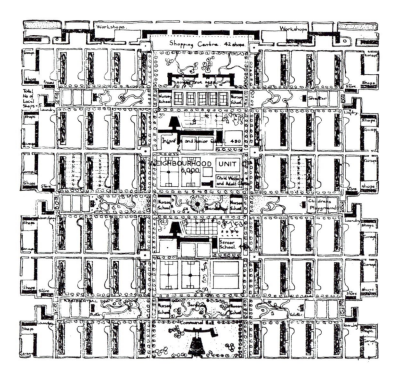

Figure 6.4
An example of a
neighbourhood unit.

that of the earlier plan. The starting point was a historic and
comparative analysis of the structure of neighbourhoods and
cities rather than an emphasis on transport: an emphasis that
would recur in Ling's later work on neighbourhood structure
for the 1943 *County of London Plan* (see Chapter 7). Despite his
strong interest in Soviet town planning practice and knowledge of the work of Miliutin and others, Ling stressed that he

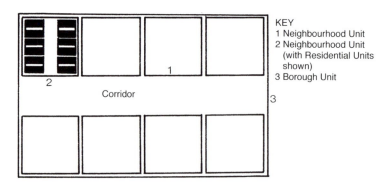

Figure 6.5
Aggregation of
neighbourhood units.

did not specifically design his framework to suit any specific preconceived model of urban form. Nevertheless, the extent to which this hierarchical schema was amenable to inclusion in a transport-led linear city plan allowed it to be accepted as one of the foundations of that plan.

Preparations

More research was started on the state of contemporary London, with reports being prepared on dwelling, work, leisure and transport. The landscape architect Christopher Tunnard, for instance, delivered sketches of how the open spaces might be consolidated into wedges penetrating back into the heart of London. Early sketch plans showed a preference for a radical reconstruction rather than a piecemeal steering of growth. The version shown in Figure 6.6, for example, is believed to date from early 1939. It schematically depicts a London comprising four major zones. At its core, running east–west along the line of the River Thames, was the historic centre which would be left largely untouched. To the east would be riverside industrial zones. The key innovation would be ten linear strips of development placed at right-angles to the historic centre. These, in turn, would be separated from one another by wedges of green space. Together, the alternating strips of urban development and open space

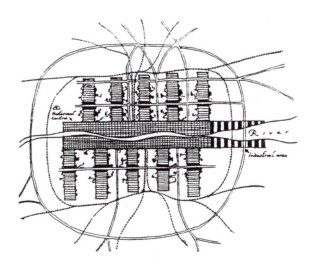

Figure 6.6
An interim design for the
MARS Plan.

would have obliterated most of north and south London. Scarcely less radical would have been the changes to the transport system. This would be rationalised by the addition of orbital road and rail networks to avoid the bottleneck of central London, with a purpose-built grid of new arterial roads to serve the linear strips and provide connection with the orbital roads.

The advent of war in September 1939, the conscription of many MARS members, and the internment of Korn in the Isle of Man as an enemy alien for 18 months brought work on the plan to a halt. At the end of 1941, an intensive burst of meetings attempted to inject greater urgency into the Committee's proceedings. At a meeting on 8 December 1941, Felix Samuely provided a summary of suggested axioms: the separation of home and workplace; major units being designed for 600 000 people; everyone able to walk to both a secondary road artery and open space in ten minutes; crossings between main and secondary arteries being on different levels with the crossings themselves in open space. The plan would be based around a new rail system that would supply the main form of mass transport along the linear strips.[37] Tellingly, the meeting then heavily criticised these proposals, with the criticisms indicating that the members of the Committee had very little previous knowledge of them. Moreover, it was recorded that: 'During the foregoing discussion it became apparent that all members were not prepared to accept the Linear Plan without further investigation'.[38] At an ensuing meeting on 2 January 1942, the lack of any real progress was indicated when Jane Drew proposed that the Committee should draw up a programme of work for the next 18 months, beginning with a statement of principles.

The turning point came in late January 1942 when Korn returned to the MARS Group after a long absence caused by his internment and the need to reestablish his affairs. Acting largely independently of the rest of the Group, Korn brought matters to a speedy conclusion. Recovering the only existing copy of the preliminary drawings to have survived bomb damage,[39] Korn put together the final plan, with Samuely supplying material on costings and on the rail proposals and Fry assisting with the drawings. The end product was published in the *Architectural Review* in June 1942, although publication of the full set of drawings of neighbourhood units awaited the appearance of Fry's book *Fine Building* (1944).[40]

The Master Plan for London

Seen in synoptic outline in Figure 6.7, the 1942 Plan super-imposed a new gridded pattern on London to produce a dramatically reconstructed city of ten million people. With even less restraint than shown in the earlier sketch (Figure 6.6), almost the entire city would have been swept away apart from a few historic buildings of national significance. At the heart of the new pattern was an east–west corridor, some 25 miles long and two wide, containing London's vital industrial commercial and administrative functions. Radiating north and south would now be 16 strips of urban development, each roughly one mile across and bordered by belts of protected countryside that would prevent sprawl and allow inhabitants easy access to open space.

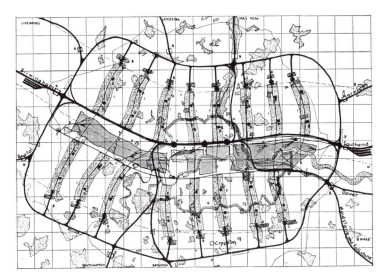

Figure 6.7
Master Plan for London,
MARS Group, 1942.

Besides recognising the authors' *a priori* commitment to the linear city, the key to understanding this pattern lies, first, in the application of a version of Ling's hierarchical arrangement of settlements and, secondly, in the primacy given to the economics and operational efficiency of transport. Taking these in reverse order, Korn and Samuely believed that the legacy of the past left London with a congested, outmoded and inefficient transport system. Railways would take priority in the reorganised system: a striking difference from the 1937 plan's emphasis on road transport. The central corridor would contain rapid through-routes as well as a high-capacity system for London's own needs, with the ten London termini reduced to three through-stations. Radiating from this were the north–south secondary rail arteries, roughly six miles long, that formed the core of the residential linear strips. Housing would extend half-a-mile on each side of the transport artery, with stations allocated to serve populations of approximately 100 000. Each of these strips would have a goods station situated at its outer edge and these would be linked by an orbital railway to ensure that goods traffic was segregated from passenger traffic.

Industry would be reorganised according to four main proposals. Heavy and port-related industry would be retained in the central corridor, albeit with housing eliminated from industrial zones. Light industry would be concentrated into a sector of north-west London and into smaller estates created at the outer edges of the city districts to balance the inward flow of traffic. Small home industries 'provided with communally controlled workshop accommodation' might be allowed in the residential areas or even the green areas.[41] Finally, some industry might be decentralised to 'satellite towns', with populations of up to 25 000, situated on extensions to the spinal transport lines of the linear residential areas.

Plans for housing provision flowed from a critique of the status quo. In the minds of Korn and Samuely, London was an amorphous sprawl with little underlying social cohesion. Such isolation would continue:

> unless there is some organisation of social life and its expression in architecture and town planning; for the visual effect on the mind is considerable. The vast crowds must be split into groups in which the individual does not feel so overwhelmed that he is forced to retire to his own home almost entirely for his social life.
>
> Only by forming clearly defined units, which in turn are part of larger units, can social life be organised.[42]

The place allotted to town planning and architecture in this enterprise was striking. The authors sketched a world in which the hierarchical organisation of social units appeared to offer the only workable pattern for the future city, a pattern that could be fostered by sensitive arrangement of the urban environment.

The suggested hierarchy, derived from Ling's earlier study, had five levels: the residential unit (for a population of 1000);

a neighbourhood (6000) that would comprise six residential units; the borough unit (50 000) made up of eight neighbourhood units; the city district (600 000) comprising 12 borough units; and the city itself (10 million). Each level would have a recognisable focus to which people could give their allegiance. Added to these calculations was a requirement that 14 acres of open-space should be supplied per 1000 dwellings, with no dwelling more than half-a-mile from its open space.

Figure 6.8 shows the proposal for neighbourhood units. While it incorporated similar ideas to those in Ling's original version (see Figure 6.4), the disposition of residential units *vis-à-vis* community services was different as was the reliance on ten-storey *unité* blocks as the sole form of residence. It was stated on several occasions in the published plan that dwellings could be either flats or houses-with-gardens,[43] but this is misleading. As Fry noted when recalling discussion about the plan: 'It was far too much biassed in favour of flats. Quite simply, we weren't looking any further.'[44] The six residential units clustered around the neighbourhood's school and local civic amenities.

In the same manner as devised by Ling, eight neighbourhood units were arranged into a borough unit of 50 000 people. In the example shown in Figure 6.9, they were arranged on either side of a central corridor containing the town hall, central park and civic buildings. Schools were placed on the edge of the built-up area so that their playing fields would merge into the parkland and countryside. The dominant impression is of a sharply bounded settlement; on one side by open space and on the other by the central rail artery. Ten such borough units comprise each of the spines ('city districts') shown previously on Figure 6.7, each with a population of 500 000. These 16 spines, plus the smaller satellite towns, would then make up the full population of ten million.

Reactions

Viewed in context, publication of material on planning and reconstruction was not an unusual event in 1942 (see Chapter 7). The reason why the 1942 MARS Plan attracted attention, and continues to intrigue researchers, lies in the extent to which a radical modernist analysis was applied to the problems of a metropolitan city.[45] As Dennis Sharp noted, it

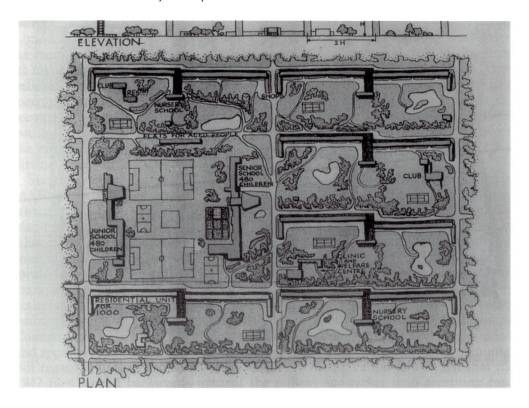

Figure 6.8
Proposal for
neighbourhood units.

'summed up, as no other plan did anywhere in the world at that time, the whole nature of the CIAM approach to a hierarchical structure for a city'.[46] Judgment about the plan, however, depended on whether it was regarded as comprising definite recommendations for London's future reconstruction or illustrative analyses of principles of land-use and transport that were applied to London as an example.

The answer to that question was far from clear from the plan itself. Other Town Planning Committee members argued that Korn and Samuely *did* believe that this was a practical suggestion for reconstruction but that they were probably alone in doing so.[47] There was broad agreement that neither had much regard for the existing London, which they regarded as formless, and saw war-time destruction as creating the opportunity for a fresh start. They also believed that the savings from greater efficiency and reduced congestion in the new metropolis would, *in the long term*, more than offset the ferocious costs of the reconstruction.[48] Indeed, years later, Korn would continue to argue that 900 000 houses accommodating four million people were built in Greater London between the two world wars, providing proof of what the building industry could do if directed towards a common goal.[49]

Such arguments gained little support elsewhere and strained the credulity even of MARS Group members. Lionel Brett, for instance, described the plan as 'characteristic of the simplicities of our time', decried the hypnotism that geometric plan-making seemed to have exerted, and argued for a 'much more sensitive use of what exists'.[50] Thomas Sharp argued that the linear city plan suffered from inadequate understanding of urban transport, the difficulty of generating civic loyalty among the prospective residents of the linear strips, from 'its extreme extravagance in public services', and from the extent of destruction necessary to realise the scheme. He concluded that it was 'not only a wild dream but also a rather bad one'.[51] Perhaps the most telling assessment was that the MARS Group itself largely excluded the 1942 Plan from its own deliberations on future planning for the Metropolis in favour of the 1943 County of London Plan which it informally 'adopted' (see following chapter).

Figure 6.9
A borough unit, comprising eight neighbourhood units arranged on either side of a central corridor containing the town hall, central park and civic buildings.

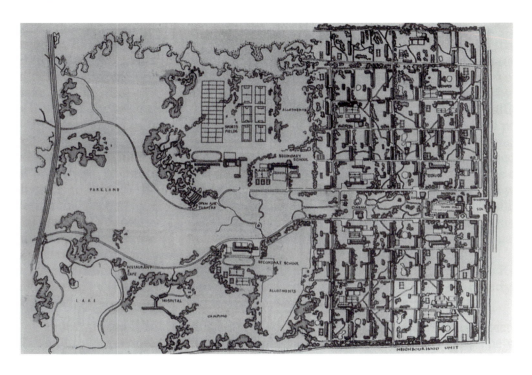

Even those who had participated in the work of the Town Planning Committee were mostly critical. Goldfinger considered the plan 'a good idea' and applauded its willingness to fly in the face of British resistance to axial planning, but regarded it as flawed in its application.[52] Ling felt the 'concept of neighbourhood structure, adopted in the new and expanding towns of the post-war period, was helped along by the MARS Plan, even if it did not develop directly from it'. At the same time the 'MARS Plan itself had no influence on the planning of London – which I can state with some authority from my own work on the County of London Plan.'[53] Peter Shepheard suggested that there was an erroneous assumption that far more of the existing London would be destroyed than was actually the case.[54] Johnson-Marshall criticised the plan for its rigidity, its disregard for the existing historical centre of London, its over-reliance on flats, and in Korn's belief:

> that it was a real solution to London's problems. That was entirely an illusion, but I could never shake Arthur from his convictions. However as a demonstration of one way of putting urban components together, it was a useful contribution.[55]

This view was echoed by Fry.[56] He emphasised that the war meant that the MARS Group had virtually ceased to operate at this time and that the Master Plan was a well-intentioned, if ill-judged, attempt to contribute to the debate about the post-war reconstruction of London.

This perspective is valuable because too much emphasis on reaction to the specific details of the plan *per se* can obscure important lessons that can be learned from viewing the 1942 Master Plan in its broader context. Despite its date of publication, the Master Plan was the product of inter-war rather than wartime thinking and the culmination of a loosely related set of experimental exercises rather than a single isolated project. These exercises reveal progression from analytical presentations about existing problems to complete plans for the future London. The initial analytic presentations helped to develop a critique of the contemporary city and applied CIAM's fourfold classification of urban functions – two important underpinnings of later work. The 1937 plan established interest in linear city notions, seeing transport as a fundamental parameter of the future city. It sketched a new urban form, adopting the neighbourhood unit as a key element in new development. Although there were few direct links of personnel or programmatic efforts to refine the earlier ideas, the

1942 plan effectively extended these notions. More specifically, by drawing on Ling's work on social units, the authors
showed how neighbourhood units could be woven into a full
hierarchical urban system for the modern city.

The use of neighbourhood units is symptomatic of a broader
point about the flux of thinking about the future city at this
time. Although historians usually associate neighbourhood
units with the Garden City and New Town Movements, the
concept was part of the common currency of planning and
architectural ideas during the 1930s. As seen in this chapter,
they had just as much appeal to the Modern Movement as a
logical way of conceptualising the structure of new settlements and as a convenient building block for constructing
them. On a related note, the MARS Plans vigorously canvassed the merits of the linear city as a possible prototype for
the urban future, but experimentation did not necessarily
mean commitment. The MARS Group may well have loaned
its name to two linear city plans, but its members felt no
specific allegiance to linear city as opposed to 'city of towers'
designs as the dominant vision of the future city. Both were
regarded as equally plausible ways of producing syntheses
that expressed modernist town planning principles,[57] even
though the final products had a quite different appearance.
The same degree of flux in planning thought, the same untidy
crossings of intellectual boundaries, would persist throughout
the war years.

7   MARKING TIME

SECRETARY: **It all sounds fine but who's going to pay for it all? I should think it will cost millions and millions.**

LORD LATHAM: **Yes, it will certainly cost a great deal, but not more than unplanned building and a lot less than war. In a way, you know, this is London's war, against decay and dirt and inefficiency. In the long run, plans such as this is [sic] the cheapest way to fight those enemies. What a grand opportunity it is. If we miss this chance to rebuild London, we shall have missed one of the great moments of history and shown ourselves unworthy of our victory.**[1]

This fragment of dialogue from the documentary *The Proud City* (1945) found Lord Latham, Leader of the London County Council, answering questions posed by the 'people of London'. The film was lightly camouflaged propaganda in favour of adopting the recommendations of the 1943 County of London Plan, an advisory plan completed for the Council by a team led by Patrick Abercrombie and J.H. Forshaw.[2] Latham's belief that the battle must be pursued with single-mindedness despite the high cost would have been perfectly familiar to cinema audiences by that time. So too would his analogy between warfare and the struggle to eliminate the city's blighted past. British Movietone News, for instance, had featured a face-to-camera interview with Arthur Greenwood, Minister of Housing, as early as April 1930 in which he announced the Labour Government's intention to declare war on the slums. 'All good men and women' were asked to support the slum clearance drive.[3] The late-1930s and early 1940s brought a spate of documentaries on housing and, later, planning that hammered home a similar message. The battle for a planned urban environment must be fought with the same single-mindedness and mobilisation of resources necessary to fight a war.[4]

These were views with which modern architects wholeheartedly concurred, although few were in any position to influence matters. Mobilisation, exile and, in some cases, internment placed careers on hold. Attempts to fly the flag for modernism were confined to small scale interventions through educational associations, exhibitions and plan-making. In this chapter, we discuss these limited initiatives, along with the advisory plans drawn up for many British cities in the mid-1940s. Few, if any, of the latter produced results that were modernist in the strict sense, but they revealed an edgeways penetration of modernist ideas about design and society that came about through the sympathies of the personnel appointed to the planning teams. This point is illustrated in particular by the two plans for London associated with Patrick Abercrombie.

Fortunes of war

The rise of fascism, the proscription of modern architecture in many European nations and the onset of war scattered the international Modern Movement. Those of Jewish extraction or on the political Left who were unable to emigrate faced persecution and death in Europe. Others who emigrated commonly encountered difficulties and indifference but, ironically, often assisted the spread of modernism in the longer term, given their extraordinary ability to find work when denied it in their countries of origin.

One of the first casualties of war was the suspension of normal international channels for meeting and exchange of ideas. CIAM's activities were abruptly terminated with the immediate cancellation of CIAM VI. Scheduled for Liège between 15 and 19 September 1939, its theme would have been 'open space (air, light, greenery)', with subsidiary themes of air pollution and the 'mobilisation' of land. The replacement Congress at Bridgwater eight years later would have a very different function and agenda (see Chapter 8). In the interim, any CIAM activities were confined to local initiatives, such as the Chapter for Relief and Postwar Planning (CRPP) founded in New York in 1944 under the presidency of Richard Neutra.

CIAM's leadership was scattered. Helena and Szymon Syrkus, Cornelius van Eesteren and Le Corbusier remained in German-occupied Europe. The Syrkuses remained in Poland, directing a clandestine office for architecture and planning until Szymon was deported to Auschwitz in 1942. He survived the war and was able to work on the plan for Warsaw's reconstruction in 1945. Van Eesteren continued as Chief Architect and Planner for Amsterdam, contributing in secret to reconstruction plans for the obliterated centre of Rotterdam and maintaining the longstanding CIAM-inspired search for appropriate symbols for town planning.

Le Corbusier spent the war in France painting and producing abortive plans for housing and town planning. Although he experienced little personal threat, there were few prospects of work given his ambiguous relations with the Vichy régime.[5] Besides working on the Athens Charter (see Chapter 3), he founded ASCORAL (Assemblée de Constructeurs pour une Renovation Architecturale) in 1942–3. Meeting in secret, ASCORAL undertook conceptual studies of housing, prefabrication, standardisation and town planning with an eye to forthcoming reconstruction.

Giedion closed the CIAM Secretariat for the duration of hostilities but stayed at his university post in Zurich. During the war, he revised the Charles Eliot Norton lectures that he had given at Harvard in 1938–9 into the book *Space, Time and Architecture*.[6] In it, Giedion examined the relationships between architecture, industrialisation, new methods of construction and new materials over a wide sweep of history. Using the conceptual frame of the *Zeitgeist*, the book attempted to show in its later sections that modern architecture might be viewed as a cultural expression of Einsteinian notions of space–time. Although this was a fanciful notion, the book was well reviewed and became one of the most cited, if least understood, books ever written about the history of architecture.

Gropius and Sert, as noted earlier, had moved to the USA. Sert left France for New York in 1939, where he set up a practice with Paul Lester Wiener and Paul Schultz. Besides completing work on *Can Our Cities Survive?* (see Chapter 3), he became increasingly involved in city planning schemes for Latin America, leading initially to his Cidade dos Motores (Motor City) plan for Brazil (1945). For his part, Gropius suffered minor restrictions as an enemy alien until he achieved American citizenship in June 1944, but worked relatively normally. Besides his activities at Harvard, he undertook prefabricated housing projects with Konrad Wachsmann and worked on new town plans with Martin Wagner.[7]

In Britain, mobilisation meant that most architects of appropriate age were conscripted into the Armed Forces. In this respect, there was a strong suspicion that they fared less favourably than related professions, such as civil engineering: 'It was hard to believe that the War Office did not think of them as expendable since very many civil engineers were retained in their positions in Britain.'[8] Others confirm that impression of the official assessment of the architect's potential contribution:

> One of the Deputy Engineers at the Ministry of Supply's Propellent Planning Department had taught us Construction when we were at Liverpool. I went to him in 1939 and said 'what can an architect do during the war?' He was an engineer and a friend of mine and he said 'nothing, what use is architecture?'[9]

Despite this, some were conscripted into positions where they were able to make explicit use of their expertise. Fry, for example, who served in the Royal Engineers, was based first in London at the War Office's Department of Fortifications and Works from 1939 to 1942. After subsequent posting to West Africa, he became Town Planning Adviser to the Resident Minister, West Africa in 1944. It would be the start of many subsequent commissions for himself and Jane Drew in Nigeria and the Gold Coast (Ghana).

The fate of the refugee architects depended on their country of origin. Many of those from Germany and Austria were interned at camps at Huyton (Lancashire) or Douglas (Isle of Man) or transported to Canada or Australia, regardless of whether or not they had been stripped of their German citizenship. These included Bruno Ahrends, Carl Franck, Eugen Kaufmann, Arthur Korn, Frederick ('Fritz') Marcus, Nikolaus Pevsner and Eugene Rosenberg. Others were not interned, usually for reasons of occupation. As an enemy alien Felix Samuely, for instance, was disqualified from projects of national security but was not interned because of his experience in air-raid protection.[10]

Once released from internment in 1941–2, the refugees drifted back into civilian life, often into war-related activities. Whatever small influence the refugees had exerted on the shape of modern architecture pre-war, their role in its future development was now minimal with the possible exception of architectural education. Although training was running at a reduced level, with many schools evacuated from London, the refugees were able to fill niches left by staff serving in the forces and to bring their expertise to bear on teaching programmes. Korn taught at the Oxford School of Architecture, Pevsner began teaching at Birkbeck College (University of London) and Walter Segal at the Architectural Association. Trevor Dannatt, then a third-year student at the Regent's

Street Polytechnic, recalled the arrival and impact of Peter Moro on the School of Architecture:

> In my third year, Peter Moro joined the School teaching staff. He brought, certainly into my architectural life, a very considerable tightening-up of attitudes, much more structured . . . He was a very severe critic and had a remarkable influence on me.[11]

Flying the flag

Mobilisation rarely meant continuous action and many architects found themselves with time to spare, particularly once their private practices had folded. As Summerson commented:

> Unlike the first World War, the second World War gave great encouragement to new ideas in architecture and the arts. Between 1939–45, a great many people found they had time on their hands . . . At the beginning of the war, there was a general shutdown, waiting for air-raids, but gradually a mini-Renaissance developed during the war years. Paperbacks, intelligent paperbacks produced especially by Penguin had just been introduced and a considerable section of the population suddenly discovered intellectual values and spheres of thought and activity which had never dawned on them. All through the war there was a certain amount of writing and lecturing which kept this interest afloat and, in fact, increased it.[12]

These activities took various forms, but can be grouped together under three overlapping headings: exhibitions, educational initiatives and publishing.

Exhibitions

After the initial hiatus lasting until mid-1941 to which Summerson referred, exhibition activity soon exceeded the pre-war levels. The subject material was adjusted to meet wartime needs, such as fostering sympathy for Allied Governments, aiding recruitment to ancillary services, encouraging people to accept restrictions, and crystallising public opinions on post-war reconstruction. Wartime exhibitions also displayed two fundamental changes from their pre-war equivalents. First, sponsorship now came from state or voluntary agencies rather than commercial organisations. Secondly, practically all wartime exhibitions were smaller than their pre-war equivalents. Some were designed for local consumption to tap the growing interest in reconstruction; others were deliberately constructed as travelling exhibitions rather than larger displays showing in one pre-determined hall. Stands were built in small panels to facilitate speedy dismantling and assembly at venues in villages and provincial towns rarely visited by peace-time exhibitions. Army camps were another important venue (Figure 7.1). The Army Bureau of Current Affairs (ABCA) arranged over 120 exhibitions in 1943 alone. Each was duplicated so that copies could tour camps at home and abroad. Somewhat larger travelling exhibitions were designed for the Council for the Encouragement of Music and the Arts (CEMA), often with extensive accompanying brochures.[13]

Supporters of modern architecture like Ralph Tubbs, Ernö Goldfinger, Misha Black, Geoffrey Jellicoe and Bronek Katz played a significant role in such activity. Goldfinger, for example, organised a succession of exhibitions that ranged through the scales and issues of interest to modern architects. Normally working in association with his wife Ursula Blackwell or

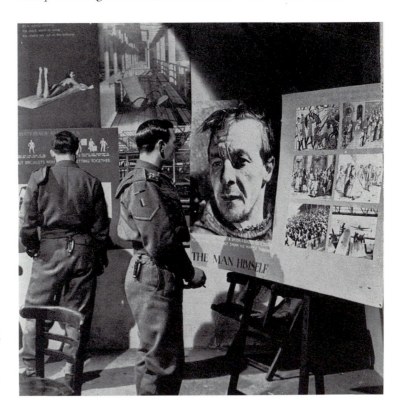

Figure 7.1
Exhibition at an Army Camp. 'The Englishman Builds', designed by Ralph Tubbs for the British Institute of Adult Education in conjunction with the Army Bureau of Current Affairs and the Council for the Encouragement of Music and the Arts.

later his partner Colin Penn, his credited exhibitions included seven for ABCA during the war years. These were: 'Cinema' and 'Food' (both 1943); 'Health Centres', 'The County of London Plan', 'Planning Your Kitchen' and 'Traffic' (all in 1944); and 'Planning Your Neighbourhood' (1945).

Besides 'The County of London Plan' exhibition (see the concluding section of this chapter), two examples show best the combination of pedagogic display and propaganda found in wartime exhibitions. The first was a local exhibition held at St Mary's Hall (Coventry) in the summer of 1940. The 'Coventry of Tomorrow' exhibition featured a model that Donald Gibson's team produced for central Coventry before the outbreak of war. It proposed a 40-acre precinct around the cathedral with a central park and clusters of public buildings. Although ideas on spatial arrangement were loosely borrowed from Le Corbusier's 'City of Tomorrow', the scheme rejected a vertical dimension and sought to face buildings in brick and stone. Models and plans such as the Architectural Association's 'Tomorrow Town' were borrowed to show modern architectural ideas in context and the exhibition was accompanied by a series of evening lectures. When the centre of Coventry was heavily damaged by the Blitz of 14 November 1940, Gibson noted that the 'seeds of a later harvest' had been sown. Councillors remembered the model and invited Gibson to collaborate with the City Engineer in producing a new plan for the city centre (Figure 7.2).[14]

The second example was the 'Living in Cities' exhibition (1942), which Ralph Tubbs designed for the 1940 Council and the British Institute of Adult Education. 'Living in Cities' was a major travelling exhibition on planning and reconstruction, that was accompanied by a Penguin paperback that sold 134 000 copies.[15] The exhibition was based on the 1938 MARS exhibition.[16] It portrayed the historical, unplanned muddle of the British city and the suburban tentacles of the diseased town that were creeping out and destroying the countryside. History showed previous models for action, such as John Nash's 'metropolitan improvements' for the Prince Regent and Haussmann's plans for Paris. After the war, the town should not be rebuilt as previously, but planned on a comprehensive basis. As Tubbs noted:

> If the cities of the future are to be places of beauty where everyone can live happily, and where everyone will have a high standard of living, it will require organisation and planning on a

very large scale, combined with enthusiasm and determination. In war, the nation unites in a common effort, everyone plays his part to hasten victory. In peace we must work together on the same scale for our common good. It must not be every man for himself but every man working to further civilisation. To succeed we must have the necessary organisation.[17]

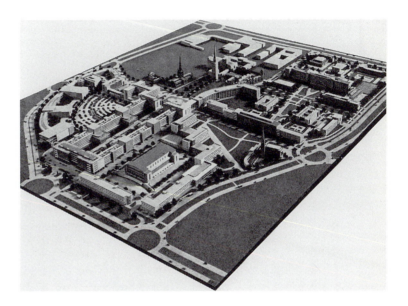

Figure 7.2
An early model for the reconstruction of Coventry, 1942.

Demolition and rebuilding would permit a new order to be created. Strips of green space might be opened up into the heart of the metropolis, in a manner reminiscent of the linear planning scheme shown at the MARS Group's 1938 exhibition. The heart of the city needed a new plan to eliminate visual chaos and impose order. Sections dealt with the home, work, transport and recreation. A stand on health pointed to the importance of medical research and preventive medicine, highlighting the importance of health centres on the Peckham model. A section on the child in the city gave ideas about the importance of play-space and of not having to walk too far to school.

There then followed clarification of 'misconceptions' that pervaded the popular view of modern architecture. The organiser was at pains to refute the ideas that modern architecture ignored tradition, meant flat roofs and white concrete walls or required everyone to live in flats. Tubbs strenuously denied that architects were trying to impose an international style, or that the city of tomorrow was a city of skyscrapers. Finally, a major sideswipe was taken at the Garden City Movement, which was also adept at organising promotional exhibitions:

> The advocates of garden cities do not face up to the problems of introducing fresh air and sunshine, trees and open space into the decayed towns of today. Dissatisfied with the existing chaos of cities, they start new centres, which are neither town nor country, but little patches of suburbia. They leave the existing cities to rot.[18]

The Modern Movement, however, were not always free to get their views across as they wished. Referring to her involvement in the 'Rebuilding Britain' exhibition at the National Gallery in February 1943, Jane Drew commented that the Royal Institute of British Architects were keen to avoid any implicit support for modernism:

> The RIBA was scared stiff that (modernist) ideas might dominate this exhibition and they watered down the whole thing by saying that we must accept the work of a wider group of architects who were tacked on to sober the thing down. Thus very little clear ideology emerged . . .[19]

Contemporary comment by Misha Black indicated further disapproval of the approach taken:

> It was a brilliant example of academic exhibition design, better finished and better in many of its details than any other wartime exhibition, but so reverent in its approach that visitors took off their hats as they entered and spoke in hushed voices. The RIBA would make no compromise with popular exhibition devices and achieved a skilful essay rather out of touch with the post-war aspirations of the common people.[20]

Educating the troops

The activities of ABCA were the tip of an iceberg. The Air Ministry, the Admiralty Education Department and the Ministry of Information were also involved in educational activities for servicemen. The Army Kinematograph Services produced documentary films for ABCA and other service agencies.[21] Perhaps one of the most innovative of organisations for soldiers serving abroad was the Service Arts and Technicians' Organisation (SATO). Its forerunner had been established in

1942 by Percy Johnson-Marshall, then serving in the Royal Engineers. Johnson-Marshall worked at Coventry on early reconstruction plans until 1941. Called up into the Royal Engineers, he was posted to India in 1942. While on the journey, he and William Tatton Brown organised seminars and an exhibition on the future of architecture. Johnson-Marshall recalled the foundation and work of SATO as follows:

> When I arrived in India by troop ship in August 1942, I was in a group of military engineers who had a large number of architects among them . . .. there were a large number of people with similar interests in the built environment and it seemed to me a good idea if something useful could be organised, since there was no real provision for study.
>
> We got together in Poona and set up an organisation originally called the Service Architects' Organisation, which we later (in 1944) widened to Service Arts and Technicians' Organisation. We brought in all the people of goodwill, progressive people, in a strictly non-political organisation. We began by organising meetings of architects, artists and like-minded people and, secondly, to form centres in various bases. So I wrote to friends like Tatton Brown and linked back to the RIBA in the person of Bobby Carter, then the Librarian, to Jaqueline Tyrwhitt, then in charge of the APRR in London, and to Colin Penn of AASTA. These three formed a small committee to help me and sent out a great deal of material. They also got the Architectural Press to send out a great number of booklets and pamphlets. We started in Poona, but then I was transferred to Calcutta, which made a much better base. We had a considerable number of architects working there and I linked up with local architects, both British and Indian. We made a large base and I enlisted the support of the Governor, Lord Casey and his wife, and we arranged activities like the attempt to help recover from the disaster that had befallen the artists of Bengal, where an artistic movement was in ruins due to famine and wartime conditions. We persuaded Lady Casey to help us arrange exhibitions. We were also able to tap the Army through its educational field, which was very deficient in India at that time. They supplied us with rooms, drawing-boards, T-squares and equipment of all kinds and we set up small ateliers. Eventually we had about 22 of these centres running. The main problem was that the people were not stationary, so I invented the idea that you did not leave a place, you always went to a place. If when you got there no activities were in progress, it was then their responsibility to start off new activities. It helped the morale of a number of people and to keep them in touch with architecture and planning activities.[22]

The shifting theatre of war led to equivalent shifts in the organisation of SATO.

> I moved to Assam at the end of 1943 and at the end of 1944 went down the length of Burma with the 14th Army. Generally, (SATO) remained fairly strong throughout the war period. We ran a number of quite large exhibitions and the organisation culminated with us creating a Polytechnic at Pegu in which William Tatton Brown played a major role. The Polytechnic was moved to Rangoon University, which we were given by the military; we ran courses and, I think, helped a number of people to come back to normality and sanity.[23]

The Polytechnics trained troops in bricklaying and local building skills that might have some use in the task of reconstruction that awaited the end of the war and demobilisation.

Publishing

At the start of Jill Craigie's film *The Way We Live* (1946), another documentary illustrating Abercrombie's city-planning endeavours, an actor peers into a bookshop in London's Charing Cross Road. As the camera dwells on an array of recently published titles, the audience sees that all deal with planning and architecture. Besides Abercrombie and Paton Watson's *Plan for Plymouth*, to which the film is devoted, the window display includes such titles as *Plan for Living: the Architect's Part*, *Planning Tomorrow's Britain*, *Rebuilding Britain: a Twenty Year Plan*, *When We Build Again*, and *Target for Architecture: a Plan for Town and Country*.[24]

These were just a small sample of the enormous outpouring of literature that addressed the task of rebuilding Britain's cities after the war. Despite wartime restrictions on paper consumption, publishing houses with an established interest in planning and reconstruction – such as Faber & Faber, the Architectural Press and Penguin – kept up a steady output of new titles. New series were launched, such as the *Rebuilding Britain* volumes published by Faber for the Town and Country Planning Association (starting in 1941), Frederic Osborne's *Planning and Reconstruction Year Book* (starting in 1942) and Paul Elek's *Architects' Year Book* (1945 onwards). Trevor Dannatt, who was assistant editor for the first volume of the *Architects' Year Book* and editor thereafter,[25] recalled that the idea for the latter series came from its Hungarian publisher Paul Elek. He had already established Year Books for an extraordinary range of niche markets that included the *Steam Boiler Year Book* and the *Aeroplane Production Year Book*. Elek

had contacted Jane Drew as a potential editor for an architectural series with an 'eye on the post war building scene'. In
terms of format, it was 'to some degree based on *Circle* . . .
[with] a number of contributors sharing a philosophical
approach. I remember Jane showing it to me as an example to
follow typographically.'[26] In her first editorial, Drew grandly
charted the Year Book's remit as to balance the text:

> with technical and aesthetic information and with the sociology
> necessary for the modern, humanitarian architect. The aim has
> been to show trends and help the forward-looking architect by
> giving him the necessary background on which his work should
> be based.[27]

Naturally, individual projects for publication continued as
time permitted. Of all topics tackled, perhaps the one that
aroused greatest interest during the war-period was the problem of the street. Shortly before the outbreak of war, the
Bressey Report had envisaged a new system of inner and
outer orbital roads, elevated cross-city roads, tunnels, multi-
level roundabouts and clover-leaf intersections.[28] Its impact
was complemented by the two books by Sir Alker Tripp, an
Assistant Commissioner for the Metropolitan Police. Tripp put
forward the theory of 'precinct planning'.[29] He pointed out, in
a manner reminiscent of Le Corbusier, that traffic conditions
had rendered the all-purpose street obsolete. It could no
longer fulfil the function of through-route as well as giving
access to buildings along its frontage. Drawing on American
concepts of hierarchical arrangement of highways and neighbourhood units, Tripp proposed a clear hierarchy of arterial,
sub-arterial and local roads. The local roads would have
limited access to sub-arterials and none to arterials. Under this
system residential, business, industrial or retailing areas would
be created, each of which would have a local system of minor
roads. Each area or 'precinct' would be a 'centre of life and
activity'.[30]

These ideas excited interest in the possibilities of the arterial
roads and techniques for ensuring rapid flows though the
system. S. Rowland Pierce, the Secretary of the RIBA's London
Regional Reconstruction Committee (LRRC), completed a
series of illustrated articles that explored the geometry and
aesthetics of multilevel crossings. Figure 7.3, for example,
shows a sketch of the junction between an elevated arterial
road and a sub-arterial road, on principles laid down by Tripp,
in a landscape hemmed in by tall buildings. Figure 7.4 shows

Figure 7.3
Sketch by S. Rowland
Pierce showing Inner
Circular Elevated Road
as proposed by Alker
Tripp.

a fuller version of these ideas. The caption reflects much about both the appeal of the imagery and the limited understanding of the consequences of mixing tall buildings with major highways:

> . . . here in a commercial and shopping area, a main arterial road crosses an important secondary street: the former provides free, fast transit without crossings and other dangerous complexities, the latter with its speed-limit traffic has covered arcades for pedestrians and shoppers and parking places for cars arranged for varying periods of time. Light, airy streets, well-lit height-zoned buildings with aspects that include space, trees and often grass. At flyover-crossroads, seen from up and down the shopping street, is an important office building – or 'community building' – for exchange, for wholesale display and exhibitions with restrooms and refreshment accommodation. Land is not wasted on internal 'light-courts', nor are the roofs unused or unusable, the attic roof and its windows have disappeared.[31]

Similar ideas mixing together high buildings, huge roadways and all possible physical indicators of the Good Life permeated essays by Aileen and William Tatton Brown. As William Tatton Brown recalled, when writing them:

> I was waiting to be called up. I was hard up for money – my practice had folded – and *Autocar* were hard up for material, after all, this was during the war and there were no new motorcars to write about. Thus, they switched on to town planning, as part of a broad concern with streets and street planning.[32]

The ideas were developed partly through the Tatton Browns'
disenchantment with the direction taken by the MARS
Group's London Plan and partly by wishing to recast Tripp's
ideas on traffic management and precinct planning into three-
dimensional form. The Tatton Browns argued that the by-laws
regulating development needed to be fixed in three dimensions:

> It is not enough to control the space between buildings. We must
> envisage the possibility of controlling the space above and below

Figure 7.4
The abstract geometry
of highways and tall
buildings in a
reconstruction design.

them in order to create new levels, on which traffic of different kinds can operate. Regulations enforcing a uniform height might be used to create a new ground level for pedestrians; in the same way regulations requiring the construction of basements of standard depth (if necessary sub-basements also) could be used to obtain new parking places at a level when much space is wasted at present.[33]

A specimen district plan showed 24-storey blocks straddling large highways. The blocks were widely spaced to allow light and the passage of air, with the spaces between interspersed with new parkland and low buildings. Powers to ensure that the lower buildings had flat roofs of similar height meant that they could carry walkways, with pedestrians able to approach buildings from roof level downwards rather than from below. Bus-stops were located close into the tall buildings and away from the fast roadways. By placing parking and garaging spaces below ground, the amount of roadway required would be less than in normal plans, given the absence of obstructions to traffic flow. Major intersections contained both roundabouts and underpasses, in arrangements seen as the urban equivalent of the clover-leaf crossings possible in less restricted spaces.

As a scheme for a new site rather than an existing city – even one that had suffered severe bombing – there were no costings for clearance and renewal. This, like other similar projects before it, was for a hypothetical city. While understandable, given that this was a spare-time project that had no major input of research, engagement with the complexities of actual city reconstruction lay in the future. Nor was there yet recognition of the potential problems of pollution and microclimate caused by this intermingling of high-capacity roadways and tall buildings. As William Tatton Brown noted: 'the traffic noise, of course, would have been terrific and it would have had to be air-conditioned. . . we (also) never realised how windy this (roof-deck) would be and how little it is used, even at the Barbican.[34]

Advisory plans

Well before the 1947 Town and Country Planning Act made plans a statutory requirement, there had been a spate of advisory city plans that might provide inspiration for the statutory plans that would follow. A few were produced by independent groups. Besides the 1942 MARS Plan (see Chapter 6), the Planning Committee of the Royal Academy unveiled another plan for London in the same year: a neoclassical curio that Lord Esher dubbed 'a period piece of academic nostalgia incorporating every cliché in the *Beaux-Arts* repertoire'.[35] In 1943 the LRRC published its interim, and only report *Greater London: Towards a Master Plan*, with the plans shown in an exhibition at the National Gallery. Its contents focused heavily on communications, favouring rationalisation of the rail system to produce broad communication corridors combining road, rail, and in some cases, canal and river.[36] Outside London, Max Lock continued the work begun in the Ocean Street Study with his *Hull Regional Survey*. Having replaced Leslie Martin as the Head of the School of Architecture at Hull University, Lock organised staff and students to carry out a survey or 'civic diagnosis' for reconstruction purposes.[37]

Most of the advisory plans, however, were commissioned by municipalities and other local authorities. These included Sir Charles Reilly's plan for Birkenhead (1944), Lutyens and Abercrombie's plan for Hull (1945), Rowland Nicholas's Manchester plan (1945), Max Lock's Middlesbrough Survey (1946) and Thomas Sharp's Exeter plan (1946).[38] Collectively, they addressed the same needs, and devised visions of cities that would be dramatically reconstructed to accommodate demands for better housing, improvement of infrastructure, alleviation of traffic congestion and functional separation of land-use. They drew upon a *pot pourri* of architectural styles, including Beaux-Arts formalism, neo-classicism, Arts and Crafts and mild modernism. Although rarely influential as planning documents they underpinned a growing consensus which looked to social improvement through a root-and-branch approach to the existing urban fabric.

Rather more influential were the two advisory plans for London: Forshaw and Abercrombie's *County of London Plan* (1943) with its important social and functional analysis; and Abercrombie's *Greater London Plan 1944* (1945), which supported the principle of planned decentralisation.[39] Neither embraced modernist approaches to London's planning, but both contained ideas that modern architects regarded as being of considerable interest. Indeed, as we will see later in this chapter, the County of London Plan looked sufficiently hope-

ful for the MARS Group to 'adopt' it in their future discussions
rather than continue with their own 1942 Plan.

The County of London Plan was given an early steer
towards disaggregating the Metropolis into component social
units by Wesley Dougill, who was an enthusiastic supporter of
neighbourhood unit planning. It was developed further by his
successor, Arthur Ling, who helped devise the cellular 'egg-
basket' diagram for which the plan is most famous (Figure
7.5). Ling had come to the team in 1941 from the City of
London Corporation. As noted in Chapter 6, Ling had conducted student research on 'Social Units' in cities and provided prototype designs used in the 1942 MARS Plan.
Recalling the cellular structure employed in the two plans, he
argued that there were very few connections between them
other than general currents of ideas:

> Abercrombie came in periodically, but the team was led by Wesley
> Dougill. Dougill unfortunately died and I eventually became
> leader in his place. The plan was produced in two years which,
> considering there was a blitz on, was a remarkable achievement
> . . . You will note that the County of London Plan starts with
> 'Social Groupings and Major Use Zones', and this is indicative of
> how much the role of existing community structures had come to
> be appreciated. There were also the various elements to be found
> in the MARS Group discussions: work, residence, transport, social
> facilities, open space and recreation, utilities. There was no other
> member of the MARS Group on the County of London Plan, but
> my previous thesis studies and participation in that Group were
> useful in considering the problems of London.

Before the County of London Plan was completed, a second
team had begun on another plan that recognised the importance of the regional context in planning London. Sir Peter
Shepheard, then only recently qualified, was appointed to the
team of 15 people who produced the plan. He recalled that
the whole rationale for doing the Greater London Plan grew
out of the County Plan. The former retained the cellular
structure, but was less restricted than the County Plan:

> It applied the same principles, although with a broader brush, but
> it was really more important in a way. The County of London Plan
> could only be done in certain ways, because things were already
> committed. In the Outer London area, things were much looser.

As part of his duties Shepheard was responsible for producing
maps and illustrations that might convey the future London to

Figure 7.5
Arthur Ling, in the guise of anonymous technician, explains ideas of neighbourhood planning found in the *County of London Plan* (1943).

the readership.[40] They drew upon the available imagery of the time without necessary commitment to one school of aesthetics or another. A drawing of flats and terraced houses near West Ham Park, for example, drew on a mild Swedish modernism (Figure 7.6). A drawing of the centre of the proposed satellite town at Ongar (Essex) consciously envisaged a precinct-style development (Figure 7.7). With regard to an aerial perspective for Ongar, Shepheard commented that its prime function:

> was to give an idea of the scale. Corbusier had drawn his great blocks with these huge spaces in between and we wanted to say that ours were not like that. That might well be part of a neighbourhood, although with a rather dreary housing layout, but there would be schools incorporated in it and open spaces and paths running through it.

Adoption and opportunism

The advisory plans were valued locally as expressing civic pride and were considered useful expositions of planning principles. For the Modern Movement, disapproval of some of the design syntheses adopted did not erode the soundness of the principle of master planning. The County of London Plan, as noted earlier, was opportunistically adopted by the MARS

Figure 7.6
Flats and houses at West
Ham Park drawn by
Peter Shepheard. The
Swedish influence in the
aesthetics of this scene,
which also permeated
Shepheard's student
thesis, are reminiscent of
the LCC's development
at Lansbury and
elsewhere.

Group, then at a low ebb and incapable of initiating new
planning ventures,[41] as a basis for their further discussions of
town planning. Indeed, the Group's Minutes clearly indicate
the distance that by 1944 they had placed between themselves
and their own linear city plan:

> Korn's offer to address the Group and answer questions on the
> MARS Plan acknowledged with thanks, but declined on the
> ground that the Plan is well-known to most members, and that
> the County of London Plan Sub-Committee had recently provided
> a forum for such a discussion.[42]

The Sub-Committee was itself formed in 1943 under the
Chairmanship of Goldfinger. It produced a limited circulation
report of 'observations' which opened with a statement noting
that it was 'one of the first plans to be sponsored by an official

Figure 7.7
A drawing of the centre
of the proposed satellite
town at Ongar (Essex)
which consciously
envisaged a precinct-style
development. Although
not realised, the design
anticipates the aesthetics
of the town centres of
the first generation of
New Towns.

body, in which modern planning principles are applied to an established social organism'.[43] The report started by discussing the plan's general approach and then using CIAM's four functions as headings for discussion. It was argued that the plan lacked a comprehensive approach for London as a whole apart from transport. Faint echoes of the 1942 MARS Plan occurred when it suggested that: 'the only other possible alternative (to the approach taken) is to disregard the historic development and present-day administrative structure of London and to suggest a radical reconstruction based only on the geographical facts of the London site and a clear recognition of the functions which London has to fulfil.'[44] The observations on the functional elements followed this emphasis on a comprehensive approach. Residential density was seen as based not on the needs of the population but an arbitrary assumption of fixed population numbers for the whole area. Open space standards were seen as too low, but could be improved

Figure 7.8
A comparative analysis of road practices, shown on a screen at the 'County of London' exhibition (1944).

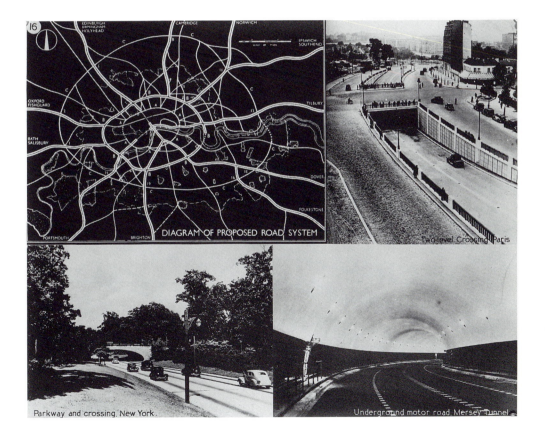

by the familiar device of opening up strips of parkland or open country penetrating deep into the city along the line of the rivers. Support was given to the principle of founding trading estates as locations for industry and moving them to the periphery. The new road pattern was criticised as having no functional justification, with ring roads that looked as if 'they were superimposed as an analogy to certain other European capitals where conditions are entirely different'.[45]

Goldfinger developed these points further through two different media. The first comprised a twenty-screen touring exhibition, accompanied by a pamphlet entitled *Your London has a Plan*.[46] The exhibition opened in January 1944 and was subsequently shown at venues throughout the capital and further afield through the twenty copies of the display material held by ABCA. Figure 7.8 shows one of the screens employed in the exhibition. It illustrated the proposed road pattern for London by images of related practices elsewhere, in the shape of photographs of a two level crossing in Paris, the Mersey road tunnel and a parkway and crossing in New York.

The second was a lavishly illustrated paperback entitled *The County of London Plan Explained* written in association with the RIBA's Librarian Edward 'Bobby' Carter.[47] The book provided an extended outline of the plan's proposals and also gave the opportunity to develop ideas generated by the Plan. The authors, for example, gave attention to the crossing points required for the Ring Roads and ways of ensuring uninterrupted traffic flows. The bird's eye view in Figure 7.9, also used in the ABCA 'Traffic' exhibition, shows the intersection

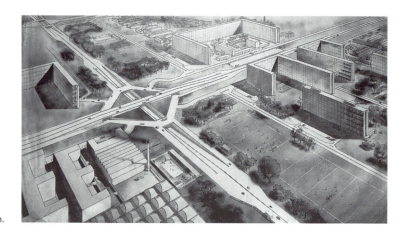

Figure 7.9
Bird's eye view of a system of crossings was devised which uses only 3–4 acres as compared with nearly 10 acres used by the clover leaf crossing. This drawing was also used in the ABCA 'Traffic' exhibition.

of two main roads, with two 10-metre carriageways, and their connection with local traffic. The dwellings were separated from the main roads by belts of open space in which playing fields, parks and allotments could be situated. The description claimed that this layout would take up only 4.3 acres as opposed to 9.4 for the full clover-leaf design that could be used where space was more abundant.

This attempt to graft more radical modernist interpretations onto the County of London Plan reveals much about the nature and use of imagery, particularly visual imagery. The Plan had various direct impacts on planning, notably through its density requirements (see Chapter 9), and various indirect impacts through its support for the principles of neighbourhood units, hierarchy and precincts. It was also a powerful and lasting focus for debate, since it could be appropriated by other groups. Carter and Goldfinger used the County of London Plan as a benign host to which a new message could be attached by means of powerfully evocative line drawings and photographs. Other groups were free to do the same from their ideological viewpoints.[48] The ensuing documents might create considerable interest and act as a starting-point for further work. Yet whatever the appeal to the urban imagination of such documents, the eventual shape of planning schemes stemmed from the specific circumstances of reconstruction and not from blind application of visionary prototypes from this or any previous era. This is a point that recurs continually as we turn to examine the immediate post-war period.

8 DREAMS AND FALSE EXPECTATIONS

Any successful training in architecture must be attuned to the spirit of the age, of that there can be no doubt. This does not merely mean that design should be 'modern' in the sense of being based on the very latest developments of structure and materials, or of embracing the very latest theories of utilization of land or development of living space. These matters are eddies in a main stream. They are constantly shifting their course; and the architect who tries to canalize them, and set his own ship to sail upon them, may find himself at any time in a backwater. What has got to be comprehended – as far as it is possible – is the main trend of development in our age; social, political, technical.

Howard Robertson[1]

The new establishment?

Whatever efforts were made, nationally and internationally, to restore professional life to normality after the disruption of war, it was impossible simply to turn the clock back. Too much had happened in the external environment in which modern architects operated for that to happen. When introducing a questionnaire sent to member groups of CIAM in 1947, for example, Maxwell Fry[2] highlighted eight specific differences in new social, industrial and political conditions of the time compared with the pre-war situation:

    (a) Increased need for dwellings through bombing and cessation of building.

    (b) Strong movement to make up the deficiencies through planned re-building of new towns and regions under Government aegis.

    (c) Similar increased need for industrial plant of all kinds.

    (d) Absence of private building while housing and industrial programmes have first priority.

    (e) Increased acceptance of mechanised and factory-made buildings, of which the success of prefabricated temporary house building programme is an example. This amounts to a revolution in method of which architects are insufficiently aware.

    (f) Increased awareness of the value of design in industry of which the 'Britain Can Make It' exhibition is an example.

(g) Very high building costs and relatively low out-put per man-hour. Effect on building programme not yet observable.

(h) State patronage of arts through agencies such as CEMA, CID, British Council etc. Growth of official architecture.

Increased state intervention through planning and patronage, acceptance of prefabrication and industrialised building methods, and growing awareness of the value of industrial design – on the surface, these all represented an enormous leap forward in official thinking towards positions long adopted by modern architects. It was hard not to feel that modern architecture's long-anticipated breakthrough was in sight.

That feeling was enhanced by changed personal circumstances. After six years of war, radical young architects returned as establishment figures. Many founded private practices that grew rapidly and played an important role in postwar architecture. F.R.S. Yorke, for instance, formalised previously informal working links with Eugene Rosenberg and Cyril Mardall (Sjöström) to form an eponymous partnership eventually known as YRM. Ove Arup had laid the basis of Ove Arup and Partners (founded 1949) and later Arup Associates (founded 1963), among the world's largest firms of consultant engineers and architects.

Others quickly rose to prominent positions in the architectural and planning offices of major cities, the National Health Service and local authorities undertaking school building programmes. The pre-war modern architects were key players in building the Welfare State. Work was now plentiful. Relations with the RIBA were described as 'excellent', with modern architects prominently represented on the Institute's Council and Committees.[3] In Lubetkin's words:

> Architecture was on ice during the war. After the war, the work that we had done, sincerely or not, realistically or otherwise, existed and could be clearly evaluated. We had made our case and established certain points that people all over the country could pick up and use. There was the breakthrough of the barrier of the RIBA; the old reactionaries were out and the doors were open to us. We were established.[4]

The general mood was infected by an optimism, about which Jane Drew observed: 'I have seen no parallel at any other time in my life.'[5] Others agreed on the extent of the consensus that the future lay in planning, despite profound differences of political orientation. As Shepheard noted:

It is incredible to read it now: that atmosphere after the war that
nurtured me and Abercrombie looks like a golden age. Churchill
was talking about a minimum wage to Bevan; Beveridge was
talking to Churchill. Everyone was talking to everyone else.[6]

At first glance, then, all the necessary preconditions were in
place for the imminent triumph of modernism at the urban
scale. That this was not the case, at least not in the short-term,
was due to the particular circumstances of Austerity and
reconstruction.

This chapter considers the transition of modern architects
back to working in the 'strange and different' world of peace-
time after the passage of six years.[7] It starts by discussing the
enormous task of reconstruction, the need to recruit skilled
individuals to work in planning the new Britain, and the entry
of trained architects into the planning process. It then considers the balance sheet for promoting the urban ideals of
modern architects in the years until 1950. Housing, despite the
hopeful signs offered by the Temporary Housing Programme,
proved a disappointment. The New Towns programme similarly
failed to deliver the high hopes that modern architects once
cherished about the possibility of building new types of city.
Internationally, too, progress was slow. CIAM was resuscitated
by a leadership whose hand was much strengthened compared with pre-1939 and held two Congresses in the late-
1940s: at Bridgwater in Somerset (1947) and Bergamo in Italy
(1949). Although well-attended, these did little more than
help the international Modern Movement to regroup and
recover their agenda.

Planning and the urban challenge

The scale of devastation in British cities was generally less
severe than those European cities caught up in the theatre of
war. Observers in the summer of 1945 reported the 'biblical
annihilation' of Hamburg, Dresden, Berlin and other German
cities. Twenty-six per cent of all buildings in Budapest and 94
per cent of the city's industrial premises were destroyed.
Warsaw saw the complete decimation of 782 out of 957
buildings classed as historical monuments, with 141 partly
destroyed. Shortly after its liberation, General Eisenhower
commented that: 'I have seen many towns destroyed during

the war, but nowhere have I been faced with such extent of destruction executed with such bestiality'.[8]

While not suffering losses on the same scale, the damage to British cities was still considerable. Industry, commerce, housing and the infrastructure had sustained severe damage and had become run-down through lack of investment, although there were considerable variations in losses from bombing. Cities like Edinburgh and Oxford suffered minor damage compared with Hull, Southampton and Coventry. Variations were also found within cities. In London, 30 per cent of the total acreage of the City and around 20 per cent in the East End boroughs of Stepney, Shoreditch, Poplar and Finsbury had suffered war damage (Figure 8.1). This compared with figures of only 4 per cent in Hammersmith and 5 per cent in the more affluent West End boroughs of Westminster, Hampstead, Fulham, Kensington and Chelsea.[9]

The most pressing problems concerned housing. Estimates were that aerial bombardment had destroyed or rendered uninhabitable 0.5 million houses and seriously damaged a further 0.25 million dwellings. Another 3 million houses had suffered lesser damage. Replacement would have posed problems in itself, but further problems were caused by the effects of population increase (a rise of one million between 1939 and 1945), a decrease in household size, and by the cessation

Figure 8.1
Hope and Glory: bomb damage as the starting point for reconstruction.

of slum clearance and other housing programmes for the duration of the war. The case for tackling these problems by comprehensive rather than piecemeal approaches was never more persuasive.

This was echoed in *Let Us Face the Future*, the Election Manifesto of the incoming Labour Government of 1945.[10] Strangely there was no mention of a new town building programme, a programme which would soon be established with remarkable speed. None the less the Manifesto gave clear recognition of the need for a massive programme of house-building and linked that requirement to the guiding principle of planning. Sections 6 and 7 contained specific commitments to generating a house-building programme; to a restructuring of the building industry, a coordinated approach to the demands of different sectors, a loose commitment to 'good town planning', land nationalisation, and the reorganisation of Ministries to streamline town planning matters.

Many of these things proved difficult to achieve. The pledge about the reorganisation of Ministries to streamline town planning matters was not honoured. Responsibility was diffused: the housing drive in England and Wales alone involving no less than four different Ministries – Health, Supply, Town and Country Planning, and the Ministry of Works. In the process, it was to involve ministers with very differing, indeed conflicting, personalities from that broad church that was the Labour Party during the Attlee years. These included Arthur Greenwood, Hugh Dalton, the former Chancellor of the Exchequer who became Minister of Town and Country Planning, his predecessor Lewis Silkin, and Aneurin Bevan, as Minister of Health.

Nevertheless, the creation of a statutory town and country planning system was not long delayed. The 1947 Act marked the beginnings of a planning system that moved well beyond development control towards actively managing and shaping the future city. It also created an enormous demand for planners. In 1946, the Town Planning Institute had only 1700 members, 20 per cent of whom were not-yet-qualified student members. This compared with over 1400 planning authorities.[11] As H.T. Cadbury-Brown remarked: 'This was a time in which the world was turning to planning, yet there was a vacuum.'[12]

It was a vacuum that architects helped to fill. Modern architects in particular were interested in the urban scale and newly-qualified architects leaving the architectural schools espoused an ideological commitment to public service. Indeed while the leading figures of the pre-war British Modern Movement tended to move into private practice or went overseas, where work was now plentiful, their younger counterparts were more readily attracted into planning jobs in the public sector. This included appointments in the municipalities or in central government agencies, such as the Ministry of Town and Country Planning.[13] Indeed by 1950, over 50 per cent of all qualified architects worked in the public sector.

There is disagreement whether, by their actions, those espousing public service were behaving as a new generation – with all that implied in terms of rekindling the revolution of modern architecture (see Chapter 9) – or were merely a 'slightly younger'[14] group who followed the established radical path. Certainly the idea of a generational shift cannot be taken too far at this stage. Some of those who qualified before 1939, like Fry, Ling and Johnson-Marshall, already possessed extensive experience in town planning. Others took advantage of accelerated courses for servicemen to acquire the necessary qualifications. For instance, William Tatton Brown took a one-year Town Planning course at the Architectural Association in 1946, with his fees paid by the Army.

Instead of a generational shift, perhaps the most noticeable change caused by the incursion of architects into the planning process was to heighten sensitivities to urban design at an important time. The presence of the architect-planners added a powerful visual imagination to the armoury of planning. The architect's ability to visualise and communicate information about three-dimensional form was added to the conventional two-dimensional language of the plan. At the same time, their relations with existing planners were not always easy or productive. Most pre-1947 planners were trained as engineers or surveyors, whereas the new emphasis on survey and analysis demanded different skills. Ling summarised the situation:

> The need for comprehensive planning after the wartime devastation led to a large number of architects being attracted into planning. There was also a new, post-war generation of planners who qualified by means of crash courses. There was a considerable amount of friction between them and the older type of planners, who had mainly worked in development control and there was some difficulty in getting the new principles incorporated into the administrative system. However, the new Town and Country Planning Act (1947) and a Reconstruction Act (1944) put

comprehensive planning on a new basis. In the beginning there
were building controls and licensing, so there weren't too many
development applications coming in. One could therefore aim to
make development control a creative rather than a negative
process. But it was not long before old habits and political
objectives returned; market forces re-asserted themselves as the
basis for development and conflict between architects and planners developed.[15]

Only in departments that espoused both a strong relationship
between architecture and town planning and a 'technological'
orientation, such as Coventry or the Hertfordshire and London County Councils, did the new breed of architect-planners
fit in easily.

Housing the nation

For many, the 'housing crisis' was the most pressing domestic
challenge facing the Government in peacetime. After a pain-
fully slow start caused by logistical problems and labour and
material shortages in the construction industry, activity picked
up in the late-1940s. By 1951, a total of 1.5 million units of
accommodation in flats and houses had been provided. The
vast proportion of this was local authority housing for rental,
with the building licence system being deliberately used to
restrict the activities of the private sector. There was little
immediate encouragement for modern architects in this
sphere of activity, notwithstanding the face of the future being
presented as forcefully as ever through exhibitions and projects. Housing exhibitions like the 'Building Now' exhibition
at the RIBA in April 1946 featured such schemes as Tecton's
Priory Green estate for the London Borough of Finsbury
(Figure 8.2). Schemes like Max Lock's unrealised project for
Hartlepool Headland would offer the prospect of mixed development of flats and houses to replace the densely packed
street network and dilapidated terraced housing of the industrial city (Figure 8.3). The moment for such projects, however,
had not yet arrived. There were few experiments with multi-
storey flats for public housing in the immediate post-war
years. Even mixed developments of flats and houses were rare
before 1950.

Instead, following the guidelines of the *Housing Manual*
(1944),[16] most of the dwellings constructed were three-
bedroom, two-storey, and primarily semi-detached houses on

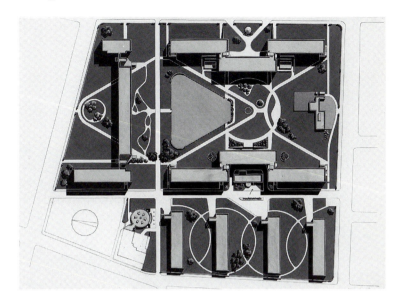

Figure 8.2
Tecton's layout plan of
the Priory Green Estate,
Finsbury, London.

cottage estates. Largely as a result of Bevan's influence, the
houses were built to the relatively generous space standards of
the Dudley Committee's report.[17] It can be argued that, given
the straitened circumstances of the time, these high standards
were partly responsible for reducing the overall numbers of
houses that could be built. Certainly Dalton increased the rate
of house-building after the reduced space standards of the
1949 *Housing Manual* were implemented.[18]

   If the municipal housing drive of the late 1940s proved
disappointing for modernists, rather more might have been

Figure 8.3
Max Lock's unrealised
project for Hartlepool
Headland, 1948.

expected from a prefabricated house-building programme that gave industrialised building methods an opportunity to show their worth. The Temporary Housing Programme was initiated in 1944. Its aim was to supply emergency wartime housing but it was subsequently extended to play a part in post-war reconstruction. The houses were produced in factories and shipped on to site for assembly – analysis of its costs indicates the programme's rationale was as much linked to providing work for factories while they diversified away from wartime as it was to housing.[19] By 1949, over 156 000 prefabricated one-storey houses ('prefabs') had been built. They were intended to last no more than 15 years and theoretically all should have been replaced by 1964. In practice only 29 per cent of the allocation for England and Wales had been removed by that date, with some redesignated as permanent housing.

The problem for the Modern Movement was that the prefabs made aesthetic connection with the wrong prototype. As constructed, they were first cousins to the homely seaside bungalow – a reviled symbol of inter-war urban sprawl and bourgeois taste – rather than continuing the traditions of Pessac or the Weissenhof (see Chapter 3). Moreover the production of the Arcon, Uni-Seco, Tarran and Aluminium Temporary Bungalows failed to justify the common assumption that wartime experience of mass-production would yield dividends when applied to housing. Neither the anticipated economic savings per unit nor increased choice of options to prospective residents materialised. Although lastingly popular with their residents, the prefabs were not a model that modernists were likely to cherish.

New Towns

The first stages of the British New Towns programme (1946–51) are now so heavily linked by historians to the ideology of the Garden City Movement that it may seem strange even including them in a study of the urban imagination of the Modern Movement. That view, however, is a retrospective judgment; at the time, it was by no means so clear that the New Towns would represent the triumph of Garden City ideals. In the first place, many of the architects involved in drawing up the plans for the first 14 New Town plans had connections with the pre-war Modern Movement.

These included Gibberd at Harlow, Gordon Stephenson and Peter Shepheard at Stevenage, William Holford at Corby, Lubetkin at Peterlee, and Lionel Brett (Lord Esher) at Hatfield and later Basildon. Secondly, the New Towns developed urban concepts that the Garden City and Modern Movements shared. Master planning, separation of function, urban hierarchy, abolition of the traditional street by segregated circulation systems, and neighbourhood units were common currency for the two movements. Stevenage and Harlow, for instance, were still considered sufficiently interesting for them to be suitable subjects for debate and a half-day excursion at CIAM VIII in 1951 (see Chapter 9).

These clear indications of interest in the New Towns in the early days belie present-day assumptions of antagonism on the part of modernists and support Fry's assertion that:

> At the beginning of the New Towns, we were very much at one with government, as witness the fact that most new towns were built by MARS Group architects. It was not until we realised that they were extended Garden Cities that our enthusiasm waned a little.[20]

Fry and others also suggested that there was no inherent reason why the New Towns had to follow in the Garden City tradition. Certainly the perspectives of satellite towns like Ongar from the *Greater London Plan* (see Chapter 7) indicate that those in Abercrombie's office thought of the satellite towns as modern cities rather than in the mould of Welwyn and Letchworth. Yet whatever they may have hoped, the general orientation of the New Towns was discouraging. When writing to Sert in mid-1947 in admiration of his Cidade dos Motores scheme for Brazil, Drew pessimistically assessed the British scene:

> Most of our work is in Africa as building in England is extremely difficult; there is a general gloomy feeling about our financial position and great shortages of material and labour. Our hopes rest with the new towns but the plans so far published do not look very exciting.[21]

In many ways, the terms of reference of the New Towns programme made it inevitable that the New Towns would conform to Garden City ideology. When the New Towns Committee was established in 1945 under Lord Reith, its remit was to consider:

the general questions of the establishment, development, organisation and administration that will arise in the promotion of New
Towns in furtherance of a policy of planned decentralization from
congested areas; and in accordance therewith to suggest guiding
principles on which such Towns should be established and developed as self-contained and balanced communities for living and
working.[22]

Explicit mention of decentralisation and self-containment
came directly from Ebenezer Howard, as did purchase and
tenure in the hands of public authorities, an ideal population
of between 30 000 and 50 000 and provision for a 'green belt'.
Although new elements were added that were either outside
Howard's agenda or things that would have met his outright
disapproval,[23] the idea that the first New Towns could have
escaped from their Garden City roots was probably wishful
thinking.

For the most part all that those retaining sympathy with
modernism could do to leaven the diet was to bring an
edgeways penetration of ideas into the increasingly uniform
model of the first generation Towns. Lionel Brett (Lord Esher)
struggled in vain to raise densities at Hatfield in order to give
the town a greater sense of 'urbanity' against the suburban
densities associated with nearby Welwyn. In later work at
Basildon, he was able to gain acceptance of a mixed development 'which was about as good as we could do'.[24] Frederick
Gibberd, who had experimented with a mixed development
of flats-and-houses in Hackney in 1945, added a ten-storey
point block of flats to the Mark Hall Neighbourhood in Harlow
New Town. Interestingly, it was presented as an attempt to
enhance the experience of the road traveller rather than in
terms of the functional need for different types of housing:

> This was placed so as to form an integral part of the design of a
> future major road. Driving along this road there will be a general
> impression of low buildings broken up by woods and tree clumps
> until the silhouette is broken by the tall block which will suddenly
> come into view in a gap in the development and will as suddenly
> fade away.[25]

The episode, however, that did most to create the lasting
impression of antipathy between modernism and the first
generation New Towns was the development plan for
Peterlee. Extensively analysed elsewhere,[26] it requires only
brief discussion here. It had been decided to redevelop the pit
villages of the East Durham coalfield by means of an inte-

grated development. A plan produced by C.W. Clarke, Municipal Engineer of Easington Rural District Council, in 1946 showed three dispersed neighbourhood units with a small District Centre. In the summer of 1947 Berthold Lubetkin was invited to become Architect-Planner of the new development, now named Peterlee after a miners' leader (Figure 8.4). The invitation came from Lewis Silkin, the Minister of Town and Country Planning. The brief was now different, looking to create a centralised development on a single site. The New Town would be an urban rather than suburban entity; compact and of higher density than those around London. It would have a comprehensive transport system that would coordinate with pit shifts and end the isolation of the pit villages by drawing the Easington area into the wider region.[27]

Figure 8.4
Lubetkin meets the miners.

Although hesitant at first, Lubetkin succumbed to pressure to take the appointment from Silkin and Dr. Monica Felton, a redoubtable socialist who was due to become first Chairman of Peterlee Development Corporation in 1948. In Lubetkin's words:

Lewis Silkin called me three times and I refused twice. The third time he said that it would not be just a New Town, but it would be for the miners, only for miners, and that there would be none of these chicken-coop or rabbit-hutch affairs but proper urban surroundings, which the miners themselves wanted. But I said 'what about materials?' because at that time there was no cement and no steel. He said that priority would be guaranteed and that materials would be made available. On that basis I accepted the commission.[28]

During the next two years, numerous development schemes were prepared. The first draft plan (shown in Figure 8.5) shows the New Town's site in relation to major collieries of the area. Bounded to the south by the deep wooded gorges known as the Denes, the main development would be concentrated in the large flat basin in the centre of the site. The New Town would have a unicellular structure rather than the multicellular structure favoured elsewhere. Plans and models were drawn up of housing urgently needed for mining families. Figure 8.6, for example, shows one of several variants of dwellings for the so-called One Hundred houses. With elevational detail that ranged from suburban to cubist, these houses and their associated outhouses could be put together in ways that retained the feel of traditional mining terraces.

The problem with these plans lay with the mining industry and with undertakings given to the National Coal Board (NCB) about development in the area. Discussions about the New Town had paid little attention to either the problem of subsidence or the NCB's future mining policy in the area. Moreover despite the NCB acquiescing in the discussion about the New Town, the Board had been given assurances before Lubetkin was even appointed that their mining policy would not be seriously compromised. They were prepared to permit development, but only on the original dispersed settlement plan drawn up by C.W. Clarke. This produced an impasse:

Everything was alright until we learned that there were five seams of coal under the site which all had to be extracted. This meant that the only thing that the National Coal Board would tolerate were isolated houses, so as to avoid subsidence. That way if they cracked, not everything would fall down. That was the very opposite of what I and the miners themselves wanted. When I got there, the cry was that they wanted a town, with large streets; they did not want a mere housing scheme. Yet that essentially is what they got. We later found that before we were appointed, Silkin's Ministry had signed a letter to the National Coal Board undertaking that the town would be developed in single units and that every one, before acceptance, would have to be accepted by the Coal Board. This was a complete reversal of all that had been agreed with us. But I still don't know whether Silkin knew about that letter, but doubt whether he did. When he was talking to me he was quite sincere in wanting the urban characteristics and he was present at the meetings with the miners that supported my views of what should be done. . . What I wanted to do was to stress the cohesion of the miners, but what has come about is very disappointing.[29]

Lubetkin's tenure as Architect-Planner ended in March 1950 and was not renewed. With his departure went the

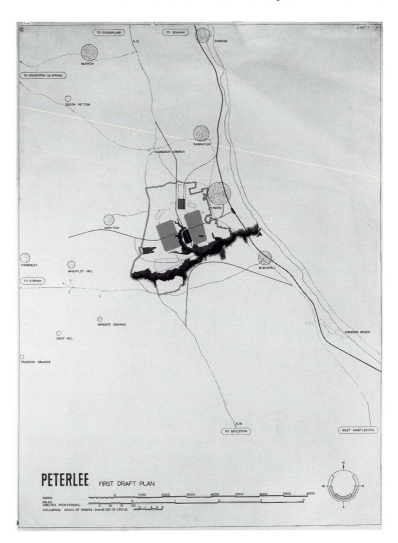

Figure 8.5
The first Peterlee draft plan.

Figure 8.6
Model of a version of the
One Hundred Houses.

'urbanistic' conception of Peterlee and the opportunity to do
something different with the New Towns programme. The
debacle at Peterlee also had all the ingredients necessary to
fuel the Modern Movement's worst suspicions about official
resistance to modern architecture and its planning ideals. In
their minds, a bold urban vision by a highly respected modern
architect was discarded not because of user needs but rather
because of the economics of coal. Suburbia had seemingly
triumphed over the city.

Recovering the agenda

Re-establishing international links was an important step in
recapturing the pre-war impetus and proving that the shared
spirit of modern architecture had survived the years of proscription and repression. Yet it was quickly realised that it was
impossible to resuscitate CIAM immediately as a fully functioning international forum. The group needed to look again
at its aims, agenda and in particular the provisions of the now-
formulated Athens Charter (see Chapter 3). Writing to CIAM
members in May 1946, for example, Giedion informed them
that:

> The Secretariat in Zurich has been reopened. By the events of the
> war contact between the groups has been loosened. The inter-

national situation demands from the CIAM more activity and therefore closer contacts. We are now trying to reorganise the CIAM according to post-war conditions.[30]

What was needed as soon as possible was to reconvene a Congress to examine the aims and purpose of CIAM and its place in the post-war world.

Richards recalled that Giedion wrote to the MARS Group to request that England stage the first post-war meeting 'because it was the country that was less disorganised from the war.'[31] A CIRPAC meeting in London in September 1946 considered various suggestions for an appropriate theme for the Congress. These included an American suggestion of 'Neighbourhood Planning', a British suggestion of 'Architecture and its relation to the Common Man' and a Swiss suggestion of 'Architecture and its relation to painting and sculpture'.[32] Discussions of potential themes and possible venues continued into 1947. In January 1947, the suggestion was that the Congress theme should be: 'The impact of Contemporary Conditions upon Architectural Expression', with an 'an old college at Winchester' being mooted as the possible site.[33] Matters were finally resolved at a CIRPAC meeting in Zurich at Whitsun (26–9 May 1947), where it was decided to hold CIAM VI at the Arts Centre in Bridgwater, Somerset between 7 and 14 September 1947. It was also resolved to break with previous practice and not to have a single conference theme. The stated reason was:

> It would be advisable – in view of the short time that remained before the Congress – to regard it as an *interim* congress and whose programme of work would only be preliminary to a full-dress congress in 1948 . . . [It was] important to know where modern architecture stood now in the various countries and what the outstanding problems really were; that the direction of future CIAM work must emerge from a study of the present situation.[34]

To some extent, this masked a tension between those who wished to maintain the town-planning thrust of CIAM activities and those who wanted to shift towards considering the aesthetics of 'architectural expression'. It was decided to have Commissions prepare reports to discuss this matter further at CIAM VI.

At one level, the Bridgwater Congress was a 'joyous reunion of the heroes of Weissenhof'.[35] A large meeting with 97 delegates (Figure 8.7) met primarily to celebrate the fact

that they had survived and to 'pick up the pieces. There were simply no rules at that stage, no set agenda.'[36] They reaffirmed the La Sarraz Declaration and listened to a series of Commission reports on topics such as town planning legislation, 'urbanism', 'architectural expression' and 'reorganisation'. Programmes of work were decided for CIAM VII. Ling, who presented the report on town planning legislation and jointly chaired the Commission on 'Urbanism', recalled the makeshift programme of this Congress:

> Fortunately the first post-war conference was at Bridgwater – as indeed was the first IFHP (International Federation for Housing and Planning) conference which was held at Hastings. I attended both of these. By this time I was working with Holford, Stephenson and Peter Shepheard at the Ministry's Planning Technique Office, which also had young enthusiasts like Colin Buchanan, Lichfield, Gordon Cullen and so on. Holford was in the process of leaving, but we gave the CIAM Congress full support and we took down to Bridgwater the models that had been made of model neighbourhoods, work done for the proposed Handbooks and so on – work which was turned into exhibition material.[37]

The 'Urbanism' Commission's report noted that the Athens Charter had given a clear line on principles to be followed for the planning of towns but that two important fields of physical planning had opened up since 1933 – the broader field of national and regional planning and the more localised field of neighbourhood planning. They regarded it as essential that CIAM reassessed its position in relation to planning at all scales from neighbourhood to regional.[38] The anticipated conflict between those who advocated a resumption of town-planning studies and those who desired to make architectural expression the new theme was resolved 'in full session where it was appreciated that CIAM must take the comprehensive view'.[39]

Two developments resulted from this decision. First, the aim of CIAM was redefined to work: 'for the creation of a physical environment that will satisfy man's emotional and material needs and stimulate his spiritual growth'. Achieving an environment of that quality involved concern with both the functional and the aesthetic:

> We must combine social idealism, scientific planning and the fullest use of available building techniques. In doing so we must enlarge and enrich the aesthetic language of architecture in order to provide a contemporary means whereby people's emotional needs can find expression in the design of their environment. We believe that thus a more balanced life can be produced for the individual and for the community.[40]

The second development was to find a framework that would allow both elements to be represented in future CIAM Congresses. To this end:

> Le Corbusier sketched a framework into which all the specific contributions from different Groups, towards the shaping of the modern physical environment, could be fitted. He was commissioned to formulate this in detail.[41]

The 'framework' was the forerunner of a *grille* (Grid) used in subsequent CIAM Congresses as a basis for comparative analysis of different planning and architectural projects (see following section).

If the potential conflict between the town planning and architectural orientations was resolved, another longer-term problem had appeared. The middle-aged faces in Figure 8.7 testified to the two decades that had passed since La Sarraz. Before the Bridgwater Congress Benjamin Merkelbach, the delegate of the Dutch group, had written to Giedion registering his concern about the 'lack of the influence of the younger generation'.[42] As a result, member organisations were asked to involve *les jeunes*, the younger generation, in national organisations with the suggestion that they might seek to involve them in the forthcoming Congress.

There was little immediate impact. Only a few younger members, notably Jacob Bakema and Aldo van Eyck, appeared at Bridgwater and their appearance was effectively linked to the political agenda of member groups. Aldo van Eyck, a protégé of Giedion's, voiced his opposition to CIAM's mechanistic viewpoint and roundly endorsed the move to express the new consciousness in architecture and the arts. By contrast, Bakema, an avowed functionalist, was seen by the Dutch group as a counterbalance to Giedion's position. Yet despite the small number of young architects involved, the problem of succession, which became integral to the story of CIAM post-1945, had firmly emerged.

Bergamo and the CIAM Grid

Two tasks were necessary before CIAM VII. One was to find an appropriate venue. The growing ideological split in Europe between East and West inevitably affected the future of CIAM: 'What will happen with CIAM we cannot ourselves control. If the world is split into two the Congress will also inevitably be separated by physical barriers escaping our control.'[43] This made all the more difficult the choice of location between Prague, the originally-preferred alternative, and Bergamo in Italy. Growing political tensions led to Bergamo being selected in early 1949; indeed Bergamo would be the last CIAM Congress that East European delegates were able to attend.

The second task required Le Corbusier and ASCORAL to contrive the CIAM Grid for the analysis of development according to scale, function and time. Despite showing a preliminary version at Bridgwater, it proved extremely difficult to find a definitive version that adequately accommodated different contexts and circumstances. Indeed it was not until January 1949 that the final version was received by member groups.[44] Using it, member groups were asked to devise analyses of urban developments at three different scales: a residential unit; a new town of around 60 000 people; and a major city undergoing change ('ville à transformer').[45]

The Grid was a ruled framework of 120 foolscap-sized 'pigeonholes' (see Figure 8.8). These were grouped for convenience of despatch and exhibition, on to eight linen folders – in other words 15 to each folder. Each pigeonhole was available for the graphic demonstration of a particular aspect

of the project, or the problem, that the author either considered necessary to its understanding or wished to draw to
the attention of other delegates. The 120 pigeon-holes were
prearranged according to a standard classification of subject
matter. The system of classification was considered under 10
main headings, numbered 10–19 and known as *Themes*. These
were:

10 Environment
11 Land use
12 Built domain
13 Equipment
14 Ethic and aesthetic
15 Economic and social influences
16 Legislation
17 Finance
18 Stages of realisation
19 Miscellaneous

There were also two further headings called the *Reactions to the
Themes*. They were:

20 Rational reactions (under three headings: the client, the
    general public and the authorities)
21 Reactions of sentiment (under same three headings)

Crucially, a further sub-classification of each theme was made
on the basis of the four established *Functions* and a miscellaneous ('divers') category:

1 Dwelling
2 Working
3 Cultivation of body and spirit
4 Circulation
5 Miscellaneous

By this device, the CIAM functional typology became a
cornerstone of the analysis. The five headings were arranged
in a column on the left of the Grid so that each of the ten
themes might be discussed in each of the five functions.[46]

The Grid was not an immediate success. In many cases,
large numbers of the cells would be blank, given the diversity
of headings. Others could present an additional linen folder to
be called an Appendix when needing more space to develop

Dreams and false expectations

			TITRE I									TITRE II	
		10	11	12	13	14	15	16	17	18	19	20	21
LES 4 FONCTIONS	HABITER 1												
	TRAVILLER 2												
	CULTIVER LE CORPS ET L'ESPRIT 3												
	CIRCULER 4												
	DIVERS 5												

Figure 8.8
CIAM grid.

anything in greater detail. Thus the pattern of used spaces would differ for each project presented. As a completely new framework, too, it would create considerable work for national delegations to present projects in the requested manner. Even CIAM's leadership were not entirely happy. Giedion's gloomy first impressions were that he could reach no definite conclusion 'as to whether town planning can be read by this procedure'. As an afterthought, he felt obliged to be more upbeat: 'it is of enormous moral importance to have this document, which is printed with the forte to impress certainly, groups and officials'.[47]

By May 1949, it was clear that only a small number of presentations would use the Grid and the official aim was scaled down: 'If we have a few examples of the Grille system, it will be enough to serve as a basis for discussion.'[48] Two of the Grids came from the English delegation. One dealt with Harlow New Town. Produced by Frederick Gibberd and his team, it demonstrated again how the British New Towns were not yet objects of scorn from the Modern Movement. The other was produced by the MARS Group and dealt with the County of London Plan.

Organised by Ernö Goldfinger with production supervised by Peter Moro, the County of London Grid was illustrated primarily by material from Carter and Goldfinger's book (see Chapter 7 and Figure 8.9).[49] The content of the Grid steered a precarious path between criticism of a plan not specifically informed by CIAM principles and support for 'a living tool in the hands of its able planners . . . [that] is constantly revised and improved in spite of great difficulties encountered'.[50] Free to apply a more critical gaze than found in the book, there were criticisms of the lack of precision and detail in the planning proposals. It was argued that certain underlying concepts were outmoded at the outset, for example, that the proposed ring and radial roads would create inextricable congestion in the centre of London. The economic basis of dispersal was criticised as was the conflict of legislative powers and the density arrangements.

Problems were encountered fitting these criticisms into the CIAM Grid. The original intention was to outline the plan's original recommendations, discuss what happened to them, and then analyse London's present planning. Any criticisms made could then lead back to criticism of the original plan.[51] This was hard to achieve: 'It was found extremely difficult to fit a critical appreciation of the London Plan into the CIAM Grid as this [the Grid] does not appear to have been designed for such a purpose.' As a result, it was agreed that the scope of the exhibit would be confined to two headings: '(1) The theme, County of London Plan (Grid numbers 10–19) and (2) Reaction to theme, MARS group criticism'.[52] Material shown under the second heading reused comments collected from the findings of one of the Questionnaires presented at the CIAM Bridgwater Congress,[53] which were shown in columns 20 and 21 of the Grid.

The Bergamo meeting in late July 1949 essentially concluded the process of recovering the agenda begun at Bridgwater. The Council of CIAM had met before the Congress and set up six Permanent Commissions which as Jaqueline Tyrwhitt observed 'sounds better than Committees'. These concerned town planning ('implementation of the Athens Charter'), 'inter-relation of the plastic arts', education, industrialisation of building construction, town planning legislation, and CIAM's social programme. The Commissions met for the first time during the Congress to plan programmes of work for report at CIAM VIII.[54]

While being described as a 'very relaxed' Congress with 'many distractions',[55] the Bergamo meeting contained heated exchanges. Helena Syrkus, one of the main authors of the plan that chose to reconstruct central Warsaw as a replica of its pre-war self, clashed with Giedion over the role of the past in urban design. This specific issue lapsed after Bergamo, since the Soviet-client governments of Eastern Europe barred delegates from attending CIAM meetings,[56] but other issues had important consequences for future Congresses.

The first was the continuing discussion about the value of the Grid. The opening session of the Town Planning Commission saw Le Corbusier advocating the Grid's value as a way to get round the mountains of paper that 'impede the progress of the town planner' and find a quick visual form of analysis.[57]

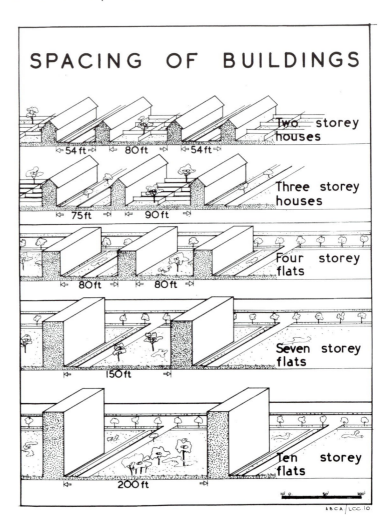

Figure 8.9
Spacing of High Buildings
in Accordance to their
Height. Original artwork
in Indian ink and tracing
paper for ABCA
Exhibition on 'County of
London Plan', included as
part of the MARS
Group's Grid for CIAM
VII (Bergamo, 1949).

The Commission examined methods other than the Grid for
exhibiting problems on urbanism, but accepted it as a tem-
plate for discussions at future meetings despite proving a blunt
tool for this Congress.[58]

Secondly, CIAM VII decided to revert to a single conference
theme provided it was wide enough to include the work of
the six Permanent Commissions. Two suggestions emerged at
Bergamo. One was to devise a document called 'La Charte de
l'Habitat' as a Charter for the meso-scale of urban life that
might be set alongside the urbanistic precepts of the Athens
Charter. The difficulty with the term 'l'Habitat' was that it had

various meanings in French and was almost untranslatable into English. Tyrwhitt noted that:

> This can be translated so variously that it has been left as it stood. It should not be transformed into a Charter for the Habitation. The MARS Group has accepted a wide interpretation of the words and is working on 'civic centres'.[59]

That interpretation, however, was so broad that it effectively created a separate theme that *rivalled* La Charte de l'Habitat as a potential focus for CIAM VIII.

Finally, and less tangibly, CIAM VII was another important step in rekindling the pioneering spirit of CIAM. Rather more than at Bridgwater, the Congress rediscovered its radical edge and the desire to move on from the doctrinal orthodoxy of the Athens Charter into new areas. As Jane Drew suggested: 'When you went to CIAM meetings and the Grids were prepared and the arguments went on until two and three in the morning at Bergamo . . . it was an electric feeling.' It was at least a note of promise after years in which the high expectations created by dreams of urban reconstruction proved slow to arrive.

9   OLD AND NEW AGENDA

As we look at a past vision of the future, what we see is the past and, in reflection, ourselves. This view may disclose how much one time may be composed of its visions of other times, how much a view of the future may place the past in time or constitute the present, how much the mirrors of time reflect upon each other so that we, standing in the midst of them, can see ourselves coming and going.

H.B. Franklin[1]

Whatever disappointments the Modern Movement experienced in the immediate post-war period due to the slow beginnings of urban reconstruction, the early 1950s finally brought expectancy to fruition. In this chapter, which completes our survey of the Modern Movement's urban imagination up to 1953, we find renewed debate over concepts and practical strategy. Ironically, just as the old agenda of modernism was resuscitated, new agenda emerged. There was a growing split between those who wanted to proceed within the same trajectory as before and those who wished to move in new directions to renew modernism's cutting edge. Active discussion recommenced on issues of philosophy, aesthetic theory and social commitment.

In charting these controversies, we again juxtapose the national and international contexts. After examining the Festival of Britain and the associated Lansbury 'Live Architecture' exhibition, we consider CIAM VIII – the 'Festival Congress' – held at Hoddesdon. Having highlighted the frictions that were appearing and considered the extent to which these mirrored a shift from one generation to another, we examine the emergence of new developments, both domestically and at CIAM IX. The final section briefly reflects on the state of the Modern Movement's urban imagination a quarter-century after the Weissenhof and La Sarraz.

Festival of Britain

The 1851 'Great Exhibition of the Works of the Industry of All Nations' in London's Hyde Park had acted as an important boost for national morale in mid-nineteenth-century Britain, temporarily obliterating the host of social and political problems that had surfaced in the 1840s.[2] Given the parlous state of the nation in the late 1940s, parallels were irresistible. The original suggestion for a centenary Great Exhibition was made by the Royal Society of Arts in 1943,[3] but gained momentum in September 1945, following an open letter of support that appeared in the *News Chronicle*. The letter, bearing the name of the editor Gerald Barry, was addressed to Sir Stafford Cripps, the President of the Board of Trade. The Board was interested in holding an exhibition to boost the export drive, but decided its purposes were better served by smaller scale events like the 1946 'Britain Can Make It' exhibition at the Victoria and Albert Museum. The idea of holding an exhibition devoted to the activities, achievements and way of life of the British people, which surfaced during discussions, was passed to the Government for further consideration. Due to the active intervention of the Lord President of the Council, Herbert Morrison, the Government decided to hold a Festival of Britain in the summer of 1951.[4]

Gerald Barry was chosen as Director General of the Festival in 1947. It was, in Jane Drew's view, an inspired appointment:

> He was a pioneer in the *News Chronicle* in having a competition for school design and . . . was a pioneer, as a patron, in supporting modern architecture. He was very unusual amongst those in authority at the time. Even the Barbican – watered down as it is now – came straight out of Gerald's philosophy . . .[5]

The war-damaged South Bank of the Thames was selected as the main exhibition site, with smaller exhibitions scheduled for venues throughout the country. Hugh Casson was chosen as the Festival's Director of Architecture and he, in turn, gathered together a group responsible for planning the site. Architects were invited to submit designs for specific buildings in the spring of 1949. The architects, engineers and others participating in designing the Festival included such stalwarts of the British Modern Movement as Peter Moro, Basil Spence, H.T. Cadbury-Brown, Jane Drew, Max Fry, Ralph Tubbs, Leslie Martin, Trevor Dannatt, Misha Black, Peter Shepheard, Ove Arup and Felix Samuely.

The Festival, which ran from 3 May to 30 September 1951, is commonly presented as the last heroic endeavour of the outgoing Labour administration: an impression reinforced by

the haste with which the incoming Conservatives cleared the
site and sold the structures for scrap. At the time, however,
much of the Festival project commanded all-party support.
With regard to the Festival Hall, for example, Trevor Dannatt
recalled:

> There was Herbert Morrison who was a great South Banker, a
> south Londoner, and former head of the LCC (London County
> Council) in the new Government. He was a profound believer in
> the South Bank being redeveloped and a protagonist who was
> responsible for the new Waterloo Bridge. Morrison was very
> influential in the whole thing becoming the success it was,
> because he could use his central government connections whilst
> his roots were in local government. Certainly, Leslie Martin
> always said in the development of the Festival Hall, there was a
> cross-party committee covering the Liberals, the Labour, the
> Conservative and LCC members.[6]

What can be said with confidence is that the Festival brought
the British public into intimate contact with modern architecture for the first time. It featured more than 30 structures
in a variety of modern styles set in landscaped surroundings.
They were arranged so that the exhibition was never seen as a
whole but only as a series of enclosures. The exhibition
buildings were arranged in two circuits; upstream illustrating
the 'Land of Britain', downstream the 'People of Britain'.[7]
There was also a Dome of Discovery housing an exhibition
illustrating 'British Exploration and Discovery'. Critics pointed
to the nostalgic, even sentimental, references to 1930s Swedish and Swiss modernism that permeated the architecture: a
corollary of the Festival's own Scandinavian-influenced 'Contemporary Style' that pervaded their interiors. There was also
the problem of the self-conscious 'showpiece' character of the
buildings:

> The problem perhaps was that the architects had been
> unemployed for five to ten years, with nothing happening. They
> were longing to do some buildings. And now suddenly here were
> all these. . . buildings and they were over-designed.[8]

Yet nostalgic, over-designed or otherwise, Ralph Tubbs's Dome
of Discovery, Powell and Moya's 'Skylon' mast (Figure 9.1)
and the rest proved popular with visitors, showing that modern architecture could create environments that were warm
and responsive as well as futuristic. It may not have yet have
been the breakthrough for the new architecture, but it did at
least prepare the public for a change in architectural style.

Figure 9.1
The Festival of Britain, 1951, by night. The illustration shows the 'Skylon', the Festival's 'vertical feature', and the edge of the 'Dome of Discovery'.

Similar observations apply to the Lansbury redevelopment in London's East End. Along with the Festival Hall, the Lansbury scheme in Poplar – a 'Live Architecture' exhibit – was the London County Council's contribution to the Festival. If the South Bank site gave people an introduction to modern architecture, then Lansbury attempted to do the same with broader principles of town planning. As Peter Moro remarked: 'There was much talk at the time about new towns, neighbourhood units and so on – it showed, at life-scale, what some of these ideas meant.'[9]

Named after the veteran Labour politician George Lansbury, the 30-acre Lansbury site was the first part of the 2000-acre Stepney-Poplar Redevelopment Area to be redeveloped. Percy

Johnson-Marshall, who came from Coventry in 1949 to lead
the LCC's planning team, recalled that they had to work with
population densities fixed by the County of London Plan:

> On arriving (at the LCC), I was handed the project for the
> reconstruction of the Stepney-Poplar area which was zoned at
> densities of 136 persons per acre and there was nothing that I
> could change in that. The Housing Committee insisted on it and
> the Valuer's Department agreed with them, since they wanted to
> get people off the housing lists. To have lowered the densities
> implied housing fewer people and that was a deeply emotive
> political issue.[10]

The scale model of the western end of the Stage 1 scheme is
shown in Figure 9.2. It comprised a mixed development of
medium-rise slab blocks of flats and houses-and-gardens,
interwoven with certain elements of the existing urban environment that were being retained.[11] As described in the LCC's
press handout:

> The buildings of varying heights will be grouped around closes
> and spaces of different sizes, each with its individual character. In
> some cases there will be children's playgrounds in the centre of
> blocks, completely protected from traffic. The layout is in fact a
> series of neighbourly groups linked together by open spaces.
> While this type of layout is new to the East End of London and
> the contrast between old and new forms of development is likely
> to prove striking, the architectural treatment of most of the
> buildings will include the use of London stock bricks and purple
> grey slates which are traditional building materials for this part of
> Poplar.[12]

The language is symptomatic of intent. The scheme presented
unfamiliar structures but retained traditional materials and
appealed to the area's reputation for 'neighbourliness', a
poignant theme recently enhanced by the experience of the
Blitz. Lansbury presented new uses of space with a pedes-
trianised shopping precinct and the semi-public open spaces
surrounding the flats, but adopted traditional modes of construction. The flats themselves, restricted by a statutory height
limit of six-storeys, adopted the gentle Scandinavian approach
to aesthetics, a subject that would shortly become a matter of
controversy within the London County Council (see below).

Figure 9.2
Lansbury redevelopment,
Stage 1. Viewed from the
western edge along
Canton Street, with the
East India Road on the
right.

The 'Festival Congress'

The suggestion that a CIAM Congress would be held in
England to coincide with the Festival of Britain was made
even before the Bergamo meeting. By contrast, the conference theme took much longer to emerge. Of the two
options that emerged at Bergamo (see Chapter 8), opinion
gradually swung in favour of the 'Civic Centre', although both
Le Corbusier and Sert believed that la Charte de l'Habitat
should be retained for later discussion.[14] This decision was
ratified by a CIAM Council meeting in New York in June 1950
which chose the theme of 'the Core of the City' for CIAM VIII
while appealing to the organisers, the MARS Group, to think
of a better title.[15]

Lack of definitional clarity bedeviled discussions of the 'Core' as much as la Charte de l'Habitat. The problem lay in its dual character. The term 'Core' was both a physical and psychological entity. As discussed at Bergamo, it was both a physical location where people could gather and a centre which gave identity to the community – 'the expression of the collective mind and spirit of the community which humanises and gives meaning and form to the city itself'.[16] This recognition of the significance of context was an important step for CIAM in moving away from a rigid functional approach, but it failed to address the problem of scale. In the words of the conference programme:

> *At each level* [author's emphasis] the creation of a special physical environment is called for, both as a setting for the expression of this sense of community and as an actual expression if it. This is the physical heart of the community, the nucleus, THE Core.[17]

The term Core, therefore, was applied to the study of settlements of any size, regardless of the major qualitative differences between the Cores of a village and a major city. The decision to treat all types of 'Core' within the same Congress effectively confined any synthesis of findings to the broadest generalities, a failing readily apparent from the contents of the ensuing conference volume, *The Heart of the City*.[18]

Ironically, the fact that this happened was partly because the CIAM Grid at last succeeded in finding a common frame of analysis for qualitatively different phenomena. The version used at CIAM VIII was greatly modified from previous versions. Prepared by the MARS Group, it comprised 24 panels laid out under six headings. These were the region, the place, and four further headings related to the Core – layout, expression, social life and realisation. Naturally, using the Grid did impose a broad conception of a town centre, which in turn might predispose the subsequent analysis. This point was made by Lubetkin, who was asked by Coates to prepare a formal Grid on Peterlee. Gently rebuffing the request, Lubetkin reflected on his experience at Peterlee:

> The 'Grid' lays down very strictly not only the method of presentation . . . but also the subject matter. From this document it appears MARS's idea of a town centre is a crystallised conception, of a definite architectural composition, in which the relations between the land-uses, and even the buildings themselves, are predetermined by the designer's will, and patiently await in this form their gradual execution.

> Whereas such an approach might make sense in the case of an existing town, whose central area is to be replanned, in the case of the projected new town (or should I say rejected?) this conception hardly applies, or at least can hardly be regarded as realistic.[19]

CIAM VIII was held at High Leigh, an isolated Victorian mansion at Hoddesdon, north of London between 7 and 14 July 1951. The remote location was significant. A much smaller Congress than either Bridgwater or Bergamo, the Hoddesdon meeting represented a determined effort to make progress on the selected theme. Prior to the Congress, Giedion appealed to the British organisers not to organise excursions: 'Otherwise I do not think that the large programme can be successfully completed. We know the harm the nice excursions did to the Congress at Bergamo.'[20] Sensing the significance of this Congress for the future of CIAM and its prospects of making any further progress in its town planning endeavours, Giedion reinforced this further in a later missive:

> I hope that my proposal to secure three days of continuous work to the congress can be accepted. I understand perfectly well that the congress visitors as well as the MARS Group members who play such an important role in the festival exposition are eager to see and discuss the problem, but I am afraid that the exhausting visit to the festival already on the second day with all the consequences may do harm to the concentrated work of the congress.[21]

Voluntarily forsaking the attractions of London's Core, the main discussions concentrated on 26 different Grids. At one extreme were Grids on the Cores of villages in Holland and Norway and a small Swedish town. Neighbourhood scale was represented by a project for a district in Chicago and Grids for the Cores of 'urban sectors' in New York, Rotterdam, Liège and Oslo. At the other end of the scale were Grids for the Cores of cities, such as Coventry, Hiroshima, Basle, Lausanne and Paris. Grids were presented of Le Corbusier's collaborative design projects for Cores of 'government centres' at Chandigarh and Bogota. Special attention was given to the Cores of New Towns. The Congress brochure[22] contained analysis of Wiener and Sert's plans for the new town of Chimbote, Peru (Figure 9.3). Other new town Grids showed Le Corbusier's abortive plan for St Dié in France (1945) and the Moroccan CIAM's scheme for the satellite town of Rabat Sale. The British contribution comprised two contrasting Grids for

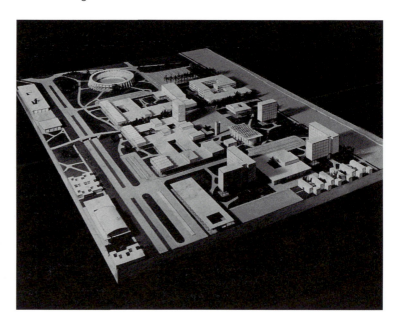

Figure 9.3
Part of the grid for
Chimbote, Peru by
Wiener and Sert.

Stevenage. One showed Stephenson and Shepheard's plans
for the Main Core of Stevenage. The other, by students of the
Architectural Association, proposed alternative development
at Stevenage by greatly increasing the density. By this means,
they hoped to achieve a greater sense of coherence and
urbanity and make the Core and countryside within walking
distance for all. A half-day visit to Harlow showed again that
the actual experience of the British New Towns remained of
interest to a conference of modern architects.[23]

There was little systematic consideration of the different
forms of the Core at Hoddesdon. Moreover, the final resolutions adopted at CIAM VIII provided little that was startling.
They stated that there should only be one main Core in each
city and that it was 'man-made'. They restated some themes
from the Athens Charter about pedestrian-vehicle separation
and demanded control of advertising. As a nod to Giedion's
concerns about the 'synthesis of the plastic arts', a resolution
supported the idea that in planning the Core 'the architect
should employ contemporary means of expression and –
whenever possible – should work in cooperation with painters
and sculptors'.[24]

These resolutions did not meet unanimous approval. Tyrwhitt, for example, recorded a series of reservations, including
her belief that the civic character and social importance of the

main Core of large cities were insufficiently stressed, primarily because all the resolutions related to smaller centres.[25] The Hoddesdon meeting also continued the awkward process of recognising the needs and potential contribution of the younger generation of architects. A CIAM Council meeting held at Hoddesdon decided that the next Congress, 25 years after La Sarraz, would be the time to 'hand over' CIAM to its younger members. Georges Candilis (Morocco) and Bill Howell (MARS) were appointed as 'CIAM Council Representatives of the Younger Generation of Architects'. Yet despite willingness, the direction of discussion at Hoddesdon remained in the hands of the established leadership. Grids for Stevenage, Chicago, New York, Providence (Rhode Island) and New Haven (Connecticut) might have been supplied by student groups, but a disproportionate number of Grids (three each) concentrated on work personally associated with Le Corbusier and Sert.

Frictions

Friction and outright animosity were nothing new for the Modern Movement. We saw in Chapter 3 the tensions and rivalries that existed just below the surface in CIAM throughout the inter-war period, the resolution of which effectively shaped the early programme of CIAM Congresses. Yet the frictions of the early 1950s were qualitatively different. On the one hand, there were the diverging experiences of the generations of architects involved. From the point of view of the older architects, the younger architects' 'starting point was different. The things that we argued about, they took for granted. It was the basis on which they began.'[26] Conversely, it was argued that changing material circumstances meant that the older architects no longer possessed the same commitment as before:

> People get tired of organisations of all kinds and somehow the enthusiasm was breaking down amongst considerable sections of its membership. If you want to put it politically, you could say that the bourgeois elements were returning to their bourgeois concepts. Many of them were building up their private practices and felt for one reason and another that they could not afford to spare the time. As well as this, there were the usual things about stages of life-cycle and life styles that deflected attention away. The simple socialist idea of making a demonstration of your own life

became more and more difficult. The interest in the worker's living also diminished as the interest in the client's way of life became paramount.[27]

Secondly, and related, there was growing disagreement about what modern architects stood for. For Ling, the split came from 'the differing emphasis placed on architecture as a private or public occupation'.[28] Johnson-Marshall noted that there was conflict between 'those who thought of architecture as a fine art and just a matter of producing plastic harmonies and so forth; and those who wanted to solve social problems'. In terms of the urban imagination, the differences between the two groups were captured by an anecdote:

> There is no doubt that there were theoretical differences. One small example from town planning: one of the policies that I had in my group when I was at the LCC was to help both the Schools of Architecture and Town Planning. Most of my group used to go and teach there in the evenings, with us having particularly close links with the Architectural Association. On one occasion, Arthur Korn invited us to participate in a neighbourhood planning exercise with the fourth year. He asked our advice and we said, 'why don't you have a look at Lansbury and do it again to see if the students can do it any better?' We can give you all the information that any consultant would need to do the job . . . and more. Anne McEwan and I offered to give our time to help. Arthur Korn, without letting us know, had brought in Mr X as one of the co-supervisors. When we turned up the students had already done something which was quite impossible to do under the conditions. We had taken the trouble to acquaint the students with all the numerous constraints that would apply in such a replanning exercise of an existing city – constraints such as the fact that there are major sewers and huge cables that cannot be removed without enormous cost. When they reached the design stage, the students had totally ignored all the design constraints. When asked why, they said that their supervisor, Mr. X, had said that they ought to start with a clean sheet and not be bothered with all the constraints. At this point, Anne McEwan and I left. This summarises in a way the differences that were present.[29]

Yet having said this, he was keen not to conflate polarisation of ideas with the notion of a generational shift in any simple causal manner, later adding that:

> The Festival of Britain absorbed modern architecture into the show. It was a very British way to behave, but it did not suit everyone. There were already others, of whom the Smithsons are

the best known, who wanted to regain a harder edge. I stress the word *regain*. They were not mere iconoclasts. They believed in the importance of history and were passionately keen to rekindle that spark that the masters like Corb and Mies had ignited. To a real extent, they were reaching back to move forwards. Certainly they were young, but there were older people who agreed with them and also younger people who didn't.[30]

New directions

Speaking on the BBC's Third Programme in June 1951, the urban sociologist Ruth Glass called for 'new ideas' about the town and a 'positive contemporary concept of [the] urban environment'.[31] Her words captured the mood of several groups whose thinking would direct debate back to the fundamentals of how modern architecture was applied to the urban scale. One centre of debate, already mentioned above, was the Architect's Department of the London County Council. Ling sketched the background to this debate:

> During the war, there was no housing built . . . and no architecture. So Forshaw, who was the Architect, concentrated on planning. Except for wartime obligations, the Planning Division, in effect, was the beginning, middle and end of the Architect's Department at that time. Forshaw looked forward to the time when the new plans, particularly in the field of housing, could be given flesh and bone by the architecture for which he was also responsible, so that the two could be brought together. At the end of the war, however, the administrators and politicians had a different idea. They considered that since the Valuer's Department was responsible for the first stage – purchasing the land for housing – and was responsible for the final stage of maintenance, rent collection etc. that the middle stage of design realisation should also come under the same Department on the same basis, it was argued, as a military operation. After a considerable battle, housing was moved to the Valuer's Department and, on the same day that it was moved, Forshaw moved over to the Ministry of Health as the chief housing architect. A new battle began for the return of housing to the Architect's Department, since that Department was actively engaged in designing the schools, and the general buildings. But it was not until 1951 and Lansbury that Matthew was able to show that he could make a contribution to housing because he was responsible for the planning side of this neighbourhood. It eventually came back. However, it had to be shown that the Architect's Department was operating it on its own. Previously we had been doing the planning layouts and

then passing them to the Valuer's Department for them to do their modified versions. On Roehampton, the schemes that were sent over from the Valuer's Department were so bad that we were able to find enough faults with them in order to delay the direction of it until the Architect's Department got housing back.[32]

The Roehampton flats became a *cause célèbre*. Two teams within the Department worked on designing housing estates at Roehampton in outer London. Those responsible for the Portsmouth Road (Alton East) estate continued the mild Swedish influences already exemplified at Lansbury in a mixed development of terrace-housing and flats. Designed in November 1951, their key innovation was the addition of thin, 11-storey, square-profile point blocks, regarded as ideally suited to a well-wooded site with varying ground levels. The idea came directly from visits to Sweden:

> Many of us were influenced by Scandinavian housing practice . . . Sweden and Denmark. I went over to Scandinavia as did some of the housing architects, such as Whitfield Lewis, Oliver Cox and Rosemary Sternstedt. They brought over, for example, the Swedish idea of the point block, a slender tower of four flats per floor, and they built a considerable number at Roehampton.[33]

Figure 9.4
Le Corbusier's unité
d'habitation, Marseilles.

The Roehampton Lane (Alton West), designed in 1953, represented a housing scheme with an altogether harder edge.

Figure 9.5
Flats at Alton West,
Roehampton.

Once again, there was an unusually direct design influence. The team responsible for the development, led by Colin Lucas, sought to replicate the appearance, particularly the concrete-work, of Le Corbusier's experimental unité d'habitation flats then under construction at Marseilles (Figure 9.4). At the same time, the internal layout differed. The rue interieure – an internal street with no natural lighting – was moved to the exterior as a traditional balcony and the dwelling units comprised five sets of 'duplex' units (maisonettes) stacked up in a slab block (Figure 9.5).

In doing so, they gave early expression to the austere style and aesthetics that became known as the 'New Brutalism'. Originally coined in 1950 as a joke by the Swedish architect, Hans Asplund, the word 'Brutalism' was appropriated with enthusiasm by younger British architects to describe their work. New Brutalism asserted the primacy of space, structure and materials displayed in their untrammelled form. As implemented at Marseilles and elsewhere, this suggested another version of 'truth to materials', with concrete bearing the marks of its timber shuttering, brickwork being unplastered, and steel frames left exposed.

The innovations seen in London were also beginning to shape social housing in cities other than London, as with Birmingham's 12-storey blocks in the Duddeston and Nechells Redevelopment Area begun in early 1951.[34] Equally, there were groups outside the public authorities that were trying to resurrect modernism's cutting edge as a force for changed aesthetic awareness and social reconstruction. The interest in mechanisation, popular cultural artefacts and the new sensitivity to landscape, for example, was stimulated by exhibitions held at the Institute of Contemporary Arts (ICA) from 1951 onwards.[35] Its 'Growth and Form' exhibition (1951), for example, was timed to coincide with CIAM VIII. Opened by Le Corbusier, it examined themes tackled by Giedion's text *Mechanisation Takes Command*.[36]

The event was also important for bringing together a pan-artistic group that was known first as the Young Group and, from November 1952, as the Independent Group. Led by Reyner Banham, then working on the thesis that would later become *Theory and Design in the First Machine Age*, its personnel included Peter and Alison Smithson, John McHale, Magda Cordell, Richard Hamilton, Nigel Henderson, Eduardo Paolozzi and Lawrence Alloway. Their work was suffused by an awareness of America, an appreciation of technology, and a vision of a future world of consumption, free from rationing, where advertising imagery was an important form of communication.[37]

Architectural commentators quickly allotted the Smithsons, in particular, a central place in the narrative of change. The Smithsons undoubtedly arrived on the scene at a propitious moment. They were representative of those who saw modern architecture as having lost its radical edge, architectural education as having drifted into complacency and CIAM 'as a corrupt parliamentary body in need of anti-oligarchic reform'.[38] They also readily appropriated the language and rhetoric of the 'heroic era' to launch their manifestos and give expression to the apparent anger and frustration of an ignored generation. Nevertheless, their real importance perhaps rested on their ability to articulate and present the new imagery of architectural modernism in post-war Britain.

Apart from designing a Mies-inspired school at Hunstanton in Norfolk (1949), they first came to prominence through their entry to the competition for new flats at Golden Lane in the City of London (1952). Most of the entries were routine exercises in mainstream modernism (for example, Figure 9.6). The competition was won by Chamberlin Powell and Bonn, but it was the Smithsons' unplaced entry that gained the more lasting coverage from the architectural press. Presented in photomontage (Figure 9.7) as well as conventional line drawing, this 11-storey scheme would have three levels of pedestrian or 'street decks'. In doing so, the Smithsons anticipated the Alton West team's transfer of Le Corbusier's rue interieure to the exterior of the block. The 'street deck' was enlarged to a 12-feet wide walkway.[39]

When explaining its value, the Smithsons revived discussion about potential sociological benefits – a style of discourse not much in evidence since inter-war debates about *die Neue Mensch*. The street deck would function socially in just the same way as a normal street, acting as a place where people could meet informally, socialise and develop group identity. In line with the 'community planners' of the day, the Smithsons argued that the street was an extension of the house. In it, 'children learn for the first time of the world outside the family; it is a microcosmic world in which the street games change with the seasons and the hours are reflected in the cycle of street activity'.[40] This quality of the street was forgotten in many housing developments but would be revived by the street-decks:

Figure 9.6
S.R. Pierce, Competition entry for Golden Lane, City of London, 1952.

It is the idea of street and the reality of street that is important – the creation of effective group- spaces fulfilling the vital function of identification and enclosure, making the socially vital life-of-the-streets possible.[41]

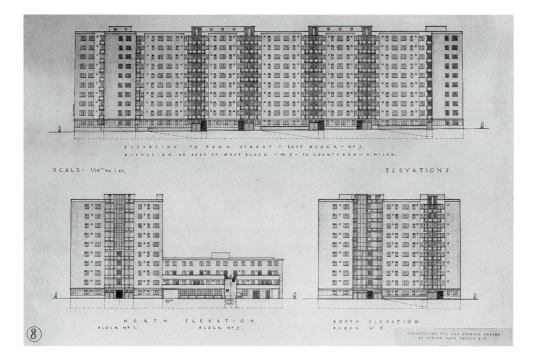

Figure 9.7
Vignette patterns of life
and sky. A. and P.
Smithson, Competition
entry for Golden Lane,
City of London, 1952.

This, in turn, was related to a theory of Urban Reidentifica-
tion, by which a community should build up a hierarchy of
associations from the house and the street to the district and
the city. Sensitive design could assist people to reidentify
themselves with their environment. They were ideas that the
Smithsons would develop further at CIAM IX.

Trouble at Aix

> I attended the Aix-en-Provence Congress, which was . . . the
> beginning of the end. It was the moment when the old guard
> somehow had lost their dynamism and interest, whereas the
> younger ones felt that the older ones were going in a different
> direction.[42]

While it is always difficult to pinpoint any moment as a
turning point from one period to another, CIAM IX at Aix-en-
Provence in July 1953 possesses credentials that are as good as
any other. The shape of the meeting was essentially decided in
May 1952 by two decisions taken at a CIAM Council meeting
in Paris. The first was that the leadership effectively back-
tracked from the suggestion that CIAM should be handed over
to the 'younger architects' or 'wound up'. No dramatic steps
would be taken at CIAM IX, but there might be a period of
transition until CIAM X, with increasing attention paid to the

work of younger architects. It was also decided to hold a discussion at CIAM IX about the ideology of CIAM, given that the range of opinions about the organisation's future were 'especially confusing for the younger generation'.[43]

The second decision was that CIAM IX would return to the theme of *La Charte de L'Habitat*. Speaking to the meeting, Le Corbusier recommended the importance of establishing a new scale for the analysis of human affairs, confiding that:

> He no longer felt we could be confident about the way men should live in this changing world. He no longer felt that he knew what 'a town' should be. The 'Habitat' is clearly an element of living space – Corbu is not sure that *urbanisme* is any longer a correct word – but how it should be organised with the other elements is less and less clear.[44]

The meeting again noted that there was no adequate English translation but 'habitat' was generally taken to be something between a housing scheme and a neighbourhood. Although a working definition of 'dwelling and its immediate environment'[45] was later supplied, the programme for CIAM IX revealed that the term had both physical, sociological, even spiritual connotations:

> The exact etymology of the word 'habitat' which has no equivalent in some languages (including English) and which gives rise, even in French, to Byzantine discussions, matters little.
>
> Habitat (L'Habitat) is not only a human shelter.
>
> It is a cell of a socially organised body.
>
> Reasoning by the absurd, the cell without the body loses all significance, in the sense which we mean the word.
>
> Habitat insures for man the accomplishment of his spatial, physiological, spiritual and emotional needs and protects him from weather and atmospheric conditions.
>
> It integrates individual and family life in the manifestations of social and collective life.[46]

The lack of specificity of this notion meant that La Charte de L'Habitat proved even more elusive than the Athens Charter; indeed the former never materialised.

CIAM IX was held at the Ecole des Arts et Métiers in Aix-en-Provence between 19 and 26 July 1953. Organised by ASCORAL, CIAM IX was easily the largest CIAM Congress, with over 500 members present. Its proceedings consisted of the work of Commissions coupled with discussion of around 40 Grids submitted, although not exclusively prepared, by the national groups. Thus, the MARS Group was responsible for gathering together six Grids but not all were by its own members. Two featured completed housing schemes at Paddington and the Pimlico estate, Westminster (Figure 9.8). There was a Grid from Hatfield New Town in Hertfordshire and a conceptual scheme entitled 'Zone' by three students at the Architectural Association (Pat Crooke, Andrew Derbyshire and John Voelcker). The final two were proposed housing projects, the Alton West estate at Roehampton and the Smithsons' Golden Lane scheme.

The Smithsons' scheme was prepared as a collaborative venture with Voelcker, and William and Gillian Howell. It was deliberately prepared 'in direct opposition to the arbitrary isolation of the so-called communities of the "Unité" and the "neighbourhood" '.[47] Rather than use the standard fourfold functional classification, the Smithsons offered their hierarchy of human associations – house, street, district and city – as a replacement. This hierarchy might reidentify people with their environment. The Golden Lane project was reused to illustrate how a housing development could be infused with a sense of communal life. Making use of Nigel Henderson's photographs of children playing in East End streets to invigorate the presentation, it provided a lightly veiled criticism of the lifeless and 'hygenic' Grids elsewhere on display at Aix.[48]

This injection of radical discontent into CIAM IX was not reflected in the official proceedings. When offered the option of change at a CIAM Council meeting at Aix, members overwhelmingly decided that continuity rather than revolutionary change was required, with places on the Council only

Figure 9.8
Pimlico estate,
Westminster (Powell
& Moya).

filled by younger members as vacancies arose. Although approved, this clearly failed to satisfy everyone. Goldfinger, a veteran of CIAM Congresses since Brussels, felt that CIAM had simply become 'a very pleasant club where we can meet and see one another', but not one capable of serious work.[49] The Smithsons, Voelcker, and William and Gillian Howell wrote a report deeply critical of proceedings at CIAM IX, noting:

> Since the 9th Congress we have tried to uncover the factors which have prevented us from reaching more definite conclusions: we attribute this failure to the following factors:
>   i. The administration of CIAM is at fault.
> ii. The accepted definitions and methods of work within CIAM are not adequate for dealing with the problems with which we are faced today.
> iii. The role of the architect/urbanist, and the particular techniques with which he works are ill-defined and need reformulation.[50]

From her standpoint, Alison Smithson complained that not only were established members reluctant to hand over the reins of power, they were also 'aloof' and unwilling to communicate, a lack of 'connective will that was to prove the rotten core of CIAM'.[51]

Taking stock

Viewed with hindsight, it is much easier now to recognise late 1953 as a key moment of change than it was at the time. European economic recovery, initially assisted by American aid under the Marshall Plan, was finally leading to rising living standards and the possibility of switching resources to investment in housing and reconstruction. In Britain, Austerity would soon end when the Conservative Government scrapped remaining areas of rationing, control of civil building and the last vestiges of the Labour Government's grander hopes for economic planning. By 1954, the progressive increase in building activity in office, school and residential sectors was adding new urgency to debates about the future city. From this point, the clearance and redevelopment machines were unleashed.

New areas of concern were already apparent. Surveying the state of architecture in January 1954, Richards indicated how much change was already on its way. Large office blocks were sprouting throughout the centre of London, landmark social housing schemes had opened for tenants and new schools were appearing. At the same time, there were causes for concern, especially that the 'human scale is lost in an infinity of repetition'.[52]

Similarly, new agenda were being created. CIAM and MARS were nearing the end of their existence. Participants in those organisations remain divided as to whether they faded away because their original purposes had been achieved[53] or because they were destroyed by a clash between the generations.[54] What is certain is that a new generation was again adding to the constellation of design and sociological imagery built up during the inter-war period. One source was the small grouping of younger architects who came together in opposition to the events of CIAM IX. From this starting point came the nucleus of an international group who met at Doorn, Holland, in January 1954 to compile the grandiosely titled Doorn Manifesto.

The Manifesto was signed by five architects: Peter Smithson, Voelcker, Bakema, van Eyck and Daniel van Ginkel and a social economist Hans Hovens-Greve. It began by recognising that the Athens Charter proposed a technique of countering the chaos of the nineteenth-century city and providing a way of understanding more clearly the potential of the twentieth century. The Doorn Manifesto was intended as a way of furthering that potential. It was argued that the Athens Charter failed to express human associations adequately. To do that properly, it was necessary to study human associations at all levels, from isolated buildings, through villages and towns to cities. A Scale of Association was superimposed on the famous 'valley section' derived from Patrick Geddes.[55] Thereafter working parties of CIAM could study human association as a first principle with the four functions as aspects of each total problem.[56]

The Doorn Manifesto in turn fostered a small but extremely influential movement in architecture. Description of that movement lies beyond the scope of this book, but we can note that the Doorn group became the core of Team X which would eventually split CIAM at its last full Congress at Dubrovnik (1956). The Smithsons, too, would become central figures in the New Brutalism Movement which in the late 1950s and early 1960s changed the appearance and representation of architecture in the private and, especially, public

sectors. Nevertheless, too much emphasis on these developments can overstate their real significance. Team X and similar
radical groups engaged in a rarefied discourse and, arguably,
'didn't talk to anyone else except themselves'.[57] The real
change came with the entry of new commercial interests into
the debate; interests for whom the Modern Movement's constellation of imagery of the future city was an important
marketing tool (Figure 9.9).

To elaborate, if the definition of propaganda is communication of messages that spread a point of view favourable to an

Ere the Swan of Avon "was mewling and puking . . ."

(FROM SHAKESPEARE'S 'AS YOU LIKE IT' ACT II, SCENE 7)

. . . the Bull Ring, Birmingham, had been a noted centre for centuries. 1964
sees this centre re-vitalised to become the most advanced development of its
kind in the world.
There's something for everyone here at the hub of the Midlands . . . shops and
stores of every kind . . . restaurants . . . cafes . . . licensed houses . . . nursery . . .
the traditional markets in a gay new setting . . . all under cover, all air conditioned
. . . music while you shop . . . colour . . . excitement . . . Car Park, Midland Red
Bus Station within the centre, and a covered passage from New Street Station.

**Further shopping projects of this kind are under development by Laing
at Blackburn, Burton-on-Trent, Chester, Rochdale and other towns and
cities in Britain.**

The Laing Development Company Ltd
65 WATFORD WAY LONDON NW4   LDL 126

Figure 9.9
The Shape of Town
Centres to Come:
Advertisement for Laing's
development of the Bull
Ring Centre,
Birmingham.

advocate,[58] then the systems builders and building contractors could scarcely have believed their good fortune. They had much to sell if only they could persuade national and local government to back their judgment and undertake the type of wholesale reconstruction central to the urban imagination of the Modern Movement. The architects, for their part, had supplied these wider commercial interests with material that met all their promotional needs. As we have seen at many points in this book, the pristine imagery devised by the Modern Movement had long possessed impeccable claims to representing *the* shape of the future. By its very nature, the imagery was also malleable. Since there was no single vision of the future city, new elements could be steadily added without causing the elegant edifice to collapse. Typologies of urban function, new housing layouts and constructional forms, neighbourhood units, new circulation systems, scales of association and the rest were readily slotted alongside existing elements and further reinforced the basic axiom that given transformations of the built environment could bring about identifiable transformations of the social environment.

Additional power was given to the design imagery by the support of an underlying, but seldom expressed, sociological imagery that promised the Good Life. The future inhabitant in the city of the Modern Movement's urban imaginings was neither lost in the anonymous urban crowd nor sitting in glorious isolation in the materially comfortable, but socially impoverished, surroundings of suburbia. Rather, members of the future society would live contentedly in their convenient, labour-saving and thoroughly functional dwellings, especially flats set in green surroundings. They would consider the home to be an anchor in their lives, but would be essentially outward-looking, seeking to participate in the wider community and use their enhanced leisure time creatively and productively. In particular, they would seek collaborative endeavours that would serve to enhance the growing mood of teamwork and fellowship in society. At the social level, therefore, these individuals were depicted as having voluntarily abandoned individualism in favour of the ties of a cooperative, harmonious and orderly society.

As with the design imagery, new elements of sociological imagery could be steadily added without destroying the plausibility of existing imagery. The advent of discussion about neighbourhood units introduced an emphasis on the local scale. Urban living could now be based around walking distances, removing the stresses of metropolitan travel for shopping or recreational purposes and enhancing the perceived value of the locality. Sensitive design would be used to create local centres which would act as foci for the community and as places that would serve a vital role in cementing civic unity. A further idea that urban society needed, indeed longed for, an organic, hierarchical social order with readily identifiable communities of different sizes was absorbed effortlessly.

Yet perhaps the most advantageous element of this constellation of imagery was that it insulated itself from criticism. The built form was held to be derived from application of rational and moral principles to the needs of society. Criticisms about the design of the future city could always be answered by reference to the needs of the future urban society; needs that the Modern Movement themselves were specifying. Seen in this way, the ideas about society can be regarded as social justifications used to legitimise cherished ideas about design. Only the lessons of experience would eventually undermine these initial premises.

These lessons, however, lay in the future. At the point at which this volume ends, the groundwork was merely in place. The visionary ideals of the previous era were being absorbed into consensual approaches shaped by the specific circumstances of reconstruction. Their influence often lay as much in providing social justifications for desired built forms as in creation of the built forms themselves. The image of the future city had long been, in Lubetkin's phrase, 'a convenient way of selling oneself'.[59] This strategy had yielded few material rewards during the quarter-century studied here, but its moment was at hand. Foundations had been laid on which modern architects and their allies in government, the building and construction industries and elsewhere could, and did, build.

NOTES AND REFERENCES

All interview transcript references are listed in full on the first occasion that they are mentioned, thereafter with identifying name followed by interview number and the relevant page of transcript in square brackets.

Chapter 1

1. Boulding, K.E. (1964) *The Meaning of the Twentieth Century: the Great Transition*, New York: Harper & Row, p.164.
2. de Certeau, M. (1988) *The Practice of Everyday Life*, Berkeley: University of California Press, pp.77–90.
3. Ross, D. (1995) 'Grand Narrative in American Historical Writing: from Romance to Uncertainty', *American Historical Review*, 100, p.651. See also Lyotard, J.F. (1994) 'A Postmodern Fable on Postmodernity', in W.J. Lillyman, M.F. Moriarty and D.J. Neuman (eds), *Critical Architecture and Contemporary Culture*, New York: Oxford University Press, pp.189–95.
4. Curtis, W.J.R. (1987) *Modern Architecture since 1900*, 2nd edn, Oxford: Phaidon, p.8. There is no room in this study to consider the complex and emotive arguments over the morality of incorporating ornamentation in building design. It was a debate that was initiated by the Austrian architect Adolf Loos in an essay entitled 'Ornament and Crime', which appeared first in 1908, and was endlessly elaborated in modernist treatises advocating ascetic approaches to design. For more information, see Banham, R. (1957) 'Ornament and Crime: the Decisive Contribution of Adolf Loos', *Architectural Review*, 121, pp.85–8.
5. Bletter, R.H. (1984) 'Expressionism and the New Objectivity', *Art Journal*, 43, p.108. See also Sharp, D. (1966) *Modern Architecture and Expressionism*, London: Longman; Gelertner, M. (1995) *Sources of Architectural Form: a Critical History of Western Design Theory*, Manchester: Manchester University Press, p.239.
6. For example, Giedion, S. (1928) *Bauen in Frankreich, Bauen in Eisen, Bauen in Eisenbeton*, translated (1995) as *Building in France, Building in Iron, Building in Ferroconcrete*, Chicago: University of Chicago Press; Hitchcock, H.R. (1929) *Modern Architecture: Romanticism and Reintegration*, New York: Payson & Clark; Pevsner, N. (1936) *Pioneers of the Modern Movement: from William Morris to Walter Gropius*, London: Faber and Faber; Giedion, S. (1941) *Space, Time and Architecture: the Growth of a New Tradition*, Cam-

bridge, MA: Harvard University Press. Giedion, in particular, was a student of Wölfflin.

7. Macrae-Gibson, G. (1985) *The Secret Life of Buildings: an American Mythology for Modern Architecture*, Cambridge, MA: MIT Press, p.xii.

8. Ackerman, J.S. (1980) 'The Design of History and the History of Design', *Via*, 4, p.13.

9. See, among others, Jacobs, J. (1961) *The Death and Life of Great American Cities*, New York: Random House; Venturi, R. (1966) *Complexity and Contradiction in Architecture*, London: Architectural Press; Stern, R. (1969) *New Directions in American Architecture*, New York: Braziller; Newman, O. (1972) *Defensible Space: People and Design in the Violent City*, New York: Macmillan; Venturi, R., Scott Brown, D. and Izenour, S. (1972) *Learning from Las Vegas: the Forgotten Symbolism of Architectural Form*, Cambridge, MA: MIT Press; Blake, P. (1974) *Form Follows Fiasco: Why Modernism Hasn't Worked*, Boston: Little, Brown.

10. Coleman, A. (1985) *Utopia on Trial*, London: Hilary Shipman.

11. Hughes, R. (1980) *The Shock of the New*, London: BBC Publications, p.164.

12. Booker, C. (1980) *The Seventies*, London: Allen Lane, p.294.

13. Ravetz, A. (1980) *Remaking Cities*, London: Croom Helm, p.54.

14. Popham, P. (1995) 'Brutalist, Original, but a Slum', *The Independent*, 2 October, p.8.

15. Campbell, B. (1993) 'The Queenies that Betrayed the Gorbals', *The Independent*, 15 September, p.24.

16. Hall, P. (1988) *Cities of Tomorrow: an Intellectual History of Urban Planning and Design in the Twentieth Century*, Oxford: Basil Blackwell, p.5.

17. Lubbock, J. (1995) *The Tyranny of Taste: the Politics of Architecture and Design in Britain, 1550–1960*, New Haven, CN: Yale University Press, p.299.

18. Kunstler, J.H. (1993) *The Geography of Nowhere: the Rise and Decline of America's Man-Made Landscape*, New York: Simon & Schuster. The quotations used in this and the next paragraph come from this text (pp.59–84). In addition, there are strong resonances in Kunstler's analysis with the strident critique put forward by Tom Wolfe: see Wolfe, T. (1981) *From Bauhaus to Our House*, New York: Farrar Straus Giroux.

19. For more discussion of the notion of ideology, see Thompson, J.B. (1990) *Ideology and Modern Culture: Critical Social Theory in the Era of Mass Communication*, Oxford: Blackwell; Eagleton, T. (1991) *Ideology: an Introduction*, London: Verso; and Barrett, M. (1991) *Ideology: the Politics of a Concept*, Cambridge: Polity Press.

20. This extends a point made by Whyte, I.B. (1993) 'Introduction' to Georgiadis, S. *Sigfried Giedion: an Intellectual Biography*, Edinburgh: Edinburgh University Press, p.vii.

21. The epithet 'elastic' was applied to functionalism by Hitchcock, H.R. and Johnson, P. (1932) *The International Style*, New York: Museum of Modern Art; quotation here from the 1966 edition, New York: Norton, p.35. For more general discussion about its nineteenth-century roots, see Various Authors (1980) 'Eugène Emmanuel Viollet-le-Duc, 1814–79', Profile 27, *Architectural Design* (3–4), pp.1–94. For usage of the doctrine in the twentieth century, see Ligo, L.L. (1984) *The Concept of Function in Twentieth-Century Architectural Criticism*, Ann Arbor, MI: UMI Research Press.

22. Banham, R. (1987) ' "La Maison des Hommes" and "la Misère des Villes": Le Corbusier and the Architecture of Modern Housing', in H.A. Brooks (ed.), *Le Corbusier: the Garland Essays*, New York: Garland Publishing, p.107; and Bückle, J.C. (1993) *Hans Scharoun*, Zurich: Artemis, p.9.

23. Banham, R. (1973) 'The Glass Paradise', in J.M. Richards and N. Pevsner (eds), *The Anti-Rationalists*, London: Architectural Press, p.191.

24. See Banham, R. (1960) *Theory and Design in the First Machine Age*, London: Architectural Press; Jencks, C. (1973) *Modern Movements in Architecture*, Harmondsworth: Penguin; and Tafuri, M. (1976) *Teorie e Storia dell'Architettura*, Rome: Laterza, translated (1980) by G. Verrecchia, as *Theories and History of Architecture*, St Albans: Granada. For a small selection of the new multidisciplinary literature, see Colomina, B. (1994) *Privacy and Publicity: Modern Architecture as Mass Media*, Cambridge, MA: MIT Press; Wigley, M. (1995) *White Walls, Designer Dresses: the Fashioning of Modern Architecture*, Cambridge, MA: MIT Press; Domosh, M. (1996) *Invented Cities: the Creation of Landscape in Nineteenth Century New York and Boston*, New Haven, CN: Yale University Press; and Reed, C. (ed.) (1996) *Not at Home: the Suppression of Domesticity in Modern Art and Architecture*, London: Thames & Hudson.

25. Banham, R. (1962) *The Age of the Masters*, London: Architectural Press, p.65.

26. Harvey, D. (1989) *The Condition of Postmodernity: an Enquiry into the Origins of Cultural Change*, Oxford: Basil Blackwell, pp.24–5.

27. This thought comes from the autobiography of Lionel Brett, Lord Esher, one of the cohort of architects interviewed for this text. See Brett, L. (1985) *Our Selves Unknown: an Autobiography*, London: Victor Gollancz, p.186.

28. The MARS Group was wound up in January 1957. In passing, it is worth emphasising that MARS was very much the *English* branch of CIAM, with its activities centred on London. Despite frequent noises about arranging provincial activities, little was done.

29. Howard, A. (1987) *RAB: the Life of R.A. Butler*, London: Jonathan Cape, p.3.

30. Interview with Sir Ove Arup, 1 December 1987. Transcript reference [T1/1].

31. Although written in 1863, these words by Charles Baudelaire retain broad acceptability in defining modernity. See Mayne, J. (1964) *The Painter of Modern Life and Other Essays by Charles Baudelaire*, New York: Da Capo Press, p.13.

32. Lowenthal, D. (1985) *The Past is a Foreign Country*, Cambridge: Cambridge University Press, pp.72–3.

33. Fletcher, R. (1988) 'Modernization', in A. Bullock and S. Trombley (eds), *The Fontana Dictionary of Modern Thought*, London: Fontana, p.540.

34. Curtis, *Modern Architecture since 1900*, p.8.

35. Berman, M. (1983) *All That is Solid Melts into Air: the Experience of Modernity*, London: Souvenir Press, p.169.

36. Collier, P. (1985) 'Nineteenth-century Paris: Vision and Nightmare', in E. Timms and D. Kelley, eds. *Unreal City: Urban Experience in Modern European Literature and Art*, Manchester: Manchester University Press, pp.25 and 42.

37. Kern, S. (1983) *The Culture of Time and Space, 1880–1918*, London: Weidenfeld & Nicolson, p.104.

Chapter 2

1. Calvino, I. (1979) *Invisible Cities*, London: Picador, p.28.

2. Polak, F.L. (1961) *The Image of the Future*, 2 vols, trans. E. Boulding, New York: Oceana.

3. For more on this distinction, see Rosenau, H. (1983) *The Ideal City*, 3rd edn, London: Methuen. Other relevant sources include Reiner, T.A. (1963) *The Place of the Ideal Community in Urban Planning*, Philadelphia, PA.: University of Pittsburgh Press; Manuel, F.E. and Manuel, F.P. (1979) *Utopian Thought in the Western World*, Oxford: Basil Blackwell; Fishman, R. (1984) 'Utopia in Three Dimensions: the Ideal City and the Origins of Modern Design', in P. Alexander and R. Gill (eds), *Utopias*, London: Duckworth, pp.95–107.

4. Houghton-Evans, W. (1980) 'Schemata in British New Town Planning', in G.E. Cherry (ed.), *Shaping an Urban World*, London: Mansell, p.103.

5. Koolhaus, R. (1994) *Delirious New York: a Retroactive Manifesto for Manhattan*, Rotterdam: 010 Publishers, p.9.

6. For more on Fordist production, see Harvey, D. (1989) *The Condition of Postmodernity*, Oxford: Blackwell; and Waites, B. (1989) 'Social and Human Engineering', in C. Chant (ed.), *Science, Technology and Everyday Life, 1870–1950*, London: Routledge, p.327.

7. Taylor, F.W. (1911) *The Principles of Scientific Management*, New York: John Wiley.
8. Hoffman, D. (1970) 'The Setback Skyscraper of 1891: an Unknown Essay by Louis H. Sullivan', *Journal of the Society of Architectural Historians*, 29, pp.181–9.
9. Quoted by Tatton Brown, A. and Tatton Brown, W.E. (1941) 'Three-Dimensional Town-Planning', part 1, *Architectural Review*, 90, p.84.
10. Cohen, J.L. (1995) *Scenes of the World to Come: European Architecture and the American Challenge, 1893–1960*, Paris: Flammarion. See also Shanor, R.R. (1988) *The City that Never Was*, Harmondsworth: Penguin, pp.16–23.
11. Ferriss, H. (1929) *The Metropolis of Tomorrow*, New York: Washburn, p.124. For a valuable discussion of Ferriss's work, see M. Tafuri (1980) 'The disenchanted mountain: the skyscraper and the city', in G. Ciucci, F. Dal Co, M. Manieri-Elia and M. Tafuri *The American City: from the Civil War to the New Deal*, London: Granada, especially pp.447–51.
12. Wells, H.G. (1899) *When the Sleeper Wakes*, London: Harper and Brothers.
13. Segal, H.P. (1985) *Technological Utopianism in American Culture*, Chicago: University of Chicago Press, p.33.
14. Reiner, *The Place of the Ideal Community*, p.45.
15. Neutra, R. (1934) 'Rush City Reformed', *La Cité*, 12 (May), pp.71–82. See also Reiner, *The Place of the Ideal Community*, pp.68–71.
16. These include freestanding Garden Cities and projects for controlled ribbon development. See Scott, M. (1969) *American City Planning since 1890*, Berkeley: University of California Press; and Collins, G.R. (1979) *Visionary Drawings of Architecture and Planning: twentieth century through the 1960s*, Cambridge, MA: MIT Press. It must be stressed that while these schemes do not fall within the scope of this chapter, the indirect relationships between this category of low-density American decentralist visions and the Modern Movement's image of the future city are legion. Moreover, as is noted in Chapter 7, the ideas of the American Garden Cities movement, especially on neighbourhood units, were likewise to have an important impact upon European modernists.
17. For example, Wright, F.L. (1932) *The Disappearing City*, New York: Payson; Wright, F.L. (1935) 'Broadacre City, a New Community Plan', *Architectural Record*, 77, pp.243–54. For commentary, see Ciucci, G. (1980) 'The City in Agrarian Ideology and Frank Lloyd Wright: Origins and Development of Broadacres', in G. Ciucci, F. Dal Co, M. Manieri-Elia and M. Tafuri *The American City: from the Civil War to the New Deal*, London: Granada, pp.293–387.
18. e.g. Barnett, J. (1986) *The Elusive City: Five Centuries of Design, Ambition and Miscalculation*, London: Herbert Press, p.84.

19. Jackson, A. (1970) *The Politics of Architecture: a History of Modern Architecture in Britain*, London: Architectural Press, p.13.

20. Velez, D. (1982) 'Late Nineteenth-Century Spanish Progressivism: Arturo Soria's Linear City', *Journal of Urban History*, 9, p.132.

21. *Ibid.*, p.136.

22. *Ibid.*, p.139.

23. Le Corbusier (1923) *Vers une Architecture*, Paris: Éditions Crés, trans. F. Etchells (1927) as *Towards a New Architecture*, London: John Rodker, p.53. For more on Garnier, see Pawlowski, C. (1967) *Tony Garnier et les Débuts de l'Urbanisme Fonctionnel en France*, Paris: Centre de Recherche d'Urbanisme; and Piessat, L. (1988) *Tony Garnier, 1869–1948*, Lyon: Presses Universitaires de Lyon.

24. Although the movement was not confined to Italy. There was, for example, a powerful Russian Futurist movement, see Crompton, S.P. (1976–77) *Russian Futurism: 1910–1916: Poetry, Manifestos, Journals and Miscellanies*, Cambridge: Chadwyck-Healey.

25. Quoted in Conrads, U. (ed.) (1970) *Programmes and Manifestos on 20th-Century Architecture*, trans. M. Bullock, London: Lund Humphries, p.36.

26. Quoted in Tisdall, C. and Bozzolla, A. (1977) *Futurism*, London: Thames & Hudson, p.121.

27. Sant'Elia, A. (1914) *Messagio*, quoted in Banham, R. (1960) *Theory and Design in the First Machine Age*, London: Architectural Press, p.129. There is considerable dispute about the true authorship of this document, see de Costa Meyer, E. (1995) *The Work of Antonio Sant'Elia: Retreat into the Future*, New Haven, CN: Yale University Press, pp.140–61.

28. The *Übermensch* was a superhuman who transcended good and evil, abandoned Christian ethics of compassion and overturned all established values. See Pehnt, J. (1995) 'The "New Man" and the Architecture of the Twenties', in J. Fiedler (ed.), *Social Utopias of the Twenties: Bauhaus, Kibbutz and the Dream of the New Man*, Wupperthal: Müller & Busmann Press, pp.14–21.

29. Quoted in Lenning, H. (1951) *The Art Nouveau*, The Hague: Mouton, p.24.

30. Pehnt, 'The "New Man"', p.16.

31. See Sharp, D.(1972) *Glass Architecture and Alpine Architecture*, New York: Praeger. With regard to the partiality to crystalline forms by non-German architects, see the comments on Ferriss above and illustrations of the work of the Dutch architect J.C. van Epen in Nooteboom, C. (1985) *Unbuilt Netherlands*, London: Architectural Press.

32. Larsson, L.O. (1984) 'Metropolitan Architecture', in A. Sutcliffe (ed.), *Metropolis, 1890–1940*, London: Mansell, p.203. See also Hays, K.M. (1992) *Modernism and the Posthumanist Subject: the*

Architecture of Hannes Mayer and Ludwig Hilberseimer, Cambridge, MA: MIT Press.

33. Quoted material from Pommer, R. (1988) ' "More a Necropolis than a Metropolis": Ludwig Hilberseimer's Highrise City and Modern Town Planning', in R. Pommer, D. Spaeth and K. Harrington (eds), *Ludwig Hilberseimer: Architect, Educator and Urban Planner*, New York: Art Institute of Chicago and Rizzoli International, pp.16–53.

34. Kopp, A. (1970) *Town and Revolution: Soviet Architecture and City Planning, 1917–35*, London: Thames & Hudson, p.115. See also Brumfield, W.C. (ed.) (1990) *Reshaping Russian Architecture: Western Technology, Utopian Dreams*, Cambridge: Woodrow Wilson International Centre for Scholars and Cambridge University Press.

35. Curtis, W. (1982) *Modern Architecture since 1900*, Oxford: Phaidon, p.142.

36. Labadié, J. (1922) 'Les Cathedrales de la Cité Moderne', *L'Illustration*, 4145, 12 August, pp.131–5. A useful commentary is found in Cohen, *Scenes of the World to Come*, pp.117–21.

37. Le Corbusier, *Towards a New Architecture*, p.58.

38. *Ibid.*, p.54.

39. Banham, R. (1960) *Theory and Design in the First Machine Age*, London: Architectural Press, p.255.

40. Interview with Ernö Goldfinger, 16 December 1986. Transcript reference [T6/5].

41. Le Corbusier (1925) *Urbanisme*, Paris: Editions Crés, trans. F. Etchells (1929) as *The City of Tomorrow and its Planning*, London: John Rodker (3rd edn (1971) quoted here, London: Architectural Press).

42. Summerson, J. (1949) *Heavenly Mansions*, London: Cresset Press, p.191.

43. Frampton, K. (1980) *Modern Architecture: a Critical History*, London: Thames and Hudson, p.155; Evenson, N. (1969) *Le Corbusier: the Machine and the Grand Design*, London: Studio Vista, pp.18–19.

44. Le Corbusier (1925) *Urbanisme*, Paris: Editions Crès, trans. F. Etchells (1929) as *The City of Tomorrow and its Planning*, London: John Rodker (version quoted here is the Revised Edition, 1987, London: Architectural Press, pp.123, 131).

45. Fishman, R. (1977) *Urban Utopias in the Twentieth Century: Ebenezer Howard, Frank Lloyd Wright, Le Corbusier*, New York: Basic Books, pp. 208–9.

46. *Ibid.*, p.211.

47. Ramazani, V.K. (1996) 'Writing in Pain: Baudelaire, Benjamin, Haussmann', *boundary 2*, 23, p.210.

48. Le Corbusier (1933) *La Ville Radieuse*, Boulogne-sur-Seine: Vincent, Fréal et Cie, translated (1966) as *The Radiant City*, London: Faber & Faber, p.7.

49. Curtis, W. (1986) *Le Corbusier: Ideas and Forms*, Oxford: Phaidon.
50. An original sketch for a cover with this name is reproduced in Ockman, J. (1985) *Architecture, Criticism, Ideology*, Princeton: Princeton University Press, p.48. It is worth recalling that *Vers une Architecture* ends with the words 'Architecture or Revolution. Revolution can be avoided.' (See Le Corbusier, *Towards*, p.289.)
51. Le Corbusier, *The Radiant City*, p.7. For a fuller treatment of this theme, see Gold, J.R. (1985) 'A World of Organised Ease: the Role of Leisure in Le Corbusier's "La Ville Radieuse"', *Leisure Studies*, 4, pp.101–10.
52. Le Corbusier, *The Radiant City*, p.64.
53. Ginzberg, M. (1926) 'Mezhdunarodny front sovremennoi arkhitektury', *Sovremennaia Arkhitektura*, 1(2), p.42, quoted in Cohen, J.L. (1992) *Le Corbusier and the Mystique of the USSR: theories and projects for Moscow, 1928–1936*, Princeton, NJ: Princeton University Press, p.35.
54. *Ibid*, p.65.

Chapter 3

1. Colquhoun, A. (1989) *Modernity and the Classical Tradition: Architectural Essays, 1980–1987*, Cambridge, MA: MIT Press, p.244.
2. *Ibid.*, pp.49–53.
3. *De Stijl* was founded in 1917. The group eventually included the painter Piet Mondrian, the architect and furniture-designer Gerrit Rietvelt, and Theo van Doesburg, whose career combined architecture, painting, poetry and literary criticism.
4. Dettingmeijer, R. 'The Fight for a Well Built City' in W.A.L. Beeren, R.W.D. Oxenaar, T. van Velzen, E.E.L. de Wilde and D. van Woerkom, *Het Nieuwe Bouwen in Rotterdam, 1920–1960*, Delft: Delft University Press, p.33.
5. The roofs actually had a low pitch, but insufficient to affect the general appearance at ground level.
6. A number of official civic delegations went to the Continent in search of ideas on housing redevelopment in the 1930s. A delegation from the city of Birmingham, for example, visited Germany, Austria and Czechoslovakia. The London County Council in 1935 sent delegations to Germany, Austria, Czechoslovakia, Holland, France and Scandinavia. Their reports were widely read and led to growing interest in the possibilities of employing flats in schemes for working-class housing. See Ravetz, A. (1974) 'From Working-Class Tenement to Modern Flat: Local Authorities and Multi-Storey Housing between the Wars', in A. Sutcliffe (ed.), *Multi-Storey Living; the British Working-Class Experience*, London: Croom Helm, p.134.

7. Figures from Rowe, P.G. (1993) *Modernity and Housing*, Cambridge, MA: MIT Press, pp.359–60.
8. Some cities, however, had launched their own social housing drives before 1924 – the most notable of which was Cologne, which built 17 500 dwellings between 1919 and 1922.
9. Housing starts reverted to the 1924 level by 1933. See Rowe, *Modernity and Housing*, p.105.
10. Zukowsky, J. (1994) 'Das Neue Frankfurt', in J. Zukowsky (ed.), *The Many Faces of Modern Architecture: Building in Germany between the World Wars*, Munich: Prestel, pp.56–8.
11. Quoted in Creese, W. (1966) *The Search for Environment: the Garden City, Before and After*, New Haven, Conn.: Yale University Press, p.316.
12. Banham, R. (1987) ' "La Maison des Hommes" and "La Misère des Villes": Le Corbusier and the Architecture of Modern Housing', in H.A. Brooks (ed.), *Le Corbusier: the Garland Essays*, New York: Garland Publishing, p.110. See also Barnett, J. (1986) *The Elusive City: Five Centuries of Design, Ambition and Miscalculation*, London: Herbert Press, p.81. For more on the aesthetic principles put forward by Sitte, see his book Sitte, C. (1889) *Der Stadtebau nach seinem Kunstlerischen Grandsätzen* (City Planning according to Aesthetic Principles), Vienna: Carl Graeser. Reissued in translation as Collins, G.R. and Collins, C.C. (eds) (1965) *Camillo Sitte and the Birth of Modern City Planning*, New York: Random House.
13. Issacs, R. (1991) *Gropius: an Illustrated Biography of the Creator of the Bauhaus*, Boston: Little, Brown & Co., p.30.
14. Norberg-Schulz, C. (1975) *Meaning in Western Architecture*, London: Studio Vista, p.380. More details are found in Pommer, R. and Otto, C.F. (1991) *Weissenhof 1927 and the Modern Movement in Architecture*, Chicago: University of Chicago Press.
15. The official poster for the exhibition shows a red cross superimposed on a picture of a cluttered Victorian living room, apparently in answer to the question 'Wie Wohnen?' (how to live?). See Friedmann, A.T. (1996) 'Domestic Differences: Edith Farnsworth, Mies van der Rohe, and the Gendered Body', in Reed, C. (ed.), *Not at Home: the Suppression of Domesticity in Modern Art and Architecture*, London: Thames & Hudson, pp.190–1.
16. Wigley, M. (1995) *White Walls, Designer Dresses: the Fashioning of Modern Architecture*, Cambridge, MA: MIT Press, pp.303–5. The polychromatic precedent, rather than the austere white-walled look, was followed in later Siedlung exhibitions, for example at the *Werkbundsiedlung* (1932) organised by the Austrian Werkbund. See Stritzler-Levine, N. (1996) *Josef Frank, Architect and Designer: an Alternative Vision of the Modern Home*, New Haven, CN: Yale University Press.
17. Blundell Jones, P. (1995) *Hans Scharoun*, London: Phaidon, p.46.

18. Behrendt, W.C. (1927) *Der Sieg des neuen Baustils*, Stuttgart: Wedekind. Behrendt was also editor of the Werkbund's magazine *Die Form*.

19. A contemporary postcard superimposed camels and other devices to liken the Siedlung to an Arab village. Another index of the antipathy is revealed by contrasting the contents of the Weissenhof with the nationalistic content of the 'Deutsches Holz' ('German Wood') exhibition that was held at Am Kochenhof, Stuttgart in 1933.

20. Considerable care is necessary when interpreting this exhibition. Many writers have reviewed its contents as if they were the same as the illustrations that appear in its catalogue, Hitchcock, H.R. and Johnson, P. (1932) *The International Style*, New York: Museum of Modern Art; 1966 edition, New York: Norton. Recent scholarship shows that this is misleading. Less than half the 58 architectural images included in the catalogue appeared in the exhibition. Seventy photographs in the exhibition were not in the catalogue. For more on the circumstances that led to this situation, see Riley, T. (1992) *The International Style: Exhibition 15 and the Museum of Modern Art*, Catalogue 3, New York: Rizzoli/Columbia Books of Architecture.

21. Matthews, H. (1994) 'The Promotion of Modern Architecture by the Museum of Modern Art in the 1930s', *Journal of Design History*, 7(1), pp.43–59.

22. Described by the organisers as 'sometimes excellent examples of sociological theory, but . . . seldom examples of sound modern building and never works of architectural distinction'. See Hitchcock and Johnson, *The International Style* (1966 edition), p.90.

23. The importance of the common ground between the two, especially in terms of the development of functionalism, was recognised in a document written in May 1938 by the Polish delegates to CIAM, Helena and Szymon Syrkus entitled 'La Geneologie de l'Architecture Fonctionelle'. Folder E2, CIAM Archive, Frances Loeb Library, Harvard University, p.5.

24. van der Woud, A. (1982) *Het Nieuwe Bouwen Internationaal/CIAM Volkshuisvesting/Stedebow*, Delft: Delft University Press, p.7.

25. Curtis, W. (1986) *Le Corbusier: Ideas and Forms*, Oxford: Phaidon, p.118.

26. Interview with Maxwell Fry, 24 November 1986. Transcript reference [T5/16].

27. Benton, C. (1987) 'The Era of Great Projects', in M. Raeburn and V. Wilson (eds), *Le Corbusier: Architect of the Century*, London: Arts Council of Great Britain, p.165.

28. In passing, it is worth noting that Moser was one of the jury members who supported the entry by Le Corbusier and Jeanneret in the League of Nations competition. Giedion, for his part, had actively canvassed for acceptance of this entry.

29. Draft and final versions of this document may be found in
    Steinmann, M. (1979) *Internationale Kongresse für Neues Bauen:
    Dokumente, 1928–1939*, Basle: Birkhäuser Verlag, pp.12–21. The
    six questions were also conveyed diagrammatically by a poster
    displayed in the chapel of La Sarraz. This is illustrated in Boe-
    singer, W. and Stonorow, O. (1964) *Le Corbusier and Pierre
    Jeanneret: the Complete Architectural Works*, vol. 1 '1910–1929',
    London: Thames & Hudson, p.175.
30. Author's translation from the 'Déclaration' of the Congrès Pre-
    paratoire d'Architecture Moderne, clauses II.1 and II.2. Quoted
    from typescript version, Folder B1, CIAM Archive, Frances Loeb
    Library, Harvard University, p.2.
31. *Ibid.*, p.3.
32. Jencks, C. (1973) *Le Corbusier and the Tragic View of Architecture*,
    London: Allen Lane, p.77.
33. Giedion, S. (1941) *Space, Time and Architecture: the Growth of a
    New Tradition*, Cambridge, MA: Harvard University Press (5th
    edn (1967) consulted here), p.696.
34. See Stritzler-Levine, *Josef Frank*; and Wilson, C. St. J. (1995) *The
    Other Tradition of Modern Architecture: the Uncompleted Project*,
    London: Academy Editions, p.13.
35. van der Woud, *Het Nieuwe Bouwen Internationaal*, p.55.
36. *Ibid.*, p.60. This was scarcely representative of the membership.
    Forty of the 105 ground plans came from Germany alone.
37. *Ibid.*, p.126.
38. The original German title was *Die Konstruktive Stadt*, which carries
    somewhat different connotations to the French *La Ville Fonctio-
    nelle*. See Pollini, G. (1976) 'Cronache del Quatro Congresso di
    Archittetura Moderna e delle vicende relative alla sua organizza-
    zione', *Parametro*, 52, p.4.
39. The maps and the symbols employed are reproduced in Sert, J.L.
    (1942) *Can Our Cities Survive? an ABC of Urban Problems, Their
    Analysis, Their Solutions, based on the Proposals formulated by the
    CIAM (International Congresses for Modern Architecture/Congrès Inter-
    nationaux d'Architecture Moderne)*, Cambridge, MA: Harvard Uni-
    versity Press, pp.7–9.
40. van der Woud, *Het Nieuwe Bouwen Internationaal*, p.126. For
    contemporary observation on the growing Soviet ideological
    objections to modern architecture, see Schmidt, H. 'The Soviet
    Union and Modern Architecture', *Die Neue Stadt*, 6–7, pp.146–8,
    reproduced in Lissitzsky, E. (1970) *Russia: an Architecture for World
    Revolution*, trans. E. Dluhosch, Cambridge, MA: MIT Press.
41. Schmidt, H. (1932) 'The Soviet Union and modern architecture',
    reproduced in Lissitzky, *Russia*, p.220.
42. Goldfinger, E. (1983) 'A meeting of minds', *Architects' Journal*, 14
    December, p.28.
43. The plans exhibited were of Dessau, Frankfurt, Cologne and
    Berlin; Oslo; Stockholm; Prague; Budapest and Zagreb; Dalat

(French Indo-China); Bandoeng (Java); Athens; Brussels and Charleroi; Paris; London; Amsterdam, Rotterdam, Utrecht and The Hague; Littoria, Como, Rome, Genoa and Verona; Warsaw; Madrid and Barcelona; Zurich and Geneva; Los Angeles, Baltimore and Detroit.

44. For example, the plans of London and its region, produced by the English MARS Group, measured more than 100 square feet in area.

45. For the former, see Giedion, *Space, Time and Architecture*, p.699; and Newman, O. (1961) *CIAM '59 in Otterlo*, London: Alec Tiranti, p.11. For the latter, see Ostrowski, W. (1970) *Contemporary Town Planning from the Origins to the Athens Charter*, The Hague: International Federation for Housing and Planning, p.159; Harvey, D. (1989) *The Condition of Postmodernity: an Enquiry into the Origins of Cultural Change*, Oxford: Basil Blackwell, p.32; and Curtis, W. (1994) *Denys Lasdun: Architecture, City, Landscape*, Oxford: Phaidon, p.40.

46. Goldfinger [T6/2].

47. Fry [T5/11].

48. Letter from Giedion to P. Morton Shand, reproduced in MARS Circular Letter III, 19 September 1933. BAL file: SaG/90/2, p.3.

49. MARS Circular Letter II, 29 August 1933. BAL file: SaG/94/1, pp.2–3.

50. A suggestion made, for example, by the Finnish architect Alvar Aalto. MARS Circular Letter II, 29 August 1933. BAL file SaG/94/1, p.4.

51. CIAM II and III led, respectively, to CIAM (1930) *Die Wohnung für das Existenzminimum* (Dwellings for Lowest Income), Stuttgart: Julius Hoffmann Verlag; and CIAM (1931) *Rationelle Bebauungsweisen* (Rational Planning for Residential Areas), Stuttgart: Julius Hoffmann Verlag.

52. 'La Ville Fonctionelle: Constatations du IVme Congrès International [*sic*] d'Architecture Moderne', typescript version. Folder B3, CIAM Archive, Frances Loeb Library, Harvard University.

53. Goldfinger [T6/2].

54. Steinmann, *Internationale Kongresse für Neues Bauen*, pp.146–59. This source also supplies details of the interchange of drafts and revisions.

55. *Les Annales Techniques* (November 1933), 44–6, pp.1183–8. The final document was crafted by Moser and Steiger.

56. See the comparison between clause 10 of the document in Steinmann, *Internationale Kongresse für Neues Bauen*, p.158.

57. For a more detailed account of the complex history of this document, see Gold, J.R. (1997) 'The myth of the Athens Charter', unpublished ms available from the author.

58. Listed as Giedion, Gropius, Weissmann, Le Corbusier, Wells Coates, Sert, Stam and Steiger in a letter sent to other members of the Committee by Steiger, 28 July 1936. Folder C1, CIAM

Archive, Frances Loeb Library, Harvard University. This was seemingly reconstituted under the chairmanship of van Eesteren during the meeting with a membership that now comprised Giedion, Gropius, Benjamin Merkelbach, Perriand, Stam, Steiger and José Torres Clavé. Minutes of the CIRPAC meeting, La Sarraz, 9–12 September 1936. BAL file: SaG/91/1.

59. Giedion had already hinted obliquely that problems had arisen in producing the edited volume from CIAM IV due to 'differences in the conceptions of northern and western countries'. Giedion, S. (1937) 'The work of the CIAM (Congrès Internationaux d'Architecture Moderne), in J.L. Martin, B. Nicholson and N. Gabo (eds), *Circle*, London: Faber & Faber, 272–8 (reprinted edition (1971) consulted here, p.275).

60. Letter from Charlotte Perriand to Wells Coates, 16 October 1936. BAL file: SaG/93/3.

61. Minutes of the MARS Group, 30 November 1937. Folder C2, CIAM Archive, Frances Loeb Library, Harvard University, pp.1–2. It was suggested that Sert could come to London in January 1938 during the time that the MARS Exhibition (see Chapter 5) was open to explain the work of CIAM and appeal for funds.

62. van Eesteren, C. (1937) 'Rapports de base', in CIAM *Logis et Loisirs*, Boulogne-sur-Seine: éditions de l'Architecture d'Aujoud-'hui, p.14.

63. The display, for example, praised the notion of the *unité d'habitation* as a form of housing that freed up open space. See Steinmann, 'Neuer Blick', p.41.

64. This compares Sert, J.L. (1937) 'Cas d'application: villes', in CIAM *Logis et Loisirs*, Boulogne-sur-Seine: éditions de l'Architecture d'Aujoud'hui, p.32 with 'Cas d'Application des Villes', *ibid.*, p.115. It is also worth noting that the spelling was not yet fixed. A CIRPAC meeting and other correspondence in 1938 refers to this document as the 'Charta' [*sic*] of Athens. See, for example, Minutes of CIRPAC Reunion for preparation of CIAM VI, 10 July 1938. BAL file: SaG/93/3.

65. CIAM, *Logis et Loisirs*. Some elements of the proceedings of CIAM V also appeared in Giedion, S. (1951) *A Decade of Modern Architecture*, Zurich: Editions Girsberger.

66. It bears this title on the Memorandum of Agreement between the author and the Harvard University Press, October 1941. Folder Cl, Sert Archive, Frances Loeb Library, Harvard University.

67. e.g. see Giedion, *Space, Time and Architecture*, pp. 720–7.

68. Giedion, S. (1942) 'Introduction', in J.L. Sert *Can Our Cities Survive?*, Cambridge, MA: Harvard University Press, p.x.

69. Sert, *Can Our Cities Survive?*, p.228.

70. Le Corbusier, *The Athens Charter*, p.26.

71. *Ibid.*, p.40.

72. The quotations that follow come from the Constatations, n.p.; Sert, *Can Our Cities Survive?*, p.247; and Le Corbusier, *The Athens Charter*, pp.64–5.

73. The quote from Sert is from *Can Our Cities Survive?*, p.246. The other quotes are from Le Corbusier, *The Athens Charter*, pp.59–61.

74. Le Corbusier, *The Athens Charter*, p.98.

75. Interview with Jane Drew, 24 November 1987. Transcript reference [T5/16].

76. Fry, E.M. (1945) 'The future of architecture', in J.B. Drew (ed.), *Architects' Year Book*, London: Elek, p.10.

Chapter 4

1. Hepworth, B. (1934) 'Manifesto', in H. Read (ed.), *Unit One: the Modern Movement in English Architecture, Painting and Sculpture*, London: Cassell, pp.18–19.

2. Orwell, G. (1962) *The Lion and the Unicorn: Socialism and the English Genius*, London: Secker and Warburg, p.85; quoted in Crick, B. (1980) *George Orwell: a Life*, Harmondsworth: Penguin, p.407.

3. The poet W.H. Auden who in 1930 wrote 'Harrow the house of the dead; look shining at/ New Styles of architecture, a change of heart', later (1966) proclaimed that he had never had any liking for modern architecture. See Bergonzi, B. (1978) *Reading the Thirties*, London: Macmillan, p.90; also Naylor, G. (1977) 'Modernism: Threadbare or Heroic?', *Architectural Review*, 162, p.107.

4. For an excellent discussion, see Saint, A. (1987) *Towards a Social Architecture: the Role of School Building in Post War England*, New Haven, CN: Yale University Press, pp.7–10.

5. Lewis, W. (1919) *The Caliph's Design: Architects! Where is Your Vortex?*, London: The Egoist Press; Edwards, P. (1986) *Wyndham Lewis: the Caliph's Design*, London: Airlift Books. For more on pre-1920 modernism, see Farrington, J. (1980) *Wyndham Lewis*, London: Lund Humphries; Howlett, J. and Mengham, R. (eds) (1993) *The Violent Muse: Avant-Garde Culture and the Aesthetics of Violence*, Manchester: Manchester University Press.

6. Quoted in Lucie-Smith, E. (1985) *Art of the 1930s: the Age of Anxiety*, New York: Rizzoli International, p.182.

7. Quoted in Curtis, W. (1975) *English Architecture, 1930s: the Modern Movement in England, 1930–9*, Unit 18, *History of Art and Design, 1890–1939*, Milton Keynes: Open University Press, p.47.

8. Blomfield, R.T. (1934) *Modernismus*, London: Macmillan, pp.v and 62.

9. Conder, N. (1949) *An Introduction to Modern Architecture*, London: Art and Technics, p.45.

10. See Swenarton, M. (1983) 'Rationality and Rationalism: the Theory and Practice of Site Planning in Modern Architecture', *AA Files*, 1(4), pp.49–59.

11. Fisker, K. and Yerbury, F.R. (1927) *Modern Danish Architecture*, London: Ernest Benn; Robertson, H. and Yerbury, F.R. (1928) *Modern French Architecture*, London: Ernest Benn; Yerbury, F.R. (1928) *Modern European Buildings*, London: Victor Gollancz.

12. Le Corbusier (1923) *Vers une Architecture*, Paris: Editions Crès, trans. F. Etchells (1927) as *Towards a New Architecture*, London: John Rodker; Le Corbusier (1925) *Urbanisme*, Paris: Editions Crès, trans. F. Etchells (1929) as *The City of Tomorrow and its Planning*, London: John Rodker.

13. Gropius, W. (1935) *The New Architecture and the Bauhaus*, trans. P. Morton Shand, London: Faber & Faber.

14. See Strong, R. (1996) *Country Life, 1897–1997: the English Arcadia*, London: Country Life Books and Boxtree, pp.106–11.

15. Lewison, J. (1982) 'Foreword', in J. Lewison (ed.), *Circle*, Cambridge: Kettle's Yard Gallery, p.5; referring to Martin, J.L., Nicholson, B. and Gabo, N. (eds) (1937) *Circle: International Survey of Constructive Art*, London: Faber & Faber. In passing, it is worth noting that this publication was produced to coincide with the exhibition of 'Constructive Art' at the London Gallery in Cork Street, although its contents were only loosely linked to those of the exhibition.

16. Published versions appeared in Carrington, N. (1933) *Design in Modern Life*, London: BBC Publications; Bertram, A. (ed.) (1937) *Design in Daily Life*, London: Methuen.

17. Young architectural students would go out armed with a ready supply of filters to render their photographs in approved manner. Christian Digby Firth, for instance, remembered his curiosity when looking at a camera belonging to his father, Francis, a student at Leeds in the mid-1930s. The camera was remarkable for the number of filters that it had. Some were actually attached to the lens mounting by cord, suggesting the frequency of use. He recalled thinking: 'why do you need to make a red picture?' Interview with Christian Digby Firth, 23 January 1987.

18. Fry [T5/6].

19. Amyas Cornell and Basil Ward are a partial exception in this list. Both started by being articled to practices in New Zealand and worked their passage as coal trimmers on a steamship to come to London in 1924.

20. Interview with Berthold Lubetkin, 26 February 1987. Transcript reference [T9/1].

21. Goldfinger [T6/1].

22. Interview with Sir James Richards, 3 December 1986. Transcript reference [T11/6].

23. Interview with Professor Arthur Ling, 30 January 1987. Transcript reference [T8/1].

24. Cherry, G.E. and Penny, L. (1986) *Holford: a Study in Architecture, Planning and Civic Design*, London: Mansell, p.64.

25. Interview with Professor Percy Johnson-Marshall, 9 and 18 December 1986. Transcript reference [T7/1].

26. Crinson, M. and Lubbock, M. (1994) *Architecture, Art or Profession: Three Hundred Years of Architectural Education in Britain*, Manchester: Manchester University Press, pp.100–8. The planning School had a complicated history, surviving Rowse's subsequent departure from the AA and later supported by an independent planning group, the Association for Planning and Regional Reconstruction (APRR).

27. The Town and Country Planning Act of 1932 offered a potential for checking ribbon development and the wholesale wrecking of old towns for commercial exploitation by empowering local authorities to regulate size, height, design and physical appearance of buildings and to reject anything 'likely seriously to injure the amenity of a locality'. These were all phrases which could be used selectively by the local planning committees, set up by the Act. Quoted in Dean, D. (1983) *The Thirties: Recalling the Architectural Scene*, London: Trefoil Books, pp.11 and 35.

28. Arup [T1/3].

29. Interview with Lord Esher, 15 April 1987. Transcript reference [T4/6].

30. Esher [T4/5].

31. Benton, C. and Benton, T. (1979) 'Architecture: Contrasts of a Decade', in J. Hawkins and M. Hollis (eds), *The Thirties: British Art and Design before the War*, London: Arts Council of Great Britain, pp.48–51.

32. Johnson-Marshall [T7/1].

33. Quoted in Dean, *The Thirties*, p.22.

34. Richards [T11/1].

35. Denby, E. (1938) *Europe Re-housed*, London: George Allen & Unwin, p.254.

36. Ling [T8/3].

37. Tatton Brown [T15/4].

38. Johnson-Marshall [T7/4].

39. Fry [T4/13].

40. Johnson-Marshall, [T7/4].

41. Interview with Aileen Tatton Brown, 5 December 1986. Transcript reference [T14/2].

42. Richards, J.M. (1940) *An Introduction to Modern Architecture*, Harmondsworth: Penguin, pp.78–9.

43. Francis Digby Firth, for example, spent six months at the Massachusetts Institute of Technology in 1935–6 studying American prefabricated constructional techniques, particularly for wooden buildings. These are reported in Digby Firth, F. (1936) *Mass Production and Low Cost Housing*, unpublished Diploma in Architecture thesis, School of Architecture, Leeds University.

44. Interview with Jane Drew, 24 November 1986. Transcript reference [T5/4].
45. Johnson-Marshall [T7/2]. He was referring specifically to two books: Mumford, L. (1934) *Technics and Civilisation*, London: Secker & Warburg; and Mumford, L. (1938) *The Culture of Cities*, London: Secker & Warburg.
46. Fry [T5/5].
47. Johnson-Marshall [T7/2–3].
48. Interview with Sir John Summerson, 4 December 1986. Transcript reference [T12/3].
49. Johnson-Marshall [T7/2].
50. Arup [T1/3].
51. Ling [T8/2].
52. Ling [T8/3].
53. Summerson [T12/9].
54. Richards [T11/11].
55. W. Tatton Brown [T15/4].
56. Coates, W.W. (1933) 'Modern Dwellings for Modern Needs' (conversation with G. Boumphrey), *The Listener*, 24 May.
57. Yorke, F.R.S. (1934) *The Modern House*, London: Architectural Press, pp.7–9.
58. Bertram, A. (1935) *The House: a Machine for Living in*, London: A. and C. Black, pp.79–80, 107.
59. Lubetkin [T9/10].
60. Lubetkin [T9/3].
61. 'Statement of Aims and Outline of Constitution', p.3, circulated to members of the Twentieth Century Group for General Meeting at Arts Club, Dover Street, London, 26 February 1931. Folder 12, Wells Coates Archive, Canadian Centre for Architecture, Montreal, Canada.
62. Letter from Wells Coates to Mansfield Forbes, 16 February 1932. Folder 12, Wells Coates Archive, Canadian Centre for Architecture, Montreal, Canada.
63. Letter from Mansfield Forbes to Wells Coates, 17 February 1932. Folder 12, Wells Coates Archive, Canadian Centre for Architecture, Montreal, Canada.
64. Glazebrook, M. (1984) 'Unit One: Spirit of the 'Thirties', in M. Glazebrook, (ed.) *Unit One: Spirit of the 30s, May-June 1984*, London: Mayor Gallery, p.9.
65. The quotations are from Read, H. (ed.) (1934) *Unit One: the Modern Movement in English Architecture, Painting and Sculpture*, London, Cassell, pp.11–13.
66. The original correspondence referred to below comes from the MARS Group Folder (MGF) held in the Library of the Architectural Association.
67. Letter from Robertson to Giedion, 20 September 1929, (MGF).
68. In passing, there remains a dispute as to whether Robertson was a full participant or merely an observer. See exchange of letters

between Wells Coates and Howard Robertson, *Architects' Journal*, 77, 10 May 1933, p.623.
69. Elgohary, F. (1966) 'Wells Coates and his Position in the Beginning of the Modern Movement in England', unpublished PhD thesis, University of London, pp.71–2.
70. Besides Coates, the other participants at the first meetings were Shand, Coates's current partner David Pleydell-Bouverie, and Fry, with whom Coates had worked at the office of the town-planning firm Adams and Thompson in 1924.
71. A copy of this document can be found in Appendix IV of Elgohary, 'Wells Coates', pp.359–62.
72. Fry [T5/3]
73. Richards [T11/4].
74. BAL file: ArO/1/5/22/ii. The related idea of a Planning Research Station would recur several times in the thinking of the time, e.g. see Cherry and Penny, *Holford*, p.66.
75. BAL file: ArO/1/1/21/i.
76. Interview with Cyril Sweett, 6 March 1987. Transcript reference [T13/2–3]. The need for discipline in pursuit of common aims was largely a fiction to which the Group paid lip-service in its early years. It was put to the test in December 1935, when the partnership of Connell, Ward and Lucas (all of whom were MARS Group members) were called before the Central Executive Committee to explain their eclectic and monumental entry in a competition for the design of new offices for Hertfordshire County Council. The attempt to call them to account foundered on realisation that the Group had no effective criteria by which it could rule on the alleged transgression of group norms. Yet the myth of discipline persisted, for example, with the Secretary Cyril Sweett still citing this as an example of the discipline brought to bear on Group members.
77. Summerson [T12/2].
78. The 1933 membership comprised 10 architects and three non-professionals. The architectural members were Wells Coates (chairman), Maxwell Fry (vice-chairman), F.R.S. Yorke (secretary and treasurer), David Pleydell-Bouverie, Ward, Lucas, Skinner, John Betjeman, Connell, and Godfrey Samuel (members). There were three liaison secretaries who were not professional architects: Shand (with national and international groups), Hastings (with the British press) and John Gloag (with British trade organisations, professional societies, and other institutions). By January 1936, the Annual Report stated membership as 58 (BAL file: ArO/1/1/1/i). In January 1938 the brochure for the New Architecture exhibition listed 71 members (MARS Group (1938) *New Architecture*, London: New Burlington Galleries, p.23). With regard to the passive membership of MARS, Cherry and Penny cite the case of William Holford who joined MARS in 1934 but attended few meetings (Cherry and Penny, *Holford*, p.59). This is

despite the fact that Holford on several occasions stood for office in the Group (e.g. BAL file: ArO/1/4/5/ii).

79. From the earliest days, it was intended to open regional groups to widen the appeal away from purely a London base. A meeting held on 19th September 1933, for example, had suggested the possibilities of opening regional groups in Liverpool, Leeds and Glasgow (BAL file: ArO/1/2/1/i). Although minor attempts were made to stimulate activities in the provinces, e.g. the 1934 Building Trades Exhibition material was shown in Liverpool, Hull and elsewhere (Elgohary, 'Wells Coates', p.83), little effectively happened to dilute the London focus.

80. Richards, J.M. (1980) *Memoirs of an Unjust Fella*, London: Weidenfeld & Nicolson, p.129.

81. Ling [T8/4].

82. Summerson [T12/13].

83. Interview with H.T. Cadbury-Brown, 16 December 1986. Transcript reference [T2/6].

84. Interview with Mrs Susan Digby Firth (Miss Kathleen Grant), 8 February 1987. Transcript reference [T3/3].

85. Skinner, F. 'Memorandum for Discussion at First Meeting', 11 February 1935, p.4. BAL file: ArO/214/1/(v).

86. Lubetkin [T9/8–9].

87. Skinner, 'Memorandum', pp.2–3.

88. Architects' and Technicians' Organisation (1936) *ATO Bulletin*, 1, p.4. BAL file: SaG/90/1.

89. It was feared that active work on construction of underground shelters would panic the civilian population living in industrial areas likely to take the brunt of German bombing. This could lead to problems with the workforce that might compromise a future war effort.

90. The figure for the ATO was estimated by Skinner. The AASTA had grown to over 2000 by 1942. Figures quoted in Jackson, A. (1970) *The Politics of Architecture: a History of Modern Architecture in Britain*, London: Architectural Press, pp.70 and 161.

91. *Ibid*, p.76.

Chapter 5

1. Swift, G. (1983) *Waterland*, London: Heinemann.

2. Louis Sullivan, for example, thought the damage inflicted by the Exposition's 'progressive meningitis' so bad that it might take half a century to recover from the blow. Quoted in Cohen, J.L. (1995) *Scenes of the World to Come: European Architecture and the American Challenge, 1893–1960*, Paris: Flammarion, p.21.

3. Cadbury-Brown [T2/4].

4. 'Statement of Aims and Outline of Constitution', p.6, circulated to members of the Twentieth Century Group for General Meeting at Arts Club, Dover Street, London, 26 February 1931. Folder 12, Wells Coates Archive, Canadian Centre for Architecture, Montreal, Canada. Additional information from Strong, R. (1996) *Country Life, 1897–1997: the English Arcadia*, London: Country Life Books and Boxtree, p.107.

5. Memorandum for Meeting of Twentieth Century Group, 3 December 1931. Folder 12, Wells Coates Archive, Canadian Centre for Architecture, Montreal, Canada.

6. BAL file: ArO/2/4/1.

7. BAL file: ArO/1/1/21/i–ii.

8. BAL file: ArO/1/1/21/ii.

9. BAL file: ArO/2/6/1.

10. BAL file: ArO/2/6/4.

11. Information from BAL file: ArO/1/2/4/ii and Lubetkin [T9/8].

12. Anon (1934) 'The New Homes for Old exhibit: the MARS contribution', *Architects' Journal*, 20 September, pp.426–7.

13. *The Times*, 12 September 1934, p.10.

14. Lubetkin [T9/7–8]

15. W. Tatton Brown [T15/6].

16. BAL file: ArO/2/14/2(ii).

17. The proposal originally came from Berthold Lubetkin (BAL: ArO/1/2/3/1).

18. In passing, it is worth noting that Wells Coates did retain an interest in the Bethnal Green project and in collaboration with a client, Randal Bell, searched for a site where the private developer could undertake a rehousing scheme that would yield an economic return. A site was found off the Mile End Road for which Coates designed a scheme in 1937 to rehouse twice as many families in modern conditions on the same site with no increase in rent. The outbreak of war prevented its implementation. See Dean, D. (1983) *The Thirties: Recalling the Architectural Scene*, London: Trefoil Books, pp.62–3.

19. BAL file: ArO/1/1/22/i.

20. BAL files: ArO/1/2/16/ii, ArO/1/5/34, and ArO/1/5/39/iv.

21. BAL files: ArO/1/5/41/iii and ArO/1/2/24.

22. W. Tatton Brown [T15/11].

23. Fry [T5/6].

24. Intermediary Report of Exhibition Committee, 1935, p.1 (MGF, Architectural Association: 26489/R L/O). The report is dated 11 April and signed by the organiser Hazen Sise.

25. Banham, R. (1960) *Theory and Design in the First Machine Age*, London: Architectural Press.

26. Meeting of 17 April 1935. BAL file: Ar0/1/2/13(i). The audience included Lubetkin and Gropius.

27. BAL file: ArO/1/3/9/ii.

28. BAL file: ArO/2/6/8/iii.

29. A copy of this document, entitled 'Modern Architecture Exhibition 1937' is to be found in the British Architectural Library (BAL file: TuR/1/1/1). Its existence is seemingly responsible for an error of interpretation on the part of Cantacuzino who asserted that the Group organised 'two exhibitions, the first in June 1937 and the second one, and more important one, entitled "New Architecture" in January 1938'. This is quite wrong: the two exhibitions were one and the same thing. The June 1937 date comes from the draft pamphlet, (p.5), which asserted that the Exhibition would be held between 14 June and 10 July 1937 at the New Burlington Galleries. As seen below, this was subsequently postponed. See Cantacuzino, S. (1978) *Wells Coates: a Monograph*, London: Gordon Fraser, p.48.

30. BAL file: TuR/1/1/1/1–2.

31. Wotton, H. (1624) *The Elements of Architecture, collected by Henry Wotton Knight from the best Authors and Examples*, London: John Brill. (The quotation comes from the 1911 reprint, London: Longmans, Green and Co., p.1.) Samuel's suggestion was first made in December 1935, see BAL file: SaG/91/1.

32. MARS Group (1938) *New Architecture*, London: New Burlington Galleries, p.8.

33. Minutes of Meeting of Executive Committee, 16 November 1937. BAL file: SaG/91/3.

34. In passing, it is also worth noting that part of the material shown was redisplayed without alteration in September 1938 at the Building Trades Exhibition.

35. MARS Group, *New Architecture*, p.6.

36. A debt had been accumulated of more than £2000 over and above the sponsorship money that had been received. Full details can be found in the Accounts Book (BAL file: ArO/2/13). A full year later (31 January 1939), a circular letter from the Treasurer, Ove Arup, spoke of the immediate threat of legal action by Beck and Pollitzer having been temporarily lifted, but appealing to members 'to do all they can to assist the Group at this critical juncture' by paying their subscriptions and all promised loans (BAL file: ArO/1/1/18/i). In the event, the costings were challenged and the debts were never fully paid. Information from Sweett [T13/7].

37. Richards [T11/12].

38. The major stands in the exhibition were designed by Ove Arup, Serge Chermayeff, Wells Coates, Francis Digby Firth, J. Earley, Clive Entwistle, Maxwell Fry, Ernö Goldfinger, Frederick Gibberd, Arthur Korn, Fred Lassere, Peter Moro, Kit Nicholson, Godfrey Samuel, William Tatton Brown, and Christopher Tunnard. The captions, hoardings and much of the catalogue were written by John Summerson. Drawings for the exhibition and catalogue were prepared by Gordon Cullen, with the poster

prepared by McKnight Kauffer. Information from BAL file: SaG/
91/3 and from interview with S. Digby Firth on 9 February 1987
who provided secretarial assistance at the time of the exhibition.
Transcript reference, [T3/2–3].

39. Students, Unit 15, Architectural Association (1938) 'The MARS
Group exhibition', *Architectural Association Quarterly*, 53, pp.386–
8.

40. Drew [T4/8], Fry [T7/6].

41. MARS Group, *New Architecture*, p.5.

42. The buildings were Bamburgh Castle, Lavenham Church (Suf-
folk), Montecute House (Somerset), the Royal Crescent (Bath),
St. George's Hall in Liverpool, and Kensal House.

43. Richards [T11/11].

44. W. Tatton-Brown [T15/9].

45. Richards [T11/12].

46. Summerson [T12/9].

47. Fry [T5/8].

48. Richards [T11/11].

49. MARS Group, *New Architecture*, p.20.

50. W. Tatton-Brown [T15/9].

51. See Le Corbusier (1935) *La Ville Radieuse*, Boulogne-sur-Seine:
Vincent, Fréal and Cie, translated (1966) as *The Radiant City*,
London: Faber & Faber, pp.321–38.

52. Moro [T10/7], Richards [T11/12].

53. W. Tatton Brown [T15/9].

54. MARS Group, *New Architecture*, p.13.

55. It is believed that the change in name was simply a matter of
avoiding confusion among a public unfamiliar with modern
architecture (W. Tatton Brown, personal communication).

56. Yorke, F.R.S. and Breuer, M. (1937) 'A Garden City of the
Future', in J.L. Martin, B. Nicholson and N. Gabo (eds), *Circle:
International Survey of Constructive Art*, London: Faber & Faber,
pp.182–3.

57. Johnson-Marshall [T7/8].

Chapter 6

1. Giedion, S. (1941) *Space, Time and Architecture: the Growth of a
New Tradition*, Cambridge, MA: Harvard University Press (3rd
edn, 1954, consulted here), p.25.

2. See Cohen, J.L. (1995) *Scenes of the World to Come: European
Architecture and the American Challenge, 1893–1960*, Paris: Flammarion, p.106.

3. Cherry, G.E. and Penny, L. (1986) *Holford: a Study in Architecture,
Planning and Civic Design*, London: Mansell, p.54.

4. Crinson, M. and Lubbock, J. (1994) *Architecture, Art or Profession: Three Hundred Years of Architectural Education in Britain*, Manchester: Manchester University Press, pp.101–2.

5. *Housing Problems* (1935), directed by A. Elton and E. Anstey. British Commercial Gas Association.

6. Max Lock Centre Exhibition Research Group (1997) *Max Lock, 1909–1988: People and Planning, an Exhibition of his Life and Work*, London: University of Westminster.

7. Rowse, E.A.A. (1939) 'The planning of a city', *Journal of the Town Planning Institute*, 25, pp.168–9.

8. Perry, C.A. (1929) 'The Neighbourhood Unit', *The Regional Plan of New York and its Environs*, vol. 3 'Neighbourhood and Community Planning', New York: New York Port Authority. For further commentary, see Elliot, E.G.S (1935) 'American Housing before the New Deal', *Town Planning Review*, 16, pp.247–53; Kaufmann, E.C. (1936) 'Neighbourhood Units as New Elements of Town Planning', *Royal Institute of British Architects' Journal*, 44, pp.165–75.

9. Information from Cocke, P.L. (1973) 'Tomorrow Town', in J. Gowan, (ed.) *Projects: Architectural Association, 1946–71*, London: Architectural Association, p.8; and Pattrick, M. (1958) 'Architectural aspirations', AA Journal, January, pp.153–4.

10. Johnson-Marshall, P. (1966) *Rebuilding Cities*, Edinburgh: Edinburgh University Press, p.116.

11. Lock, M. (1946) *The Middlesbrough Survey and Plan*, Middlesbrough: Middlesbrough Corporation. Further allusion to this advisory plan is found in Chapter 7.

12. Saint, A. (1987) *Towards a Social Architecture: the Role of School Building in Post-War England*, New Haven, CN: Yale University Press, pp.3–4.

13. These are illustrated in Astragal (1933) 'Notes and Topics', *Architects' Journal*, 17 August, pp.196–7; and Sert, J.L. (1942) *Can Our Cities Survive?: an ABC of urban problems, their analysis, their solutions*, Cambridge, MA: Harvard University Press, p.170.

14. BAL file: Ar0/1/58/ii.

15. BAL file: Ar0/1/2/16/ii.

16. Minutes for 1 July 1936. BAL file: Ar0/1/2/20/ii.

17. BAL file: Ar0/1/4/6/ii.

18. BAL file: Ar0/1/2/25/i.

19. BAL file: Ar0/1/3/9/i.

20. William Tatton Brown (personal communication, 5 June 1994) noted that:

> Hastings was a very modest self-effacing man who liked to work through other people – such as J.M. Richards, Gordon Cullen and the Tatton Browns. We would none of us thought of these ideas without him. . .and no one would have heard about them without the publicity which he was able to give in the Architectural Press.

21. W. Tatton Brown [T15/1].
22. CIAM (1937) *Logis et Loisirs*, Paris: Les Congrès Internationaux d'Architecture Moderne, pp.79–80.
23. See Ex-Serviceman AJ/47485 (A.T. Edwards) (1933) *100 New Towns for Britain*, London: Simpkin Marshall.
24. William Tatton Brown (personal communication, 5 June 1994) stressed that this and the illustrations that follow (Figs 6.1–6.3) were polemical diagrams illustrating principles of city design rather than actual town plans.
25. W. Tatton-Brown [T57/7], revised by personal communication, 5 June 1994.
26. Fry [T7/12].
27. They included, at various times, Elizabeth Denby, Jane Drew, Ernö Goldfinger, Percy Johnson-Marshall, Bronek Katz, Arthur Korn, Arthur Ling, Aleck Low, Godfrey Samuel, Felix Samuely, Robert Shaw, Peter Shepheard, William Tatton Brown, Christopher Tunnard.
28. Letter from A. Korn to MARS Group's Central Executive Committee, 15 February 1938. Reprinted in Sharp, D. (1971) 'Concept and interpretation: the aims and principles of the MARS Plan for London', *Perspecta*, 13, pp.164–5.
29. Letter from William Tatton Brown to J.L. Sert, 7 August 1938. Folder C2, CIAM Archive, Frances Loeb Library, Harvard University.
30. Letter from William Tatton Brown to J.L. Sert, 31 August 1938. Folder C2, CIAM Archive, Frances Loeb Library, Harvard University.
31. Hastings also lost sympathy with the new direction. See Fry, E.M. (1971) 'The MARS Group Plan of London', *Perspecta*, 13, p.164.
32. Korn had been Secretary of the pan-artistic *Novembergruppe* in 1924, which included Mies van der Rohe, Walter Gropius, Max and Bruno Taut, and Erich Mendelsohn.
33. Sharp, D. (1966) *Modern Architecture and Expressionism*, London: Longman, p.167.
34. Ling, A.G. (1938) 'Social Units', unpublished Diploma thesis, Department of Town and Country Planning, University College, University of London.
35. Ling [T8/6].
36. Ling [T8/9].
37. BAL file: Ar0/2/10/1.
38. BAL file: Ar0/2/10/1/i.
39. Percy Johnson-Marshall [T7/8] recalled that:

> I was in my flat in the centre of Coventry and it suffered a direct hit from a bomb. The windows were shattered. I had the MARS Plan rolled up with quite a number of other plans on the wall, in rolls, and several slivers of glass went through it. And then I got a desparate

message from Arthur Korn saying that I had the only extant copy, because a bomb had destroyed all the others.

40. Korn, A. and Samuely, F.J. (1942) 'A Master Plan for London', *Architectural Review*, 91, pp.143–50; Fry, E.M. (1944) *Fine Building*, London: Faber.

41. Cited in Sharp, 'Concept and interpretation', p.168.

42. Korn and Samuely, 'A Master Plan for London', p.145.

43. e.g. *Ibid.*, p.148.

44. Fry [T7/12].

45. Among a large literature, see Carter, E. (1962) *The Future of London*, Harmondsworth: Penguin; Houghton-Evans, W. (1975) *Planning Cities: Legacy and Portent*, London: Lawrence and Wishart, pp.98–102; Fischer, K.F. (1994) 'MARS, Academy and Abercrombie: British plans and their Continental counterparts', unpublished paper read to the International Planning History Conference, London, April; Marmaras, E. and Sutcliffe, A. (1994) 'Planning for post-war London: the three independent plans, 1942–3', *Planning Perspectives*, 9, pp.431–53.

46. Sharp, D. (1972) *A Visual History of Twentieth Century Architecture*, London: Heinemann/Secker and Warburg, p.155.

47. Johnson-Marshall [T7/12].

48. There is not room here to provide a detailed analysis of the plan's costing proposals and balance sheet. See Korn and Samuely, 'A Master Plan for London', p.144.

49. Korn, A. (1955) *History Builds the Town*, London: Lund Humphries, p.90.

50. Brett, L. (1942) 'Doubts on the MARS Plan for London', *Architects' Journal*, 96, 9 July, pp.23–5. William Tatton Brown (personal communication, 5 June 1994) argued that Hastings wholeheartedly concurred with this view.

51. Sharp, T.W. (1940) *Town Planning*, Harmondsworth: Penguin, pp.59–64.

52. Goldfinger [T6/3–4].

53. Ling [T8/6].

54. Interview with Sir Peter Shepheard, 15th March 1996. Transcript reference, [T18/4]. In passing, it is interesting to note that Korn himself did not hold that view:

> While the Plan was being prepared, we thought that London was going to be knocked down; we didn't expect to see a brick standing. I remember Arthur Korn saying that 'it may not be as bad as all that. In the first war, I was on the other side and I got stuck in Mechelen – Melline. The shells came from all directions, but after four and a half years, there was still Melline'.

55. Johnson-Marshall [T7/12].

56. Fry [T5/12].

57. Johnson-Marshall [T7/8].

Chapter 7

1. Dialogue from the film *The Proud City* (1945), dir. R. Keene. Greenpark Productions in association with the Film Producers Guild for the Ministry of Information.
2. Forshaw, J.H. and Abercrombie, P. (1943) *County of London Plan*, London: Macmillan.
3. Arthur Greenwood, Minister of Housing, interviewed by British Movietone News, April 1930.
4. Gold, J.R. and Ward, S.V. (1997) 'Of plans and planners: documentary film and the challenge of the urban future, 1935–52', in D.B. Clarke (ed.), *The Cinematic City*, London: Routledge, pp.59–82.
5. Le Corbusier's activities in World War II are a controversial, if not to say embarrassing matter for some architectural historians, as can be seen by comparing the treatment in Jencks, C. (1973) *Le Corbusier and the Tragic View of Architecture*, London: Allen Lane, pp.130–3 with that of Baudoui, R. (1990) 'Between regionalism and functionalism: French reconstruction from 1940 to 1945', in J.M. Diefendorf (ed.), *Rebuilding Europe's Bombed Cities*, Basingstoke: Macmillan, pp.33–5. There is little doubt, however, that Le Corbusier collaborated with the Petain regime during 1941–2 over discussions of reconstruction and plans for Algiers. While he later distanced himself from such dalliance, it is fairer to see the period of collaboration as a manifestation of Le Corbusier's opportunistic politics rather than search for excuses.
6. Giedion, S. (1941) *Space, Time and Architecture: the Growth of a New Tradition*, Cambridge, MA: Harvard University Press.
7. Gropius, W. and Wagner, M. (1943) 'A Programme for City Reconstruction', *Architectural Forum*, 79, pp.75–80.
8. Johnson-Marshall [T7/13].
9. Interview with Sir Peter Shepheard, 15 March 1996. Transcript reference [T18/4]. It should be stressed that there was a deliberate element of irony in this assessment; Shepheard was immediately offered a position designing factories for the Department.
10. Benton, C. (1995) *A Different World: Emigré Architects in Britain, 1928–1958*, London: RIBA Heinz Gallery.
11. Interview with Trevor Dannatt, 26 February 1996. Transcript reference [T17/2].
12. Summerson [T12/10].
13. Black, M. (1945) 'Exhibitions, 1943–1944', in J.B. Drew (ed.), *Architects' Year Book*, London: Paul Elek, pp.97–106.
14. Johnson-Marshall, P.E.A. (1966) *Remaking Cities*, Edinburgh: Edinburgh University Press, p.116.
15. Tubbs, R. (1942) *Living in Cities*, Harmondsworth: Penguin.
16. Tubbs at this time was Secretary of the Group.

17. *Ibid.*, p.25.
18. *Ibid.*, p.49.
19. Drew [T5/14]. For more information, see Richards, J.M. (ed.) (1943) 'Rebuilding Britain', *Architectural Review*, 93, pp.86–112.
20. Black, 'Exhibitions', p.98.
21. A good example being *Town and Country Planning* (1945). Army Bureau of Current Affairs Magazine Series, Army Kinematograph Services for War Office.
22. Johnson-Marshall [T7/13–14].
23. *Ibid.*
24. Respectively: Paton Watson, J. and Abercrombie, P. (1943) *A Plan for Plymouth: the Report prepared for the City Council*, Plymouth: Underhill; Williams-Ellis, C. (1941) *Plan for Living: the Architect's Part*, Rebuilding Britain Series, 5, London: Faber & Faber; *Planning Tomorrow's Britain*: Simon, E.D. (1945) *Rebuilding Britain: a Twenty Year Plan*, London: Victor Gollancz; Bournville Village Trust (1941) *When We Build Again: a Study Based into Conditions of Living and Working in Birmingham*, London: George Allen & Unwin; and Stephenson (1944) *A Plan for Town and Country*, London: Pilot Press.
25. The series lasted until 1960 and produced ten volumes.
26. Dannatt [T17/8].
27. Drew, J.B. (1945) 'Editor's Foreword', in J.B. Drew (ed.), *Architects' Year Book*, London: Paul Elek, p.5.
28. Bressey, C. and Lutyens, E. (1937) *Highway Development Survey (Greater London)*, London: HMSO.
29. Tripp, H.A. (1938) *Road Traffic and its Control*, London: Edward Arnold; Tripp, H.A. (1942) *Town Planning and Road Traffic*, London: Edward Arnold.
30. Tetlow, J. and Goss, A. (1965) *Homes, Towns and Traffic*, London: Faber & Faber, pp.53–4.
31. Pierce, S.R. (1943) 'Excerpts from a Post-War Guide to the Metropolis of Britain', *Architect and Building News*, p.69. See also Pierce, S.R. (1942) 'Control: an exploratory survey', *Architect and Building News*, 24 April, pp.55–7.
32. W. Tatton Brown [T15/7]. The material was first published in *Autocar* (11 July, 18 July and 25 July 1941). Subsequent and revised publication in Tatton Brown, A. and Tatton Brown, W.E. (1941–2) 'Three-Dimensional Town Planning: parts 1 and 2', *Architectural Review*, 90, pp.82–8; 91, pp.17–21.
33. Tatton Brown and Tatton Brown, 'Three-Dimensional', part 1, p.84.
34. W. Tatton Brown [T15/7].
35. Esher, L. (1981) *A Broken Wave: the rebuilding of England, 1940–1980*, London: Allen Lane, p.95; see original comments in Brett, L. (1943) 'The new Haussmann', *Architectural Review*, 93, pp.23–6.

36. London Regional Reconstruction Committee of the Institute of British Architects (1943) *Greater London: Towards a Master Plan. The Second Report of the Reconstruction Committee*, London: RIBA. For discussion, see Marmaras, E. and Sutcliffe, A. (1994) 'Planning for post-war London: the three independent plans, 1942–3', *Planning Perspectives*, 9, pp.431–53.
37. Max Lock Centre Exhibition Research Group (1997) *Max Lock, 1909–1988: People and Planning, an Exhibition of his Life and Work*, London: University of Westminster.
38. Lutyens, E. and Abercrombie, P. (1945) *A Plan for the City and County of Kingston-upon-Hull*, Hull: Brown; Nicholas, R. (1945) *City of Manchester Plan*, Manchester: Jarrold; Wolfe, L. (1945) *The Reilly Plan: A New Way of Life*, London: Nicholson & Watson; Lock, M. (1946) *Middlesbrough Survey and Plan*, Middlesbrough: Corporation of Middlesbrough; and Sharp, T. (1946) *Exeter Phoenix: a Plan for Rebuilding*, London: Architectural Press.
39. Forshaw and Abercrombie, *County of London Plan*; and Abercrombie, P. (1945) *Greater London Plan, 1944*, London: HMSO.
40. The three illustrations referred to in the next section are found in Abercrombie, *Greater London Plan*, between pp. 170 and 171.
41. There were suggestions that the Group might draw up 'typical plans' for expansion of a small town like Knutsford (Cheshire) to accommodate a post-war population of about 50 000. Minutes of a Group meeting, 8 December 1943 and Minutes of a meeting at the Café Royal, 5 June 1944. BAL file: SaG/95/1.
42. Minutes of Executive Committee, 29 September 1944. BAL file: SaG/95/1.
43. Goldfinger, E. (1944) 'Observations on the County of London Plan, *MARS Report*, 2, London: MARS Group, p.1.
44. *Ibid.*, p.2.
45. *Ibid.*, p.14.
46. Blanco-White, J., Coppock, R., Best, M., Gibson, D.E., Thompson, W.H. and Denby, E. (1943) *Your London has a Plan*, London: Association of Building Technicians.
47. Carter, E.J. and Goldfinger, E. (1945) *The County of London Plan Explained*, Harmondsworth: Penguin.
48. For an excellent background discussion, see Young, K. and Garside, P.L. (1942) *Metropolitan London: Politics and Urban Change, 1837–1981*, London: Edward Arnold, pp.243–55.

Chapter 8

1. Robertson, H. (1944) *Architecture Arising*, London: Faber & Faber, p.5.
2. Fry, E.M. 'A New Architectural Statement Questionnaire', circulated to members of the MARS Group, January 1947. BAL file: ArO/1/1/28.

3. Letter from M. Hartland Thomas to Godfrey Samuel, 10 November 1946. BAL file: SaG/95/1.
4. Lubetkin [T9/10].
5. Drew [T5/14].
6. Interview with Sir Peter Shepheard, 15 March 1996. Transcript reference [T18/13].
7. Sweett [T13/11].
8. All quoted material in this paragraph from Diefendorf, J.M. (ed.) (1990) *Rebuilding Europe's Bombed Cities*, Basingstoke: Macmillan, pp. 1, 79 and 155.
9. Young, K. and Garside, P.L. (1942) *Metropolitan London: Politics and Urban Change, 1837–1981*, London: Edward Arnold, p.225.
10. The Labour Party (1945) *Let Us Face the Future: a Declaration of Labour Policy for the Consideration of the Nation*, London: The Labour Party.
11. Ward, S.V. (1994) *Planning and Urban Change*, London: Paul Chapman, p.111.
12. Cadbury-Brown [T2/7].
13. For example, the Research and Techniques Division of the Ministry led by William Holford. An outgrowth of an earlier body established in 1942, it drew in a group of younger architects that included Gordon Stephenson, Peter Shepheard, D.H. Crompton and Myles Wright. See Cherry, G.E. and Penny, L. (1986) *Holford: a Study in Architecture, Planning and Civic Design*, London: Mansell, pp.88–134.
14. Esher [T4/4].
15. Ling [T8/14].
16. Ministry of Health and Ministry of Works (1944) *Housing Manual*, London: HMSO.
17. Dudley Report (1944) *The Design of Dwellings: Report of the Sub-Committee of the Central Housing Advisory Committee*, London: HMSO.
18. Ministry of Health (1949) *Housing Manual*, London: HMSO.
19. See Vale, B. (1995) *Prefabs: a History of the UK Temporary Housing Programme*, London: E & F.N. Spon. For contemporary assessments, see Casson, H. (1946) *Homes by the Million*, Harmondsworth: Penguin.
20. Fry [T5/14].
21. Letter from Jane Drew to J.L. Sert, 31 July 1947. Folder E3, Sert Archive, Frances Loeb Library, Harvard University.
22. Houghton-Evans, W. (1975) *Planning Cities: Legacy and Portent*, London: Lawrence & Wishart, p.93.
23. *Ibid.*
24. Esher [T4/12].
25. Gibberd, F. (1953) 'The Design of Residential Areas', in Ministry of Housing and Local Government *Design in Town and Village*, London: HMSO, p.30.

26. Allan, J. (1992) *Berthold Lubetkin: Architecture and the Tradition of Progress*, London: RIBA Publications, pp.448–518. This highly perceptive book is also a valuable source on Tecton's activities.

27. *Ibid.*

28. Lubetkin [T9/11].

29. Lubetkin [T9/12].

30. Circular letter to CIAM members from Sigfried Giedion, May 1946. BAL file: GoEr/314/2.

31. Richards [T11/14].

32. Meeting of CIRPAC, London 26–8 September 1946. BAL file: SaG/95/1.

33. MARS Memorandum, January 1947. BAL file: GoEr/314/2. The point about Winchester is found in a letter from Giedion to Sert, 18 January 1947. Folder C4, CIAM Archive, Frances Loeb Library, Harvard University.

34. Hartland Thomas, M. 'Memorandum' to MARS Group members, 25 June 1947; and Richards, J.M. 'CIRPAC Meeting at Zurich', undated. Both in BAL file: GoEr/314/2.

35. Reyner Banham, quoted in Landau, R. (1992) 'The End of CIAM and the Role of the English', *Rassegna*, 52, p.40.

36. Cadbury-Brown [T2/6].

37. Ling [T7/16].

38. BAL file: GoEr/312/12.

39. Report from Mark Hartland Thomas to the MARS Group, dated 2 October 1947, p.2. BAL file: GoEr/314/2.

40. Anon (1948) 'MARS: the aims of CIAM', *Architects' Journal*. From proof version, BAL file: GoEr/314/2.

41. Report from Mark Hartland Thomas to the MARS Group, dated 2 October 1947, p.2. BAL file: GoEr/314/2.

42. Quoted in Bosman, J. (1992) 'CIAM after the War: a balance of the Modern Movement', *Rassegna*, 52, p.10. His reasons were not simply altruism; he specifically wanted Bakema to attend. Bakema believed in a more pragmatic functionalist approach that might counterbalance Giedion's proposal to study the relations between architecture and art.

43. Letter from Sert to Giedion, 15 July 1948. Folder C5, CIAM Archive, Frances Loeb Library, Harvard University.

44. Letter from Coates to Goldfinger, 24 January 1949. BAL file: GoEr/314/2.

45. Minutes of Meeting of the CIAM 7 Committee, MARS Group, 31 January 1949. BAL file: GoEr/314/2.

46. Some further notes on the folders indicate how these grilles were constructed. The eight folders had 15 cells (each with long dimension of foolscap taken horizontally). In other words, there were three vertical columns of five panels. Six of the themes (10, 11, 12, 13, 14 and 18) had complete folders to themselves. Themes 15, 16 and 17 shared the same folder: 1 vertical column or 5 panels each. Somewhat awkwardly, the remaining theme

(19) shared a folder with the two reactions (20 and 21). These notes were taken from Clive Entwistle's 'Notes on methods of applying the grid', circulated with minutes of the Meeting of the CIAM 7 Committee, MARS Group, 31 January 1949. BAL file: GoEr/314/2.

47. Letter from Giedion to Sert, 26 January 1949. Folder C6, CIAM Archive, Frances Loeb Library, Harvard University. It is a typewritten letter with the more upbeat afterthought added by hand.

48. Letter from Giedion to Sert, 12 May 1949. Folder C6, CIAM Archive, Frances Loeb Library, Harvard University.

49. A detailed listing of the plates used is found in written description of the layout, 27 June 1949. BAL file: GoEr/312/12. The grid itself in its various sections (folders) is available in BAL box: GoEr/313.

50. From introductory panel, County of London Plan Grid. BAL box: GoEr/313.

51. Minutes of the first Meeting of the Sub-Committee, 31 March 1949. BAL file: GoEr/312/12.

52. Report of the CIAM 7, London Plan Group, 4 May 1949. BAL file.

53. This is the Questionnaire to which Maxwell Fry was alluding in the opening section of this chapter.

54. IFW (Ian F. Warwick), (ed.) 'A précis of a report of the Seventh Congress of CIAM held at Bergamo in North Italy', draft and unpublished report circulated to members of the MARS Group, 16 October 1949. The first three pages are initialled by Jaqueline Tyrwhitt. BAL file: GoEr/312/12.

55. *Ibid.*, p.2.

56. A reconstructed version of Syrkus's speech is found in Ockman, J. (1993) *Architecture Culture, 1943–1968*, New York: Columbia University Press, pp.121–2.

57. Le Corbusier 'The CIAM Grid', presentation to opening session, CIAM VII, Bergamo. Folder C6, CIAM Archive, Frances Loeb Library, Harvard University.

58. Notes by Denys Lasdun, final report of the First Commission dated 29 July 1949. BAL file: GoEr/312/12.

59. Unsigned preparatory document, 30 July 1949, but amended in hand by J. Tyrwhitt. Folder B6, CIAM Archive, Frances Loeb Library, Harvard University.

Chapter 9

1. Franklin, H.B. (1962) *Future Perfect: American Science Fiction of the Nineteenth Century*, New York: Oxford University Press, p.402.

2. Billinge, M. (1993) 'Trading History, Reclaiming the Past: the Crystal Palace as Icon', in G. Kearns and C. Philo (eds), *Selling Places: the City as Cultural Capital, Past and Present*, Oxford: Pergamon Press, p.103.

3. This patronage was not surprising given that the Royal Society of Arts, originally founded in 1754, was intimately involved in the 1851 exhibition.

4. Information from Summerson, J. (1956) 'Introduction', in Arts Council of Great Britain *'45–55: Ten Years of British Architecture*, London: Arts Council, p.15.

5. Drew [T5/15].

6. Dannatt [T17/9].

7. Summerson, 'Introduction', p.16.

8. Shepheard [T18/15].

9. Moro [T10/10].

10. Johnson-Marshall [T7/20].

11. This included some existing housing (to the left of Figure 9.2) and a Welfare Building (centre of picture) which were awkwardly integrated into the scheme.

12. Quoted in Gaskell, S.M. (1986) *Model Housing: from the Great Exhibition to the Festival of Britain*, London: Mansell, pp.121–2.

13. Minutes of a Joint Meeting of the Executive Committee and the CIAM 7 Sub-Committee on 10 March 1949. BAL file: GoEr/312/12.

14. See, for example, correspondence cited by Bosman, J. (1992) 'CIAM after the War: a Balance of the Modern Movement', *Rassegna*, 52, p.11.

15. Formal Notes on CIAM Meeting, New York, 5 June 1950. Folder C7, CIAM Archive, Frances Loeb Library, Harvard University.

16. Giedion, S. (ed.) (1951) *A Decade of New Architecture*, Zurich: Editions Girsberger, p.40.

17. Quoted in Sert, J.L. (1952) 'Centres of Community Life', in Tyrwhitt, J., Sert, J.L. and Rogers, E.N. (eds), *The Heart of the City: Towards the Humanisation of Urban Life*, London: Lund Humphries, p.3.

18. Tyrwhitt et al, *The Heart of the City*. In passing, it is worth noting that the book was provisionally called 'The Core of the City'. That title was endlessly discussed, with 'The Core of the Community' and 'Centres of Community Life' offered as options before the final title was decided. Correspondence between Sert and Tyrwhitt. Folders C7 and C8, CIAM Archive, Frances Loeb Library, Harvard University.

19. Letter from Lubetkin to Wells Coates, 21 February 1951, quoted in Allan, J. (1992) *Berthold Lubetkin: Architecture and the Tradition of Progress*, London: RIBA Publications, p.511.

20. Letter from Giedion to Coates, 1 May 1951. Folder C7, CIAM Archive, Frances Loeb Library, Harvard University.

21. Letter from Giedion to Wells Coates, 19 May 1951. Folder C8, CIAM Archive, Frances Loeb Library, Harvard University.

22. MARS Group (1951) *CIAM VIII, London 1951: the Core*. BAL file: GoEr/314/3.

23. Interestingly, delegates met Gibberd at the Lawn, the solitary tower block, where they looked at plans before visiting areas under construction.

24. 'Summary of Needs at the Core, CIAM 8, Hoddesdon', quoted in Ockman, J. (1993) *Architecture Culture, 1943–1968: a Documentary Anthology*, New York: Rizzoli, p.136.

25. Letter from Tyrwhitt to Sert, 1 August 1951. Folder C9, Frances Loeb Library, Harvard University.

26. Johnson-Marshall [T7/17]

27. Johnson-Marshall [T7/17–18].

28. Ling [T8/8]

29. Johnson-Marshall [T7/17].

30. *Ibid.*

31. Reported in Glass, R. (1951) 'Town planning and the social scientist', *The Listener*, 14 June, pp.951–2.

32. Ling [T8/13].

33. Johnson-Marshall [T7/21].

34. Glendinning, M. and Muthesius, S. (1994) *Tower Block: Modern Public Housing in England, Scotland, Wales and Northern Ireland*, New Haven, CN: Yale University Press, p.55.

35. Founded in 1946 to promote the cause of modernism in art and design, the ICA increased its coverage of architecture from 1951 onwards.

36. Giedion, S. (1948) *Mechanisation Takes Command: a Contribution to an Anonymous History*, New York: Oxford University Press.

37. For more on the Independent Group, see Robbins, D. (ed.) (1990) *The Independent Group: Postwar Britain and the Aesthetics of Plenty*, Cambridge, MA: MIT Press; and Massey, A, (1995) *The Independent Group: Modernism and Mass Culture in Britain, 1945–59*, Manchester: Manchester University Press.

38. Banham, R. (1966) *The New Brutalism*, London: Architectural Press, p.47.

39. In fairness, the Smithsons were not the only entrants to offer this innovation. It was also found in the entry by Jack Lynn and Ivor Smith, later the project architects for Park Hill in Sheffield.

40. Smithson, A. and Smithson, P. (1970) *Ordinariness and Light: Urban Theories 1952–1960 and Their Application in a Building Project 1963–1970*, London: Faber & Faber, p.45.

41. *Ibid.*, p.52.

42. Johnson-Marshall [T7/16].

43. Letter from Le Corbusier, Giedion and Tyrwhitt to CIAM delegates, 14 May 1952. Folder C10, CIAM Archive, Frances Loeb Library, Harvard University. A valuable guide to the positions

taken by different participants is found in Bosman, 'CIAM after the War', pp.15–16.

44. Letter from Tyrwhitt to Sert, 13 May 1952. Folder C10, CIAM Archive, Frances Loeb Library, Harvard University.

45. Respectively: Notes for Special Meeting of MARS Group at Building Centre, 5 June 1952 and Minutes of AGM, 11 May 1953. Both in BAL file: GoEr/312/5.

46. Bodiansky, V. (1953) 'For a Charter of Habitat', in 'L'Architecture d'Aujord'hui' (1953) *Contribution a La Charte de l'Habitat*, Aix-en-Provence: CIAM, n.p.

47. From a paper written at Aix and reproduced by the Congress Secretariat for the delegates. Taken from Smithson, A. (1982) *The Emergence of Team 10 out of CIAM*, London: Architectural Association, p.7.

48. Quoted in Landau, R. (1992) 'The End of CIAM and the Role of the British', *Rassegna*, 52, p.11.

49. Address given by Goldfinger to the Building Centre, 20 October 1953. BAL file: GoEr/315/1.

50. Smithson, A., *The Emergence of Team 10 out of CIAM*, p.10.

51. Quoted in Landau, 'The End of CIAM', p.41.

52. Richards, J.M. (1954) 'Preview', *Architectural Review*, 115, p.8.

53. Richards [T11/15].

54. Cadbury-Brown [T2/7].

55. An idea which Geddes himself probably derived from Elisée Reclus. The 'valley section' equated the path of human development with the path from the rural economy of the remote rural upland through the small market town to the great city located downstream.

56. Smithson, A., *The Emergence of Team 10 out of CIAM*, pp.33–4.

57. Shepheard [T18/15].

58. Barber, W.E. (1976) 'Propaganda', in *Dictionary of American History*, vol. 5, New York: Charles Scribner's Sons, p.433.

59. Lubetkin [T9/7].

INDEX